4) Unique
different
+ better

BENCHMARKING

The Experience
Economy

The Search for
Industry Best Practices
that Lead to
Superior Performance

BENCHMARKING

The Search for Industry Best Practices that Lead to Superior Performance

Robert C. Camp

Productivity Press

BENCHMARKING

The Search for Industry Best Practices that Lead to
Superior Performance

Robert C. Camp

Library of Congress Cataloging-in-Publication Data

Camp, Robert C., 1935-
   Benchmarking: the search for industry best practices that lead to
superior performance / Robert C. Camp.
     p. cm.
   Bibliography: p.
   Includes index.
   ISBN 978-1-56327-352-0
   1. Organizational effectiveness. 2. Performance. 3. Business
intelligence. 4. Research, Industrial. I. Title.
HD58.9.C36   1989
658.4'7—dc19

Acquisitions Editor: Jeanine L. Lau
Production Editor: Tammy Griffin
Cover design by Walzak Design. Set in Century Schoolbook by DanTon
  Typographers.

ISBN 0-87389-058-2 (ASQC Quality Press)
ISBN 0-527-91635-8 (Quality Resources)

Printed in the United States of America
07   1

ASQC Quality Press
American Society for Quality Control
611 East Wisconsin Avenue, Milwaukee, Wisconsin 53202

Quality Resources
A Division of The Kraus Organization Limited
902 Broadway, New York, New York 10010

This book is dedicated
to the early pioneers of Xerox Benchmarking
who had to find their way
through undocumented territory.

Table of Contents

List of Figures

List of Tables

Preface

Benchmarking is the search for those best practices that will lead to the superior performance of a company. Establishing operating targets based on the best possible industry practices is a critical component in the success of every business. Traditional target-setting methods have failed U.S. managers and blind sided them to foreign competition. The Japanese term *dantotsu,* which means striving to be the "best of the best," incorporates the essence of the process they use to establish competitive advantage. We Americans have no such word, perhaps because we always assumed we were the best. We cannot assume that anymore.

The benchmarking process, establishing operating targets based on best practices, is being used increasingly by U.S. industry. Benchmarking is a positive, proactive, structured process which leads to changing operations and eventually attaining superior performance and a competitive advantage. Investigating and incorporating best industry practices leads to profitable, high inventory turn, return on asset results.

This book demonstrates how to conduct investigations to ensure that your operation is based on industry best practices. Using a case history approach based on the distribution function, this book shows: (1) how to structure and conduct investigations, (2) how to analyze and measure the opportunity for change, and (3) how to implement an action plan to achieve significant benefits.

How do you set objectives, goals, and targets in an unbiased manner? Many techniques have been tried. One is a simple extrapolation of the past: "We did it that way last year, and we'll do it again next year." Perhaps a slightly more enlightened way is to extrapolate the past, but to modify for known conditions: Increase for known activity, adjust for accepted inflation planning factors, and add a further adjustment for needed productivity. The latter is a common approach for establishing future budgets.

In today's marketplace, these approaches are certain to lead to disaster. And they have. U.S. manufacturers glibly believed they knew what was required to remain competitive, and they felt they could rely on establishing their goals and targets on these simplistic, extrapolation methods. "If we were doing well, then why not simply project our current good approaches into our future approaches toward budgets, resources, methods, practices, and processes?"

Belief in this outmoded approach was dispelled by the invasion into the U.S. marketplace of substantially less expensive, and many times higher quality, Japanese-produced goods. Why were shocked

U.S. manufacturers caught off guard? Because the Japanese did not accept the notion that goods and services could be competitive by simply mimicking the past. They recognized that new methods, processes, and practices had to be uncovered, and more important, they recognized that the best of these had to be combined to provide a competitive advantage. They had to find the best of the best, and the best of the best had to fit together logically.

How did they accomplish seeking out the best of the best and then adapting them to their situation? Their study trips abroad are legion. They came in droves to the United States and saw firsthand the methods being used. They did not limit their trips and investigations to their own industry but visited a wide cross section of industries. They knew they might find methods in one industry directly useable by another, or useable with minor adjustments. They knew the methods found in seemingly unrelated industries could provide a competitive advantage. A proven technology found in one, such as bar coding in the grocery industry, could be immediately used. Installed in the control processes for manufacturing typewriters, they could outpace other typewriter manufacturers who used only manual, serial number control in their own operations and continued to believe they had the best.

The practice of widely searching for new ideas for methods, practices, and processes not limited to one's industry was probably not consciously given a name. The process, however, was repeated time and time again and involved sifting, synthesizing, and adapting processes to fit their specific needs. Ideas were hotly debated for usefulness, observations were carefully documented, either written or recorded on film. The process was constant, consistent, and comprehensive.

That process of consistently researching for new ideas for methods, practices, and processes, and of either adopting the practices or adapting the good features, and implementing them to obtain the best of the best is what is now known as **benchmarking.** This book is a description of that process. Benchmarking is industrial research or information gathering that allows a manager to compare his or her function's performance to the performance of the same functions in other companies. Benchmarking identifies those management practices the function should use to attain superiority. Taken from the land surveying term for a mark used as a reference point for elevation or direction comparisons, the practice of comparing performance between organizations is commonly referred to as benchmarking.

Here is a text that will tell you, by relating the benchmarking process to a specific example, how benchmarking is done. The example used is the benchmarking experience of a logistics or distribution function of a large manufacturer. It includes the experience of the author in conducting benchmarking activities over the past seven years. Examples of successful investigations are described such that it becomes a how-to book that answers the question posed by many visitors who have asked, "How do I do benchmarking?"

Benchmarking is a positive, proactive activity that is the missing ingredient in the kit bag of U.S. marketing and manufacturing firms to correctly establish its goals, objectives, and targets. Its focus is on the search for best practices that will lead to superiority. What manager is not interested in the structured search for industry best practices? This subject can be discussed at any professional gathering and be a topic of even generic discussions between competitors.

It is a new way to establish operating targets — not how they have been established in the past, but established based on the best of the best practices, constantly reviewed and updated to ensure the best and most structured way to obtain long-term superiority. Benchmarking is what the Japanese have done to attain an advantage at the expense of the U.S. middle manager's operation.

Acknowledgments

The author acknowledges the
many individuals who have
contributed to the process of
benchmarking, the co-authors
of the Harvard Business Review article
which was the inspiration for
this book, and Xerox Corporation
for permitting publication
of this important business topic.

The contents of this text
have been donated to assist in the development
of the internal
Xerox Benchmarking for Quality Workshop Training Program.

BENCHMARKING

**The Search for
Industry Best Practices
that Lead to
Superior Performance**

CHAPTER 1 INTRODUCTION

Historical Perspective

Managerial Perspective

Benchmarking Defined
- Formal definition
- Webster's definition
- A working definition

What Is Benchmarking?
- What it is, what it is not
- Benchmarking and targets

Key Process Steps
- Planning
- Analysis
- Integration
- Action
- Maturity

How to Get Started in Benchmarking

Summary

Quick Reference Guide 1.1. How to Get Started in Benchmarking

1

INTRODUCTION

How to Achieve Effective Goals and Objectives

Traditional target setting methods have failed U.S. managers and blind sided them to competition. Only the approach of establishing operating targets and productivity programs based on industry best practices leads to superior performance. That process, being used increasingly in U.S. business, is known as **benchmarking.**

Two ancient truths convincingly illustrate why benchmarking is so vitally needed. One saying is over 2,500 years old and originates in China. It is hard to say how old the other is, but it originated in and is successfully practiced in Japan.

In the year 500 B.C., Sun Tzu, a Chinese general, wrote, "If you know your enemy and know yourself, you need not fear the result of a hundred battles." Sun Tzu's words could just as well show the way to success in all kinds of business situations. Solving ordinary business problems, conducting management battles, and surviving in the marketplace are all forms of war, fought by the same rules — Sun Tzu's rules.

The other truth is a simple word of unknown age. It is the Japanese word *dantotsu,* meaning striving to be the "best of the best." It is the very essence of benchmarking. We in America have no such word, perhaps because we always assumed we were the best. But world competitive events have smashed that notion forever. We cannot assume anything anymore. Benchmarking moves us past that assumption.

Benchmarking is a positive, proactive process to change operations in a structured fashion to achieve superior performance. The benefits of using benchmarking are that functions are forced to investigate external industry best practices and incorporate those practices into their operations. This leads to profitable, high-asset utilization businesses that meet customer needs and have a competitive advantage.

Benchmarking is firmly based on Sun Tzu's urging to view and understand not only the internal company world, but more importantly to assess the external constantly. Only coupled with the constant search for *dantotsu,* the "best of the best" methods and practices innovatively applied to business processes, will U.S. industry revitalize itself. The purpose of benchmarking is to ensure that probability of success.

The basic philosophical steps of benchmarking, listed as follows, are fundamental to success:

- **Know your operation.** You need to assess the strengths and weaknesses of the internal operation. That assessment must be based on the understanding that competitors will analyze your operation also to capitalize on the weaknesses they uncover. If you do not know the operation's strengths and weaknesses you will not be able to defend yourself. You will not know which operations to stress in the marketplace and which will require strengthening.
- **Know the industry leaders or competitors.** In a similar fashion you will only be prepared to differentiate your capabilities in the marketplace if you know the strength and weaknesses of the competition. More importantly, it will become clear that only the comparison to and understanding of the best practices of industry or functional leaders will ensure superiority.
- **Incorporate the best.** Learn from industry leaders and competition. If they are strong in given areas, uncover why they are and how they got that way. Find those best practices wherever they exist and do not hesitate to copy or modify and incorporate them in your own operation. Emulate their strengths.
- **Gain superiority.** If careful investigations of best practices have been performed, and if the best of those best practices have been installed, then you will have capitalized on existing strengths, brought weaknesses to match the marketplace, and gone beyond to incorporate the best of the best. This position is clearly a position of superiority.

Benchmarking is the formalized and more disciplined application of these very basic steps to operational improvement and the achievement of superiority. The generic benchmarking process is shown in Figure 1.1.

The generic benchmarking process makes several important points that will help early understanding of the process. First, benchmarking can be divided into two parts, practices and metrics. Practices are defined as the methods that are used; metrics are the quantified effect of installing the practices. Each can be investigated by the process. The tendency is for managers to work to determine the metrics or quantitative targets to quickly internalize the realization, good or bad, of what the organization will find from benchmarking against the external environment. This is a visceral approach to getting the bad news over quickly.

Benchmarking should be approached on the basis of investigating industry practices first. The metrics that quantify the effect

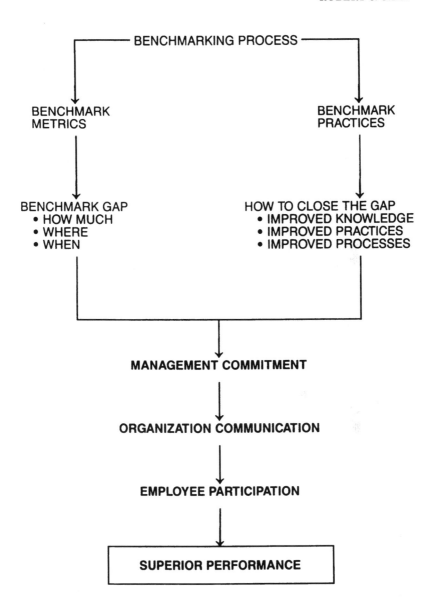

FIGURE 1.1. GENERIC BENCHMARKING PROCESS

of the practices can be obtained or synthesized later. One cannot determine why the gap exists from the metrics alone. Only the practices on which the metric is based will reveal why. The reverse is not always possible, and it could mislead or defeat the purpose of benchmarking.

Benchmarking is an understanding of practices. Once they are understood they can be quantified to show their numeric effect. Perhaps more important, once a metric is determined it will immediately beg the question "why?" Benchmarking is on soundest ground to have the practices understood to answer the question "why" up front. The contribution to the credibility of the findings is immeasurable.

The final point is that the benchmarking process and the benchmark findings must be understood by the organization to obtain commitment to take action to change. There are several ways to accomplish this. They will be described later.

Essential to the benchmarking process are both carefully designed communications to the organization and concerted management support. These are critical to such a radical new way of doing business as benchmarking. There is also a definite place for employee involvement in benchmarking. The findings need to be implemented. What better way to do so smoothly than through the efforts of those closest to the work process. They are the most knowledgeable about how to adopt and implement the findings directly or adapt them to the work conditions.

The sum of these major actions is what leads to superior performance.

Historical Perspective

The chronology of benchmarking mentioned here is that of Xerox Corporation. Xerox was fortunate to have discovered and applied benchmarking early in its drive to combat competition. It could just as well have been that of any other major industrial firm. The experience of Xerox, however, illustrates the need for and the promise of benchmarking.

In 1979, Xerox initiated a process called competitive benchmarking. Benchmarking was first started in Xerox Manufacturing Operations to examine its unit manufacturing costs. Selected product comparisons were made. Operating capabilities and features of competing copying machines were compared and mechanical components torn down for analysis. These early stages of benchmarking were called product quality and feature comparisons.

Comprehensive benchmarking was formalized with the analysis of copiers produced by the Xerox Japanese affiliate, Fuji-Xerox, and later other Japanese manufactured machines. These investigations confirmed the substantially higher U.S. manufacturing costs. When the manufacturing cost was completely analyzed it revealed that competitors were selling machines for what it cost Xerox to make them. U.S. manufacturing quickly shifted to adopt these externally set benchmark targets to drive its business plans.

Because of manufacturing's success in identifying competitor's new processes, new manufacturing components, and costs of manufacturing, senior management directed that benchmarking be performed by all business units and cost centers. At first only a few of the operating units used benchmarking, but by 1981 it was adopted as a corporate-wide effort. At the 1983 annual meeting of shareholders the chief operating officer announced that his number one priority was to achieve leadership through quality. Benchmarking was one of the three components of that effort. Benchmarking, along with employee involvement and the quality process, was seen as central to achieving quality in all products and processes. Benchmarking was visualized as the process of understanding customer requirements, and employee involvement was viewed as the process by which benchmarking would be implemented.

Prior to benchmarking, most unit cost and other targets for asset management and customer satisfaction were set internally by using standard budgeting procedures with adjustments for some assumed level of productivity and judgments about what would satisfy customer needs. This process was essentially a projection of past practices into the future. There was little concentration on targets established by the marketplace or by leadership firms with superior functional practices.

Most nonmanufacturing operations before 1981 made comparisons primarily with other internal operations. For example, managers compared the productivity of different regional distribution centers, or per pound transportation costs between regions. When directed to perform benchmarking, after-sale support functions — maintenance, repair service, distribution, invoicing, and collection — found it difficult to identify the analog to the successful product analyses performed in the benchmarking activities of manufacturing. That is to say, there was no machine or physical product to tear down. Therefore, these functions, as well as others, came to recognize that their product was incorporated and delivered through a process. The process was seen as that which needed to be detailed and later compared with the external environment. This later comparison would reveal methods and practice differences which could then be used to determine the benchmark.

Competitors' processes were therefore looked at operation-by-operation and step-by-step. In logistics, for example, that meant deciding on the major deliverables for transportation, warehousing, inventory management, and other processes. These were then compared to competitor functions to determine their key methods and practices. In the service organization the practices of dealers were examined; in the invoicing operations the practices of banks were investigated; in order entry the electronic transmission of orders from drugstores was considered.

While these early nonmanufacturing benchmarking efforts against direct product competitors were partially successful, it became clear that focusing on competitors' practices only could divert attention from the ultimate purpose; that is, superiority in each business function and, therefore, in the marketplace. Benchmarking solely against competitors may also uncover practices that are not optimal and not worthy of emulation. In addition, competitive benchmarking may lead to meeting the competitor's position, but it will not lead to creating practices superior to those of the competition. When these shortcomings are coupled with the obvious fact that getting information about competitors is difficult, other methods of benchmarking need to be pursued. This realization has led to the understanding that there are several ways to benchmark and that they each have their usefulness. What is fundamental is recognizing that benchmarking involves uncovering best practices wherever they exist.

Managerial Perspective

In their continuing search for greater effectiveness, organizations have compared both overall performance and individual unit performance with that of others for many years. Comparisons are made most frequently within a company. These inward orientations tend to reinforce feelings of superiority and foster not-invented-here excuses. Comparisons with outsiders, however, may expose best industry practices and encourage the adoption of those practices. The practice of comparing performance between organizations, referred to as benchmarking, is a disciplined search for and establishment of a standard to which internal operations can be compared.

Benchmarking as discussed here is industrial research or intelligence gathering that allows a manager to compare his or her function's performance to the performance of the same function in other companies. Benchmarking identifies those management processes, practices, and methods the function or cost center would use if it existed in a competitive environment. Benchmarking is an indicator of what a business function's performance should or could be.

Although benchmarking should be an ongoing, continuous process, it is often only initiated when a business is losing market share, when profit levels are declining, or when customer dissatisfaction is high. This often happens because when a business is not in danger, there can be disincentives to improve operating costs and profits. Internal performance as opposed to competitive gain may be stressed to satisfy personal goals and ambitions. Rapid sales growth can mask inadequate performance in functions of the business.

Cost centers by their very nature leave a motivational void. They buffer the function from competition. Further, when performance to budget is stressed, time is often spent arguing about the size of the budget, not stressing improved performance. If profit generation was stressed, time would be spent generating revenue, controlling expenses, and anticipating the competitive environment. Benchmarking is the only way to overcome these deficiencies and force individual business functions to constantly test their ability to be competitive and profitable as measured by the external environment.

In benchmarking the manager's goal is to identify those companies, regardless of industry, which demonstrate superior performance in functions to be benchmarked so that their practices, processes, and methods can be studied and documented. A well-executed benchmarking investigation can provide a manager with detailed information about the best functional practices in the industry. These practices can then be used or modified to establish a long-term competitive advantage in the marketplace.

Benchmarking can benefit a company in several ways:

- It enables the best practices from any industry to be creatively incorporated into the processes of the benchmarked function.
- It can provide stimulation and motivation to the professionals whose creativity is required to perform and implement benchmark findings.
- Benchmarking breaks down ingrained reluctance of operations to change. It has been found that people are more receptive to new ideas and their creative adoption when those ideas did not necessarily originate in their own industry.
- Benchmarking may also identify a technological breakthrough that would not have been recognized, and thus not applied, in one's own industry for some time to come, such as bar coding, originally adopted and proven in the grocery industry. In these

9

instances it is more important to uncover the industry best practices than to concentrate on obtaining comparative cost data. The business unit can determine for itself what cost levels could be achieved if it incorporated the benchmark practices in its own operations.

- Finally, those involved in the benchmarking process often find their professional contacts and interactions from benchmarking are invaluable for future professional growth. It permits the individuals to broaden their background and experience. It makes them more useful to the organization in future assignments.

Benchmarking Defined

There are several bases on which to define benchmarking as an activity. Benchmarking has a formal definition which has wide application to all business functions. Webster's definition is also informative. Perhaps even more important is the need for a working definition.

Formal Definition

The formal definition was derived from experience and successes of the earliest days of applying benchmarking techniques in the manufacturing area:

Benchmarking is the continuous process of measuring products, services, and practices against the toughest competitors or those companies recognized as industry leaders. (David T. Kearns, chief executive officer, Xerox Corporation)

There are several considerations in this definition requiring further description.

Continuous process. Benchmarking is a self-improvement and management process that must be continuous to be effective. It cannot be performed once and disregarded thereafter on the belief that the task is done. It must be a continuous process because industry practices constantly change. Industry leaders constantly get stronger. Practices must be continually monitored to ensure that the best of them are uncovered. Only those firms that pursue benchmarking with discipline will successfully achieve superior performance. In an environment of constant change complacency is fatal.

Measuring. The term benchmarking implies measurement. Measurement can be accomplished in two forms. The internal and external practices can be compared and a statement of significant differences can be documented. This is a word statement measurement of the industry best practices that must be implemented to achieve superiority, although qualitative in nature. It describes the opportunity for change to best practices.

The practices can be quantified to show an analytical measurement of the gap between practices. It quantifies the size of the opportunity. This metric is often the single-minded measurement that most managers want. While it is important and traditional to strive to obtain analytically derived benchmark metrics, it will become apparent that both must be pursued. Practices on which the metrics are based should be pursued first. Benchmarking is not just an investigation of the metrics of the external business function, but an investigation to determine what practices are being used to ensure effectiveness and eventually superiority and which practices achieve the metrics. Benchmarking is not just a study of competition but a process of determining the effectiveness of industry leaders by measuring their results.

Products, services, and practices. Benchmarking can be applied to all facets of a business. It can be applied to the basic products and services. It can be applied to the processes that go into manufacturing those products. It can be applied to all process practices and methods that are in support of getting those products and services effectively to customers and meeting their needs. Benchmarking goes beyond the traditional competitive analysis to not only reveal what the industry best practices are, but to also obtain a clear understanding of how best practices are used.

It will be the view here that most business activities can be analyzed as processes. Most business activities have a beginning, an end, and a main activity. There is an output from the process that is what the next customer wants, whether that customer is internal or an external, end user or consumer of the output or product. A study of business processes and their methods and practices will be the main objective of the benchmarking approach.

Companies renowned as industry leaders. Benchmarking should not be aimed solely at direct product competitors. In fact it could be a mistake to do so since they may have practices that are less than desirable. Benchmarking should be directed at those firms and business functions within firms that are recognized as the best or as industry leaders, such as banks for error-free document processing. The company serving as a benchmark partner is not always obvious. Careful investigation is needed to determine which firms to seek as benchmarking partners and why. Fortunately there are ways to uncover who and why they should be chosen.

In the formal sense benchmarking is an ongoing investigation and learning experience that ensures that best industry practices are uncovered, analyzed, adopted, and implemented. It focuses on what best practices are available. It ensures an understanding of how they are performed. And finally, it determines the worth of the practices or how well they are performed.

Webster's Definition

The Webster's dictionary definition is also informative. It defines a benchmark as:

> *A surveyor's mark. . .of previously determined* position *. . .and used as a reference point. . .standard by which something can be measured or judged.*

Both definitions serve to reinforce the benchmark as being a standard for the comparison of other objects or activities. It is a reference point from which others are to be measured.

Outside of land surveying where a benchmark is well understood and accepted, there is only one other common use of the term. The computer industry has used the term to mean a standard process for measuring the performance capabilities of software and hardware systems from various vendors. The standard then serves as a basis of choice between the alternative offerings, each of which can have different features and functions, but meet the overall requirements by a different mix of capabilities.

Benchmarking used in the dictionary sense serves as a standard, but one which may change over time to reflect the real conditions of the business world, namely that business practices must change over time to remain competitive.

A Working Definition

The definition of benchmarking, as seen from the perspective of one who has been involved in the process over a number of years and exercised the process many times, incorporates the previous definitions. But it goes beyond to emphasize some important considerations not included in these definitions. The working definition preferred for benchmarking is:

> *Benchmarking is the search for industry best practices that lead to superior performance.*

This definition is preferred because it is understandable by operationally oriented business units and functions. If they know their operations thoroughly, then the search to ensure that the best of proven practices are incorporated is a clear objective. The definition covers all possible business endeavors whether a product, service, or support process. It is not necessary to include them by specific reference.

The focus is on practices. It is only the change of current practices or methods of performing the business processes that overall effectiveness will be achieved. It stresses practices and the understanding of practices before deriving a benchmarking metric. Benchmarking metrics are seen as a result of understanding best practices, not something that can be quantified first and understood later.

The definition concentrates on achieving superior performance. In this regard it pursues *dantotsu,* the best of the best practices, best of class, or best of breed. That is, those best practices that are to be pursued regardless of where they exist — in one's own company, industry, or outside one's industry. It is only this view that will ensure superiority rather than parity.

The definition is proactive. It is a positive endeavor. It is one calculated to obtain cooperation of benchmarking partners. There should be few professionals who would object to constantly seeking best practices. There should be a constant sharing of ideas and debating about how the industry is going to constantly improve itself. This will only occur if the search is open and seen as benefiting both benchmark partners.

Benchmarking should be approached on a partnership basis in which both parties should expect to gain from the information sharing. The discussion of practices and methods, especially among noncompetitors, can only result in both parties gaining from the investigation and discussions. Even competitors can gain in discussions that appropriately skirt proprietary and sensitive topics. The concentration solely on best practices permits that objective to be achieved.

Benchmarking as a term should motivate managers because it is a positive activity, perceived as a mechanism for improving operations to proactively search for best practices. It will be only through the test of finding the best of the best in industry that any manager will be able to justify his or her own operation and assure that he or she has performed to the ultimate standard.

Benchmarking is the most credible of all justifications for operations. There can be little argument about a manager's position if he or she has sought the best in industry and incorporated it in his or her plans and processes.

What Is Benchmarking?

There should be some understanding of what benchmarking is and is not, and its relationship to target setting. There are many misconceptions of what benchmarking is and these should be clearly understood and reinforced. What benchmarking is not should be quickly dispelled. Likewise, since benchmarking involves setting new directions, its relationship to targets should be understood also. These should give a better understanding of where benchmarking fits into the overall planning scheme.

What it Is, What it Is Not

Benchmarking is not a mechanism for determining resource reductions. While that may occur because many operations do not emulate best industry practices, it does not necessarily mean a reduction. Resources will be redeployed to the most effective way of supporting customer requirements and obtaining customer satisfaction as a result of benchmarking activities. It may be that benchmarking will require a resource increase, both people and spending, as a result of more correctly determining true customer satisfaction levels and needs from benchmarking activities.

Benchmarking is not a panacea or program. It must be an ongoing management process that requires constant updating — the collection and sifting of external best practices and performance into the decision making and communications functions at all levels of the business. Benchmarking must have a structured methodology to ensure successful completion of thorough and accurate investigations. However, it must be flexible to incorporate new and innovative ways of assembling difficult-to-obtain information. The benchmarking process steps can be applied repetitively, yet be adaptable. The benchmarking process must keep those conducting the studies aware of new avenues of approach and information sources while accomplishing the basic task.

Benchmarking is not a cookbook process that requires only looking up ingredients and using them for success. Benchmarking is a discovery process and a learning experience. It requires observing what the best practices are and projecting what performance should be in the future. Through it, information can be gathered that will permit setting performance goals which are realistic in the context of the external business environment by ensuring that best, feasible, proven practices are incorporated into business operations.

Benchmarking is not a fad, but a winning business strategy. It assists managers in identifying practices that can adapted to build winning, credible, defensible plans and strategies, and complement new initiatives to achieve the highest performance goals — namely, superior performance.

Benchmarking is a new way of doing business. It forces an external view to ensure correctness of objective setting. It is a new management approach. It forces constant testing of internal actions against external standards of industry practices. It promotes teamwork by directing attention on business practices to remain competitive rather than personal, individual interest. It removes the subjectivity from decision making.

Benchmarking and Targets

Benchmarking is basically an objective-setting process. Benchmarks, when best practices are translated into operational units of measure, are a projection of a future state or endpoint. In that regard their achievement may take a number of years to attain. The benchmarks may most importantly indicate the direction that must be pursued rather than specific operationally quantifiable metrics that are immediately achievable. A benchmarking study may indicate that costs must be reduced and customer satisfaction levels increased or return on assets increased. In addition, the concentration on best practices supports the general direction that must be pursued with specific insights into how the benchmarks can or should be attained. The conversion of benchmarks to operational targets translates the long-term actions into specifics.

Targets are more precise although their quantification should be based on achievement of a benchmark. Furthermore, a target incorporates in it what realistically can be accomplished within a given time frame, usually one yearly budget cycle or business plan horizon. Considerations of available resources, business priorities, and other operational considerations convert benchmark findings to a target, yet steadily show progress toward benchmark practices and metrics. The significant difference between a complete benchmark definition and a target is that a carefully conducted benchmark investigation will not only show what the benchmark metric is but also how it will be achieved.

Key Process Steps

The benchmarking process is displayed in Figure 1.2. The individual steps will be covered in more detail in later chapters. The L. L. Bean case study in Chapters 3 through 12 takes readers through each step in a real-life application. The key ways of conducting a benchmarking investigation through to successful conclusion will also be detailed.

It is important, however, to have a general understanding of the generic phases and some understanding of their rationale. The benchmarking process consists of five phases. The process starts with a planning phase and proceeds through analysis, integration, action, and finally maturity.

Planning Phase

The objective of this phase is to plan for the benchmarking investigations. The essential steps are those of any plan development — what, who, and how.

What is to be benchmarked? Every function of a business has or delivers a product. The product is the output of the business process of the function, whether a physical good, an order, a shipment, an invoice, a service, or a report. Benchmarking is appropriate for these and all other outputs. The products therefore must first be determined.

To whom or what will we compare? There are business to business, direct product competitors. These are certainly prime candidates to benchmark. But they are not enough. Benchmarking must be conducted against leadership companies and business functions regardless of where they exist. Only in this fashion will superiority be ensured.

How will the data be collected? There is no one way to conduct benchmarking investigations. There is a process. There are an infinite variety of ways to obtain required data, and most data are readily and publicly available. A certain level of inquisitiveness and ingenuity is required, but a combination of methods that best meets the study needs will most often be productive. Sources of information are limited only by one's imagination.

What will be important is to recognize that benchmarking is a process not only to derive quantifiable metric goals and targets but more importantly to investigate and document those best industry practices which permit achievement of the goals and targets. A benchmarking study should concentrate on practices and methods. Their effect can always be quantified. (See the L. L. Bean case study in Chapters 3 through 5.)

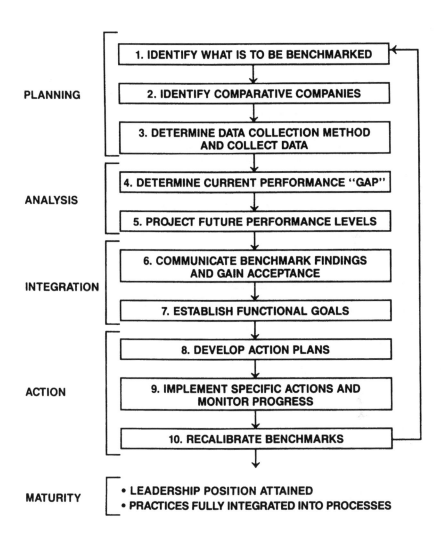

FIGURE 1.2. BENCHMARKING PROCESS STEPS

Analysis Phase

After determining what, how, and who is to be benchmarked, actual data gathering and analysis must be accomplished.

The analysis phase must involve a careful understanding of current process practices as well as those of benchmarking partners. The benchmarking process is, after all, a comparative analysis. What is desired is an understanding of internal performance on which to assess strengths and weaknesses. Is the benchmarking partner better? Why are they better? By how much? What best practices are being used now or anticipated? How can their practices be incorporated or adapted for implementation?

Answers to these questions will be the dimensions of any performance gap: negative, positive, or parity. The gap provides an objective basis on which to act — to close the gap or capitalize on a positive one. The gap, however, is a projection of performance and therefore will be one which changes as industry practices change. What is needed is not only an understanding of today's practices but where performance will be in the future. It is important that benchmarking be a continuing process so that performance is constantly recalibrated to ensure superiority. (See the L. L. Bean case study in Chapters 6 and 7.)

Integration

Integration is the process of using benchmark findings to set operational targets for change. It involves careful planning to incorporate new practices in the operation and to ensure benchmark findings are incorporated in all formal planning processes.

The first step is to gain operational and management acceptance of benchmark findings. Findings must be clearly and convincingly demonstrated as being correct and based on substantive data. Credible data can be supported by deriving data and information from several sources to support the findings. Based on the findings action plans can then be developed.

Benchmark findings must be communicated to all organizational levels to obtain support, commitment, and ownership. This essential step can usually be accomplished through a variety of communications approaches. The key to the process will be the conversion of benchmark findings into a statement of operational principles to which the organization can subscribe and by which actions for change will be judged. These principles place the organization on notice that they are the rules by which the organization will improve itself to meet customer needs and eventually to attain superiority. (See the L. L. Bean case study in Chapters 8 and 9.)

Action

Benchmarking findings and operational principles based on them must be converted to action. They must be converted to specific implementation actions and a periodic measurement and assessment of achievement must be put in place. People who actually perform the work tasks are most capable of determining how the findings can be incorporated into the work process. Their creative talents should be used to perform this essential step.

In addition, any plan for change should also contain milestones for updating the benchmark findings themselves, since the external practices are constantly changing. Therefore provision should be made for recalibration. Also, an ongoing reporting mechanism is needed. Progress toward benchmark findings must be reported to all employees. This feedback is especially necessary to those who assist with the implementation. They will want to know how they are doing. (See the L. L. Bean case study in Chapters 10 and 11.)

Maturity

Maturity will be reached when best industry practices are incorporated in all business processes, thus ensuring superiority. Superiority can be tested in several ways. In some instances services are sold to external customers in addition to serving the internal customer. If the now-changed process were to be made available to others would a knowledgeable businessperson prefer it? That becomes a powerful confirmation of a benchmark. Needless to say if other companies benchmark your own internal operations that also would be confirmation.

Maturity also is achieved when it becomes an ongoing, essential, and self-initiated facet of the management process. It becomes institutionalized. It is done at all appropriate levels of the organization, and not by specialists. While knowledgeable specialists may exist to consult on the most productive approaches for benchmarking, only when the focus on external practices becomes the responsibility of the entire organization will benchmarking truly have achieved its objectives of ensuring superiority through incorporation of best industry practices.

How to Get Started in Benchmarking

Those who initially are exposed to the subject of benchmarking often ask how they can get started. The author's preferred way is to have them read this text completely and implement and practice the 10-step benchmarking process. But for those who cannot spare the initial time and want a quick primer, Quick Reference Guide 1.1 is provided. It is broken down into two sections. The first section covers initial and somewhat general information gathering, but sound steps in the investigation process. The second section discusses information gathering in the unit's own functional area or area of interest.

To get started in the process of benchmarking there are some proven first steps. One must determine what to benchmark, assuming there is agreement that the next steps will be directed to gathering available data. This may come from library research and contacting internal personnel and sources. Those shown in Quick Reference Guide 1.1 are easily initiated approaches and should be done early in any benchmarking investigation. The guide gives initial target areas to turn to in these starting steps.

The focus of the second area of investigation is more external and on a specific function or area of interest. The information comes from periodicals about the function, associations that represent the function, service bureaus that offer services surrounding the function, and consultants who are knowledgeable about the function. Initial contact with these external sources starts the process of ensuring that all available public information is covered and relevant information is documented. These require a higher level of effort to get underway and should be approached based on sound planning and careful understanding of the scope of the investigations. It also includes two unique sources: industry experts and software vendors. The reason for these will become evident with descriptions in later chapters.

While the guide is not to be inclusive, it does give quick reference to the initial steps found to be productive. A more thorough approach can be tailored following in-depth study of the text and time to define a careful benchmarking investigation. Starting with the guide will provide a faster start and nothing will be lost in the process. The guide is, however, only a guide. It cannot substitute for exercising the full 10-step process. *Caveat emptor* benchmarkers!

Summary

Successful benchmarking is based on achieving several important factors and management behaviors. It requires management commitment to make tough decisions to base operational goals on a concerted view of the external environment. There must be a willingness on the part of those performing benchmarking to learn from others. There needs to be a realization that internal operations cannot always have the best answer for every problem. They can and should learn from others and constantly measure themselves against the best in the industry. This text describes the necessary skills to conduct successful benchmarking activities. Creativity in extending the basic process will enhance what is covered here to achieve truly superior benchmarking results.

Benchmarking is a continuous process of measuring against the best. Goals are based on the benchmark findings to achieve superiority. Progress is measured periodically to update the organization's position toward achieving the benchmarks. Benchmarking results in process practices and measurable goals based on what the best in the industry is doing and is expected to do. The approach contrasts sharply with the rather imprecise, intuitive estimates of what needs to be done to characterize current searches for productivity. Benchmarking is the rational way of ensuring the organization is satisfying customer requirements and will continue to do so as customer requirements change over time. Benchmarking ultimately reflects an attitude to strive for excellence in every business endeavor.

QUICK REFERENCE GUIDE 1.1

HOW TO GET STARTED IN BENCHMARKING

A. Information Sources — Getting Started

- Focus on an Area/Element that Needs to Be Pursued

  Examples:

    1) Order entry
    2) Service dispatching
    3) Warehouse storage

- Contact a Business Library
  - Request a search of information produced in the last three to five years for your topic of interest
  - Library will identify articles/sources from

    1) External reports
    2) Public magazines
    3) Industry journals
    4) Annual reports

- Contact Internal Experts
  - Market research
  - Competitive analysis
  - Functional experts

- Survey Internal Reports/Studies
  - Special studies
  - Surveys
  - Market research

B. Information Sources — Specific/Functional

- Subscribe/Monitor Trade Periodicals

- Professional Associations
  - Newsletters
  - Seminars (especially speakers/tours)
  - Bibliographies
  - Special libraries

QUICK REFERENCE GUIDE 1.1 (CONT.)
HOW TO GET STARTED IN BENCHMARKING

- Service Agencies/Bureaus in the Business Function
  - Ask if they can share anonymous experiences from their client companies

    1) Industry practices or methods
    2) State-of-the-art methods/practices

- Consulting Firms
  - Functional experts
  - Ask if they are aware of particular breakthroughs/ practices in a specific area

- Industry Experts
  - Department heads of noncompetitors
  - Teachers/professors at schools/universities

- Systems Software Development and Hardware Vendors
  - Ask about their experiences working in your functional area

CHAPTER 2
WHY BENCHMARK?

Objectives of Benchmarking

Benefits of Benchmarking
- Meeting customer requirements
- Establishing effective goals and objectives
- True measure of productivity
- Becoming competitive
- Industry best practices

Success Factors

Quick Reference Guide 2.1. Success Indicators for Benchmarking

WHY BENCHMARK?

How to Attain Superior Performance

This chapter covers why benchmarking should be considered and used. There are reasons why one should benchmark and a better understanding of the more important reasons will permit managers to carefully direct their investigations to obtain the full measure of benefits.

This chapter also reviews the objectives or purposes for benchmarking. They are primarily derived from the need to establish more realistic goals and objectives. While there are many benefits to be derived from benchmarking, some tangible and some intangible, the more important tangible benefits of benchmarking are covered. The intangible benefits such as the self-motivating features of benchmarking in its mature phase — which encourages managers and organizations to search for best practices out of their own initiative — are mentioned throughout the text at appropriate points.

There are five more important benefits:
1. More adequately meeting end user customer requirements.
2. Establishing goals based on a concerted view of external conditions.
3. Determining true measures of productivity.
4. Attaining a competitive position.
5. Becoming aware of and searching for industry best practices.

To aid in the proper use of the benchmarking process a set of success factors is also reviewed. They permit measuring the progress toward and achievement of benchmarking benefits.

Benchmarking should have objectives that are clearly understood and agreed to by a functional management team before there is a commitment to supporting benchmarking activities. The agreement will forestall possible misunderstandings about the data and information gathered from investigations and the treatment of the materials afterward. Likewise the benefits to be derived from benchmarking will set expectations on the part of the management team. Preparations for successful use of benchmarking findings can be planned for early. This will aid in the difficult implementation phase when organizations must be prepared for and buy into new, changed practices.

Objectives of Benchmarking

Benchmarking is first a goal-setting process. But, more importantly, it is a means by which the practices needed to reach new goals are discovered and understood. These are probably the most basic and fundamental outputs of benchmarking. Their understanding will be the central theme stressed and reinforced through examples to implant these tenets firmly in the mind of the reader.

Beyond the basic goal-setting objective of benchmarking the motivational worth of benchmarking also is significant. When fully integrated into the responsibilities, work processes, and reward system of the organization, it empowers and encourages the organization to move forward to realistic goals and change existing work practices which otherwise would have to be dictated.

Benchmarking legitimizes goals and targets by basing them on an external orientation. Ownership of and commitment to the benchmark is assured through agreement of the practices on which they are based. Agreement on the practices ensures attainment of the benchmarks. Benchmark findings marshall resources to concentrate on solving basic business practices and basic problems of the business that impede success.

When a cross section of people in the organization, including those from the operational organizations, are involved in the benchmarking process it focuses attention of the entire organization on the correct business goals. It challenges, in a productive, planned fashion, those individuals and organizations to concentrate on what will make operations more successful in the marketplace and eventually attain superior performance.

Benefits of Benchmarking

There are many ways to describe the benefits to be derived from benchmarking. In the succeeding chapters, examples from the logistics function and other business functions such as order entry and billing, and other industries as well as case studies and quick reference guides will describe many. The reader will be able to extrapolate these examples to others that they may see from their own unique functional viewpoint. The basic benefits are derived from meeting customer requirements, establishing goals, measuring true productivity, becoming competitive, and ensuring that best industry practices are included in work processes. These are each discussed in the next section.

A comparison of the reasons for benchmarking along with a contrast of the results expected with and without this approach is shown in Table 2.1.

While one can debate the adjectives and descriptions used to highlight the differences between using traditional approaches and benchmarking in each of the five categories, it has been the observation of the author that the statements are more correct than not. The further understanding of benchmarking and its application covered in later chapters should confirm these observations in the mind of the reader. The comparisons should give the middle management ranks of most large organizations no small amount of anxiety over what they truly have accomplished in attempting to become productive and attain a leadership position.

Meeting Customer Requirements

It is helpful to think about meeting customer requirements by considering a business function as an overall process made up of many smaller processes. A function's effort to satisfy the end user's customer requirements is made up of many distinct internal processes. Each individual process should satisfy its customer's requirements until ultimately the external customer is satisfied. The typical individual work process, whether delivering a physical product or service, to a customer is composed of three basic steps: There is an input, a processing step, and an output. The output, either product or service, is expected to satisfy the process' next customer in line and eventually the end user's requirements. That output, for example, can vary from providing the features and functions of an office product, to the options on an automobile, to how customer inquiries and complaints are handled. The end result is that the output is something of value and meets the needs of the next customer in the process or those of the ultimate consumer.

If the focus of the organization were strictly internal it would attempt to rely on its own perceptions of what the customer wants. This internal focus will not develop practices and strategies that will meet the needs of the end user customer. Only an external focus will assure that customer requirements are determined, documented, and eventually implemented. Benchmarking is the process for uncovering what those needs are by searching out best industry practices.

If best industry practices are uncovered, by definition they are a statement of more adequately meeting customer requirements. This is because one criterion of a widely accepted practice is that it exists because it serves a need, a customer need. Therefore, understanding the work practices of industry leaders results in close conformance to what customers want or require. Under-

29

WITHOUT BENCHMARKING	WITH BENCHMARKING
Defining customer requirements	
Based on history or gut feel	Market reality
Perception	Objective evaluation
Low fit	High conformance
Establishing effective goals and objectives	
Lacking external focus	Credible, unarguable
Reactive	Proactive
Lagging industry	Industry leading
Developing true measures of productivity	
Pursuing pet projects	Solving real problems
Strengths and weaknesses not understood	Understanding outputs
Route of least resistance	Based on best industry practices
Becoming competitive	
Internally focused	Concrete understanding of competition
Evolutionary change	New ideas of proven practices and technology
Low commitment	High commitment
Industry best practices	
Not invented here	Proactive search for change
Few solutions	Many options
Average of industry progress	Business practice breakthrough
Frantic catchup activity	Superior performance

TABLE 2.1. KEY REASONS FOR BENCHMARKING AND CONTRASTING RESULTS

standing the work process outputs and benchmarking them against the best in the industry reveals true customer requirements. The best practices would not exist if they were not preferred by users or consumers.

Benchmarking confirms the belief that there is a need for change. It does this in the context of seeking to satisfy customer requirements in order to remain competitive — and in order to do it right the first time.

Establishing Effective Goals and Objectives

Benchmarking is an alternative to the traditional way of establishing goals and objectives. It is believed to be the most effective way to accomplish those results. While goal setting is an ongoing evaluation process, the concentration on the external environment as the basis for those goals is the only effective way of accomplishing that task.

There are other goal-setting procedures. Extrapolation of past trends and practices is one common approach. But these methods have generally failed managers because the external environment was changing at a pace significantly faster than projected. The competitive marketplace of the past few years has proven the risks of prior goal-setting exercises.

Benchmarking forces a continual focus on the external environment. It also forces that focus at all levels of an organization — not just the strategic direction but at the work process level. Therefore, all functions and work units are attuned to the external world on a timely basis. Not only does benchmarking assure this focus, but it also constantly validates and adds credibility to the goal-setting process by its concentration on the best in the industry.

There is no more credible basis for goals than their being based on the industry best. This simple basis for goal setting ends all internal target debates. If goals are based on the industry best, not only do they meet customer needs, they are also unarguable.

One example is embodied in the inventory management measurement metric or statistic used in selected industries. There are essentially two ways to state industry performance in a summary statistic. One is months of forward supply. It is the number of months of inventory deemed necessary to prevent risks of future forecast demand errors. It is a stockpiling metric. The other metric is inventory turns. Turns are the number of times an inventory must be completely replenished to meet customer usage. It is a velocity metric.

The goals and objectives of the industry, and therefore its

associated practices, can be known by which metric is used. A months of supply metric is primarily used by industries not pressed by customer needs. Stockpiling usually results from a lack of focus on the causals of the inventory amount and profile. A turns metric however reflects velocity of customer needs. It incorporates an explicit requirement that all components of inventory be stocked by a conscious matching to customer needs to attain high turns.

The inventory effectiveness can be judged solely on the metric selected without knowing the specific measurement data because the alternative metrics drive different performance levels. If the benchmark findings reveal that the industry practice is to use turns rather than months of supply, that in itself reveals a great deal about the efficiency of the industry. It also ensures more realistically meeting customers needs.

There are behaviorial benefits to using benchmarking for goal setting also. If performance levels are driven to those of the functional leader in a field or profession, then the entire energies of the organization must be turned to that single focus. The result is that a benchmarking process will also promote directly, or as a by-product, the effective teamwork of the organization by concentrating on external practices. The reviews, sifting of findings, debate about applicability, and modification for implementation is a healthy process which brings all viewpoints to concentrate on what's best for the business and eventually on a consensus of what should be done. While the review process may be lengthy, the resulting commitment to common, unambiguous, credible goals makes implementation substantially easier.

Benchmarking confirms what you want and need to change. It does this in the context of determining the right goals, objectives, and measurements on which to judge performance.

True Measure of Productivity

True productivity is derived when workers at all levels are solving real problems of the business. That is, they are concentrating on understanding their outputs and how these satisfy the next in line users or ultimate customer. The process comes from an appreciation of what the organization does well and an understanding of how other organizations do those things not done well better. Benchmarking is the process for obtaining these basic understandings and converting them to action which results in true productivity.

Benchmarking is a proactive way, therefore, of affecting change. The organization understands its strengths, recognizes its weaknesses, and knows how the external world performs those practices which require modification better. Benchmarking restores ownership at the source for goals that ensure customer satisfaction, including quality, cost, and timeliness.

Becoming Competitive

Benchmarking provides an increased awareness of products, costs, markets, and processes that ensure that effective plans are developed to deliver them. It is the route to competitive advantage. The constant external focus and testing of ideas, methods, practices, and their incorporation in plans and programs for their delivery is the single approach for ensuring long-term competitiveness. To become competitive one must understand the competition. The focus on the direct product competitors is one focus of benchmarking. Benchmarking in its most thorough application goes beyond looking solely at competitors and uncovers the best practices wherever they may exist, in any industry. The canvassing for proven practices and technology across a wide spectrum of industries is what brings ultimate competitiveness. A competitive leadership position means that process strengths have been capitalized on wherever they have been practiced.

The benchmarking process by its nature challenges the current way of doing business by bringing in new ideas and practices from the outside. These new practices are used to build functional strategies and business plans from knowledge gained in benchmarking. They are later converted into commitments to resources and action plans in the budgeting cycle. This process of external view, findings, strategy formulation, and plan commitment is what ultimately results in becoming competitive.

Often U.S. industry has not changed until the pain of competition was felt severely. This approach has proven disastrous. By that time either life-threatening surgery had to be performed, or the lead time to change never permitted catching up to the competitor's pace. Benchmarking helps recognize the pain before it occurs.

The principal way benchmarking does this is by basing a pro forma, future, desired state picture on benchmark findings of industry best practices. Benchmarking is the basis for developing a picture of how the operation should look after the change to attain superior competitive performance. In this fashion it is a powerful way to marshall the energies of the operation to become competitive and to exceed the competition.

Is this useful?

Industry Best Practices

Benchmarking processes bring about an awareness of the external world. Its greatest value is in learning about practices used by others that are better than those currently in place internally. The outside findings are used directly or used to modify, improve, or adapt external practices to provide useful internal change and improve efficiency and effectiveness. It is a process to find a better way, rather than an attempt to reinvent the proverbial wheel.

The concentration on identifying industry best practices also breaks down the not-invented-here syndrome, since finding proven best industry practices already in operation effectively negates an argument of not being useable. Benchmarking effectively develops new ways of doing business and challenges the business-as-usual myopia. It is a structured way to study other organizations and to adopt industry best practices to complement internal operations and incorporate creative new ideas. The combination of internal review of operations, structured benchmarking, creative innovation, and business judgment all lead to improved strategies and satisfied customers.

The concentration on uncovering industry best practices through benchmarking is the sure route to superior performance. By not focusing benchmarking efforts solely on one's own industry, there is a greater chance of a breakthrough in business practices and implementation of proven technologies used by the best of the best.

Success Factors

What makes benchmarking successful is both the use of the benchmarking process to its fullest extent and the support of management. In fact, management involvement is essential to benchmarking. This is because benchmarking directly affects the goals to which management commits.

Management involvement is essential when it comes to ensuring that requirements are understood for the benchmarking outputs. Action plans later based on these outputs will have higher probability of success. This requires participation by management teams on the basic plan for benchmarking, and progress reviews at which alternative approaches to accomplish the investigations are debated. In addition, assistance in getting access to needed information and resources to complete the benchmarking task are essential. Not only does management need to understand the benchmarking plan and potential output, but also to remove barriers and obstacles to success.

The management team must be kept informed and have an opportunity to discuss the results of benchmarking investigations before acceptance of the benchmark findings. In addition, through this process management says that it appreciates and accepts new and creative approaches to accomplishing the work outputs.

The accomplishment of these basic management responsibilities is as crucial to the successful accomplishment of benchmarking as any other endeavor, and probably more so since benchmarking will initially be new to the organization. Careful attention at this embryonic stage is essential.

Factors for successful benchmarking are outlined in Quick Reference Guide 2.1.

It is important to understand what makes benchmarking successful. In this fashion the practices that successfully support benchmarking can be stressed and acted on to ensure they are in place early and detractors can be hedged or eliminated. In this way the benchmarking investigations will be conducted in the most positive environment and success will be enhanced.

There is no more crucial indication of potential for success in benchmarking than strong, concerted, and interested support by management. This sends a clear signal to the organization that benchmarking is worthwhile. Others had best take notice. Commitment by management can take many forms, from reviewing the plans for benchmarking to making benchmarking a specific part of the improvement plans for the organization. With these action plans management sets the expectation levels for benchmarking throughout the organization and legitimizes it. These actions are all in addition to the direct benefits of benchmarking, namely practicing the 10-step process and uncovering best practices.

Prior to any benchmarking investigation, there should be a clear understanding of the many work processes in the function. Management's interest in reviewing these, much like the process czar mentioned in Chapter 11 (Step 9), is an indication of interest in the basic processes of the operation and the need to improve them throughout. Inquisitiveness by management as to why practices and methods are what they are and questions about how they can be improved sets the stage for benchmarking. Obviously, questions about how others perform is the kind of questioning on which benchmarking is based.

But this is not enough. It is one thing to understand current practices and question how others perform in similar circumstances; it is another to take action on the benchmark findings. The willingness to change and adapt is perhaps the final act of commitment and support by management. It should encourage the eventual institutionalization of benchmarking and indicate to the organization that this is how work will be performed and how the achievements of the organization be measured in the future.

Management must also take the lead in impressing on the organization that competition is constantly improving and it is necessary to get out in front to stay ahead. This will not be a popular position to champion for it means continuing reliance on change and search for best practices, but it is a reality of the marketplace confirmed through benchmarking. The commitment to improvement must be to watch the productivity improvement pace of the industry as well as to close the now-identified benchmark gap. A further level of effort, that is "shooting ahead of the duck," is required to outdistance the competition.

It has already been stressed that benchmarking is based on focusing on industry best practices and approaching benchmarking investigations on a shared basis. Benchmarking partners should be those leading companies in the industry or functionally best operations that are recognized leaders. The successful approach will be to derive benchmarking data and information from these sources using the 10-step benchmarking process.

Beyond these steps, which are covered in this book, an openness to new ideas, creativity in finding information, and innovativeness in applying the benchmarking findings to current processes must exist to derive the full measure of opportunity from benchmarking. The benchmarking effort cannot be a one-time event. It must be continuous over a somewhat extended time period to see the results. Eventually, as the organization becomes more adapted to the process, it will be performed at all levels of the organization and at the initiative of the affected individuals. They will actively seek external information on which to compare themselves and change their operations. It will no longer have to be programmed, but will happen out of their own initiative. It will become institutionalized in the organization.

QUICK REFERENCE GUIDE 2.1
SUCCESS INDICATORS FOR BENCHMARKING

- An active commitment to benchmarking from management.
- A clear and comprehensive understanding of how one's own work is conducted as a basis for comparison to industry best practices.
- A willingness to change and adapt based on benchmark findings.
- A realization that competition is constantly changing and there is a need to "shoot ahead of the duck."
- A willingness to share information with benchmark partners.
- A focus on benchmarking first on industry best practices and second, on performance metrics.
- The concentration of leading companies in the industry or other functionally best operations that are recognized leaders.
- Adherence to the 10-step benchmarking process.
- An openness to new ideas and creativity and innovativeness in their application to existing processes.
- A continuous benchmarking effort.
- The institutionalization of benchmarking.

CHAPTER 3
WHAT TO BENCHMARK
(STEP 1)

Mission Statement
  • Output deliverables
  • Performance measurement
  • Testing the appropriateness of outputs to be benchmarked
  • Level of detail

Understand and Document the Work Process

Selection Criteria

The L. L. Bean Experience

WHAT TO BENCHMARK

Benchmarking Outputs

Identifying what is to be benchmarked, or the benchmarking outputs, is often one of the most difficult steps in the process. However, there is a way to arrive at benchmarking outputs in a logical, well-thought-out manner. This chapter will discuss how to develop what the benchmarking deliverables or outputs should be. They are determined from the basic mission of the organization or business unit and can logically be broken down to the output elements that should be the basis of a benchmarking investigation.

The chapter also will cover how to test the appropriateness of the outputs and the level of detail necessary to ensure a complete and thorough investigation. Key to this approach is the need to define and document adequately one's own operation, process, and methods. This permits the understanding of the differences found through benchmarking external practices. The selection criteria to consider when determining what to benchmark is also covered.

This chapter introduces the first part of a mini case example that is continued at the end of each of the chapters covering the 10-step benchmarking process. The example is that of a benchmarking experience of a Xerox logistics operation with its counterpart at L. L. Bean. The example focuses on the warehousing operation of L. L. Bean and provides a step-by-step example of the rationale for and conduct of a benchmarking study. While the case study concentrates on a logistics example, the analogy to any other business function should be readily apparent to the reader. Many more examples drawn from the logistics function and order processing and fulfillment operation are cited throughout the text to expand on applications of the benchmarking process.

What to Benchmark

The key to determining what should be benchmarked is to identify the product of the business function. The product may not be readily apparent. In a manufacturing operation there is a physical, visible, quantifiable product that is the output. It is whatever is being manufactured or assembled. It can be seen, measured, and compared to other competing products. But what is the product for a function that provides a service? Or for that matter, for one internal function serving another, such as logistics or the billing and collection of invoices? The customers for these functions are not necessarily obvious, much less their outputs.

While the power of benchmarking covered here will be primarily focused on business processes and practices, many other things can be benchmarked. Among them are a physical product produced or a service provided, or the level of customer satisfaction desired. Benchmarking in this sense is used to develop a standard or measure against which to compare. The distinguishing feature of a benchmark is that it is based on best practices found externally. Other candidates for benchmarking are shown in Table 3.1.

The objective here is to identify the products of the function and to do so by also identifying who wants these products. Who are the customers for the function's products?

The Mission Statement

To attack the problem, it is best to start at a high level of evaluation. There are at least two ways to bring greater clarity to functional product or output definition. One is to start at a high

---

Customer Requirements
  Products
  Services

Products Manufactured
  Copiers
  Repair Parts

Services Provided
  Repair Services
  Financing

Critical Success Factors
  Customer Satisfaction Level
  Delivery Service
  Unit Costs
  Asset Utilization

Products Purchased
  Components
  Material Handling Equipment

Processes Used
  Order Entry
  Customer Inquiry/Problem
    Resolution
  Warehouse Fulfillment
  Billing
  Collection

TABLE 3.1. CANDIDATES FOR BENCHMARKING

strategic concept level and cascade down to an individual deliverable. The other is to evaluate a list of questions that may reveal the function's products or problem areas in need of benchmarking.

Usually a function will have a mission statement that summarizes the major purpose of the organization. For a logistics organization that mission statement may look like the one in Table 3.2. It may vary from industry to industry and by product type but it is a statement of the reason for the organization's existence.

From the mission statement can be derived typical deliverables expected by customers of the function. This is the first step in breaking down the initially defined, broad purposes to the specific outputs to be benchmarked. There is no magic in this cascading process, only good mental energy.

In a logistics function typical strategic deliverables are: (1) the level of customer satisfaction expected, (2) the inventory level to be maintained or turns to be attained, and (3) the unit cost or cost level to be achieved. These are the traditional, high-level deliverables that are the bases for managing a logistics function. They are the deliverables that require the managerial trade-offs to satisfy customers, both external and internal. Next, these deliverables must be further subdivided and cascaded to a lower level to further define more specific outputs to be benchmarked. These will be covered by way of example in succeeding tables and figures.

One way to assist this effort is to approach the problem from a different perspective. And that is to pose a set of questions that may reveal current issues facing the function. A set of starter questions is shown in Table 3.3. The objective is not only to ensure that the logical deliverables of the function are benchmarked, but also the current and perceived future problem areas. All of these, products and problem areas, are candidates for benchmarking.

MISSION

To be the logistics operation of choice for the firm's marketing function for product classes A, B, and C by achieving superior levels of customer satisfaction at lower cost and increased inventory turns.

TABLE 3.2. TYPICAL LOGISTICS FUNCTION MISSION STATEMENT

The Output Deliverables

With the mission statement and logical deliverable outputs defined, a solid starting point has been established to further break down the outputs to specific items to be benchmarked. At this point a judgment must be made as to how far and to what detail the output to be benchmarked will be further defined.

The purpose for starting at a high level is that at some point the results of the detailed benchmarking studies must be summarized to show the aggregate effect. The most appropriate way is to display these against major deliverables, but how far to break them down is not quite so clear. Should a deliverable such as unit cost be subdivided into labor expense spending, and further to employee absenteeism per person — and the latter benchmarked?

That is a judgment that can only be determined from knowledge

---

- What is most critical to business success?
  - Customer satisfaction?
  - Inventory turns?
  - Expense to revenue ratio?

- What areas are causing the most trouble?

- What are the major deliverables of this area?
  - Its reason for existence?

- What products are provided to customers?

- What factors are responsible for customer satisfaction?

- What problems have been identified in the operation?

- Where are competitive pressures being felt?

- What performance measurements are being tackled?

- What are the major cost components?

TABLE 3.3.   QUESTIONS THAT MAY INDICATE A NEED
FOR BENCHMARKING OR DEFINE
BENCHMARK OUTPUTS

of the industry, of the function and of the effect of those outputs on cost. With trial and error, a reasonable set of outputs can be defined. They also can be further expanded or contracted as necessary during the benchmarking investigations.

In a logistics function, with distinct product lines that have different customer satisfaction support requirements and network echelon structures, it would be logical to break down the major deliverables by these distinct cost determining drivers. Such a further definition might (1) divide unit cost into four to six measures, depending on the major steps in the delivery process from source to customer, and (2) break the customer satisfaction measures and inventory turns into three to four levels, depending on logical product classes or classes of similar support requirements. Such a breakdown would appear as shown in Table 3.4 and serve to summarize not only the benchmarks but progress toward them as well as a target date for achievement. This latter presentation chart format could also serve as a summary statement for management review purposes. It is one that is derived logically from an accepted mission statement.

Performance Measurement

Are there other approaches to defining detailed deliverables? Certainly! One of the most obvious is what current measurements are incorporated in existing reporting systems. Benchmarking may require development of measures in addition to currently reported metrics. The current measurement system should be a logical start because units of measure and other operating statistics will be well understood already. Any difference between current measures and a benchmark can be judged within the context of experience with current measures to determine the severity of the gap.

The current performance measurements may of themselves directly indicate what should be benchmarked. However, a caution is in order. It is possible that the current measurement system is heavily financially oriented. Not enough of the data and information may reveal operationally stated outputs. It may not, for example, without going to a secondary level of detail, reveal the outputs per man-hour or units per vehicle or cost per pound that are the operational measures that eventually will need to be benchmarked and for which changed methods and practices must be understood and implemented to affect the cost base.

Furthermore, the reporting may not be inclusive enough. What is desired is the ability not only to cascade the outputs from the major deliverables, but also to have the outputs logically and analytically summarize the major deliverables. Deliverables usually go beyond financial measurements alone.

UNIT COST	1983	1984	1985	Benchmark	Benchmark Achievement
PRODUCT LINE "A"					
$/Mile	$1.10	Superiority	Superiority	$1.00-$1.20	Now
$/Delivery	$8.00	$7.60	$7.50	$6.50-$7.50	1986
• "A" Items	$4.70	$3.90	$3.80	$3.50-$4.00	1986
• "B-C" Items	$10.70	Parity	Parity	$9.50-$10.50	1984
PRODUCT LINE "B"					
$/Piece	$3.60	$3.25	Parity	$2.90-$30.00	1985
PRODUCT LINE "C"					
$/Line item	$2.60	$2.40	Parity	$2.20-$2.30	1985
CUSTOMER SATISFACTION LEVEL					
P/L "A," % Faultless Deliveries	NA	NA	NA	NA	NA
P/L "B," % Delivered from First Echelon	85%	Parity	Parity	85-90%	Now
P/L "C," % Delivered Next Day	75%	Parity	Parity	TBD	Now
INVENTORY INVESTMENT					
P/L "A"	NA	NA	NA	NA	NA
P/L "B," Turns	2.2	2.4	2.7	3.4-2.4	1986
P/L "C," Turns	3.2	3.3	3.4	TBD	TBD

NA = Not Applicable/Available
P/L = Product Line

TABLE 3.4. STATEMENT OF BENCHMARK OUTPUTS (SECOND LEVEL OF DELIVERABLE DEFINITION)

Testing the Appropriateness of Outputs to Be Benchmarked

How do we know if the outputs to be benchmarked are appropriate? Outside of the logical cascade and build-up structure a further test can be based on a question asked of each. If a questionnaire was developed with the outputs, and data gathered based on the questionnaire, would logical, useable answers be obtained? Benchmarking by its nature is a comparative process and at some point comparative data will be obtained. Obtaining information is expensive, and the process, whether through questionnaires or other data-gathering vehicles, will need to be tightly reasoned to obtain the data and information in an efficient manner.

More importantly, do the questions asked or the areas of discussion to be explored directly describe the business methods and practices on which the benchmark will be based? Underlying a quantified benchmark is a process, method, or practice that must be understood to later take action to install or modify and have it implemented. Therefore, the questions or outputs stated in question format must stand the test of deriving useable data. Can the data obtained be used at a later date to quantify the effect of installing a new or changed business practice in the current operation?

Furthermore, is there a function, unit, area, or manager ultimately responsible and a customer for the new practice or method change? If an external firm was visited and information obtained about a new practice, who would want to know about it? How to get acceptance of the change will be discussed later, but for the moment, the appropriateness of the outputs to be benchmarked should also stand the scrutiny of whether or not there is a customer for the data and information. Benchmarking investigations should be directed toward someone who can and must take action to implement the change.

Level of Detail

The level of detail for the deliverables breakdown is a matter of judgment — a breakdown low enough to quantify the benefit of the practice change but high enough to summarize the impact to management. A set of outputs that is another level below function deliverable for a logistics operation is shown in Table 3.5. Further detail would be designed and incorporated into a questionnaire, which will be discussed later.

SUMMARY MEASUREMENTS (by commodity or product class, and further significant breakdowns, if desirable)

- Unit cost, example; cost per piece, line item, or order
- Service level, example; percent fill rate from first echelon
- Inventory level, example; inventory turns, or months of forward supply

NETWORK STRUCTURE

- Number of distribution centers
- Location of distribution centers
- Operations performed

PRODUCT CLASS "A" TRANSPORTATION

- Consolidation/redistribution practices
- Delivery operations to customers by volume band
- Service level, inside delivery, or other special delivery functions
- Returns, removal, disposal

PRODUCT CLASS "A" WAREHOUSING

- Use of contract or general commodities carrier and storage at local level
- Number and location of carriers and operating practices
- Packaging/dismantling practices

PRODUCT "B" TRANSPORTATION

- Ability to consolidate with other materials to obtain full truckload quantity shipment
- Unique use of couriers, air freight air carriers, UPS, or other movement for replenishment
- Distribution practices, including use of contract public warehouses and depots

PRODUCT "B" WAREHOUSING

- Material handling practices including conventional, semiautomated, or automatic storage/retrieval systems
- Number and location of field distribution centers, or market located centers
- Type operation — manned, unmanned, emergency order only, or full line supply

REPLENISHMENT PLANNING AND CONTROL

- Service level standards and actual performance by echelon
- Inventory levels by echelon

SYSTEMS

- State-of-the-art systems implemented for order entry, material planning, warehouse control, and transportation
- Key productivity features

TABLE 3.5. MAJOR LOGISTICS BENCHMARKING OUTPUTS AND DATA ELEMENTS DESIRED

Outputs or deliverables should be documented to a level of detail necessary for cost analyses, analyses of key tasks, hand-offs, and measurements. The outputs are actionable by the operation if change is required. Eventually a comfort level for detail will be achieved. More detail can always be defined. The results should be checked to ensure they support summary deliverables.

Still, a further way to identify outputs is to convert the problems, issues, and challenges faced by the functions into problem statements. If the problem statement is then used to develop an Ishikawa cause-and-effect diagram, the problem causes and major cause areas are direct indicators of what should be benchmarked. An Ishikawa diagram also is useful in developing a comprehensive questionnaire. One is shown in Figure 3.1, which was developed for the analysis of return on assets.

The diagram states the problem in the right-hand box. In this case the statement is that there is a need to increase return on assets. The causals are divided into major contributors: the two that are a function of profit margin (management practices and cost reductions) and the two that affect asset turns (network structure and inventory practices). Supporting causals are then listed under each major category; there are a total of 14.

This type of analysis, derived from brainstorming activities to obtain a starting set of causals and later confirmed by factual data gathering, is an excellent method to get a start on not only outputs to benchmark but also the questions and problem areas that form the basis for a questionnaire. The causals become the outputs that require benchmarking.

Understand and Document the Work Process

Before embarking on any benchmarking investigation of process practices it is important to understand and document the function's own internal work process first. This effort should involve documenting the process steps and the practices used as well as defining the critical measurements used.

There are several work process evaluation techniques that can be used which standardize this effort. They analyze a process as having an input, output, and process step. The interrelationships of sequential process steps are rationalized. The resulting analysis readily reveals where measurement is appropriate and what units of measurement are logical.

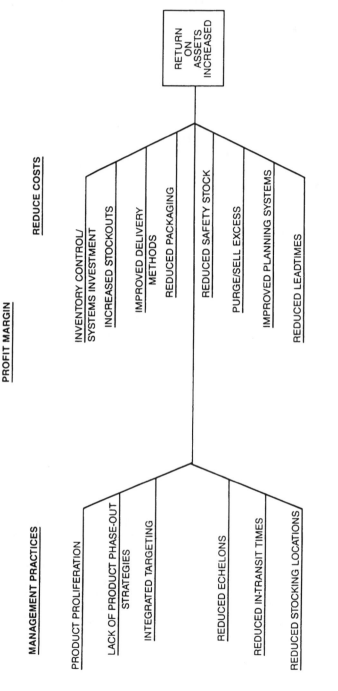

FIGURE 3.1. ISHIKAWA CAUSE-AND-EFFECT DIAGRAM

An important phase of documenting the process beyond thorough understanding of the process steps is determining the unit of measure to be used. The units of measure, expressed as ratios, are the key metrics that the benchmarking investigation will want to uncover for any new industry best practices. Knowing these in advance allows preparation of a questionnaire or plans for a site visit to incorporate them and ensure their documentation. They will be used later on to determine the size of the benchmark gap.

The metrics selected should be the agreed on true indicators of the process performance. They most likely should cover unit cost, customer satisfaction level, and appropriate asset measurements. If measurements are not clear or are difficult to obtain, two alternatives are possible. One, the process practices benchmarking will in and of itself become a mini case study. The comparison between internal and external industry best practices will be adequate to permit quantification after the fact. Or, if as is the case in some business functions, there are industry-wide standard scales for their activities, then internal and external practices can be measured for progress on the scale. Interview feedback on how the benchmark partners view where they are on the scale will provide an adequate measurement.

Selection Criteria

The criteria for selection of what to benchmark should be considered early in the formulation of the study. These have to do with the reasons for the processes existence and their overall importance to the business function.

The reasons for existence can be judged by the critical nature of the process and practices associated to customer satisfaction. How important is it in the internal supplier-customer chain or in satisfying end users or consumer needs? Ultimately a process exists for this purpose only and whether it should be benchmarked depends heavily on answering this question. Benchmarking is the mechanism to ensure that customer needs are satisfied by industry practices. It is logical to start there.

Further criteria would determine how important the decision for improving a practice is and how applicable benchmarking is to the decision. The strategy and plans for a business function may reveal specific areas in need of benchmarking because little is known about how the external world or industry handles a specific item. The importance of plans and strategy also is a relevant criterion. Finally, there is the need for benchmarking expressed simply to solve a given problem. Then one must ask how significant is the problem to be benchmarked in relation to other places where benchmarking resources could be directed.

The L. L. Bean Experience

Prior to the benchmarking experience with L. L. Bean, the Xerox logistics function had developed a comprehensive mission statement and list of deliverables. The primary functional outputs or deliverables were further defined by supporting detailed deliverables that were of interest to benchmark.

Where would the logistics function start its benchmarking activities? Furthermore, what prioritization would define where initial benchmarking efforts should be directed and be most productive? The example of the experience with L. L. Bean is indicative of the first steps to be taken by a firm interested in benchmarking industry best practices.

Historical productivity levels in the logistics function had been in the three to five percent range, but it was also clear that the level was not going to be adequate and that further cost-effectiveness would be required. Productivity would have to increase in the face of industry price changes and the requirement to maintain profit margins. The reflection of this company-wide scenario cascade to the logistics function resulted in the following analysis and prioritization.

The inventory control area had recently implemented a new planning system based on benchmarking best practices after consulting with a leading expert in the field. The transportation function was capitalizing on opportunities presented by deregulation. Thus, warehousing was seen as the next major functional area in need of improvement. That realization was being further fostered by the distribution center manager's rising concern about not keeping up with industry changes. These concerns had been heightened from contacts and presentations at professional association conferences and seminars. There were indications of a latent need for change increasingly being felt throughout the logistics function.

In particular, the picking area was seen as the greatest bottleneck in the receiving through shipping process cycle. This led the logistics function to prioritize its benchmarking efforts on identifying and concentrating work on warehouse productivity and more specifically materials handling as most critical to long-term effectiveness and desire for superior performance. The problem could be further broken down into two major areas of investigation: (1) streamlining the flow of materials through the warehouse, principally a matter of layout and equipment design, and (2) better utilizing the now-established design on a daily and hourly basis, as orders were received, to minimize the travel distance to pick, pack, and ship an order.

The logical steps for improving warehouse productivity were not always clear and approaches emphasizing layout, equipment, or efficient use of labor were hotly debated. A new technology for materials handling, automated storage and retrieval systems (ASRS), had been vigorously proposed as a solution. ASRS is primarily used for raw material and assembly unit storage to feed production or assembly operation. ASRS warehouses were readily available for study by the logistics engineering group responsible for material-handling improvements.

The logistics function did have the ability to investigate this recent innovation for its applicability to finished goods. However, evaluations usually showed that the heavy initial investment could not be justified for the variety of size, shape, and weight usually found in finished goods. A different means of improving warehousing and materials-handling productivity would be needed. But what?

The need for benchmarking and what to benchmark were therefore defined to be the investigation of best industry practices for a picking operation first, but eventually the entire receiving to shipping process cycle. It was not assumed that the best practices would be found in the same industry or even that the best practices desired for each step (receiving, picking, packing, and shipping) would be found at one firm. The investigation launched a search for best practices wherever they existed with the challenge to adopt, adapt, and combine the best of the best, and thereby ensure superior performance.

CHAPTER 4
IDENTIFYING COMPARATIVE COMPANIES (BENCHMARKING PARTNERS) (STEP 2)

Information Source Priorities

Determine the Best Competitor or Functional Industry Leader

Types of Benchmarking
- Internal benchmarking
- Competitive benchmarking
- Functional benchmarking
- Generic benchmarking

Identifying the Best Firms
- Public data bases
- Professional associations
- Other sources

The L. L. Bean Experience

IDENTIFYING COMPARATIVE COMPANIES (BENCHMARKING PARTNERS)

Industry Best Leaders

This chapter introduces one very important aspect of benchmarking, namely the identification and use of information sources. The chapter is about identifying companies against which to benchmark. At the same time several important information sources are also described. The next chapter will discuss data collection methods. Those already described here will not be repeated. This chapter then should be viewed as covering not only the process of identifying benchmark companies or operations but also the review of selected, primary information sources.

This chapter is a fundamental one for a different reason. The basic types of benchmarking are described. There are several bases on which to benchmark — at least four are of interest here. Benchmarking can be conducted against internal operations, external direct product competitors, industry functional leaders, and generic processes. Some are easier to conduct than others, yet at least one — benchmarking against product competitors — is compulsory. Each should be examined for its worth in yielding desired information. Table 4.1 compares some of the key characteristics for conducting the different types of benchmarking.

BENCHMARKING OPERATION	RELEVANCE	DATA COLLECTION EASE	INNOVATIVE PRACTICES
Internal Operations	X	X	
Direct Product Competitors	X		
Industry Leaders		X	X
Generic Processes		X	X

TABLE 4.1. KEY BENCHMARKING CHARACTERISTICS

These can be judged, at least initially, in terms of relevance of the data to the operation, ease of data collection, and the potential for uncovering innovative practices. The internal and direct product comparisons are going to be those seen as having the most relevance. It keeps the benchmarking activities within the same industry. Product to product comparisons of features or business function activities are comparable. It may not, however, be the most revealing of comparisons because there is no assurance that internal functions have best practices installed.

All but the product competitors have a level of data collection ease that is not impeded by sensitive matters if not confidentiality. The industry leaders and, even more so, generic processes are more difficult to benchmark because the benchmarker must have a level of insight to see the possibilities of incorporating the practices in internal processes. The true benefit of the last two types of benchmarking is the potential for uncovering innovative practices not found in one's own industry. This is what holds the opportunity for finding proven technology in operations elsewhere or that of a major breakthrough.

Information Source Priorities

There is a natural tendency, when benchmarking is to be conducted, to immediately contact several companies to set up visits. Experience has shown that this can be a serious mistake and waste valuable resources. Information sources through which to conduct benchmarking are extensive. Those information resources should be tapped first, before conducting visits or using any other approach to benchmarking. The benefit is that the information searches will not only catalog existing information, but also further help define the investigation, make it more focused, and pinpoint information of highest priority.

Benchmarking and the associated information gathering can be compared to weaving a "fabric" of information. There may be many threads already available. The more serious part of benchmarking, site visits, or major studies should be directed toward those information gaps or missing threads that are most crucial. The information already available in the public domain should be tapped first to source companies to benchmark against and to assemble as much information about them that is available.

There is a second reason for conducting information searches before direct contact: Tapping the data and information already available may develop leads to other sources of information. One obvious example is through the references cited in most journal publications. In this fashion there are assurances that all available information is assembled first. Specific site visits most often but not always associated with the prime method of benchmarking should be used only after other sources are exhausted or at least investigated. The information-gathering process should be approached as ongoing. Experience will tell when diminishing returns have been reached and site visits are worth being conducted. This approach will also ensure the maximum effectiveness of the visits.

Determine the Best Competitor or Functional Industry Leader

At some point benchmarking must assess the comparative advantage or disadvantage of those firms in the same industry. This is called competitive benchmarking. However, direct product competitors may not be the sole benchmarking focus. Competitors may have practices that are not the best and not desirable of emulating. It is more appropriate to consider the competitor in broader terms. What is the firm, function, or operation that will have best practices against which to benchmark? In the truest sense, there is no "competitor" for a business function like logistics or processes such as order entry or invoicing.

What is desired are comparable operations where best practices, methods, or processes are used. With this broader definition of a "competitor" a search can be conducted to truly find the best against which to benchmark.

However, some caution is in order. There needs to be some level of comparability. For example, customer satisfaction levels and product-handling characteristics should be similar. Usually the primary business performance drivers should be similar. This usually means measures of customer satisfaction should be comparable. High customer satisfaction firms should be benchmarked against high customer satisfaction internal operations. Product characteristics should also be comparable, at least for the purposes of the primary function being performed by the operation. This usually means, at least for a logistics operation, that the size, shape, weight, and handling sensitivity are comparable. While there may be some learning value of comparing operations that only handle liquids to those of strictly packaged goods, it is more probable that packaged goods to packaged goods comparisons will be more productive.

If possible, the benchmarking investigations should stay within the same industry. However, the industry may be defined quite broadly such as the electronics industry or office products industry. For example, the electronics industry may cover manufacturers of cameras, copiers, and supplies. The risk in defining the industry too narrowly is that technical breakthroughs and proven technology may be overlooked by not investigating operations of dissimilar product manufacturers.

The grocery industry was the first to use the bar code for automatic data capture and to prove the technology. That practice now has been widely spread to diverse operations, from bar coding blood samples and hospital patient records to warehouse documents and individually stocked items. While a level of comparability should be structured to identify the firms of most interest against which to benchmark, other more broadly defined operations may hold potential as well, and should not be overlooked.

Finally, some consideration should be given to the firm's structure. An integrated marketing manufacturer can, with difficulty, be compared to a manufacturer that markets through distributors and retailers. Adjustments can be made during the analysis to ensure comparability, but the most value will be derived from similarly structured firms and operations. Unless, of course, the focus of the investigation is to reveal those very basic structural differences between manufacturers and distributor channels.

The benchmarking investigations should focus on firms with some level of comparability. The investigations should also uncover best practices wherever they exist, even if in dissimilar industries. These considerations are shown in Table 4.2.

Types of Benchmarking

There are at least four types of benchmarking that can be conducted: (1) benchmarking against internal operations, (2) benchmarking against external direct product competitors, (3) benchmarking against external functional best operations or industry leaders, and (4) generic process benchmarking. Each has benefits and deficiencies and may be more appropriate in certain circumstances than others. Examples of comparative companies in the office products industry for the three external benchmarking types are shown in Table 4.3.

CONSIDER "COMPETITOR" IN THE BROADEST TERMS

- What firm, function, or operation has the best industry practices

- Comparable operations where best practices, methods, or processes are used

ENSURE COMPARABILITY

- High customer satisfaction firms should be measured against high customer satisfaction firms

- Product characteristics should be generic for the process. That is, packaged goods should be measured against packaged goods

STAY WITHIN THE SAME INDUSTRY

- Define the industry broadly

- The electronics industry is an example

WHERE ARE BUSINESS PRACTICE BREAKTHROUGHS FOUND OR LIKELY TO OCCUR?

- Uncover innovative practices wherever they exist

- Even in dissimilar industries

TABLE 4.2.   DETERMINING THE BEST COMPETITOR OR FUNCTIONAL LEADER

Internal Benchmarking

In most large multidivision or international firms there are similar functions in different operating units. One of the easiest benchmarking investigations is to compare these internal operations. This may involve comparisons of logistics operations for different divisions or between Canadian, U.S., European, and Far East operations. Data and information should be readily available and problems of confidentiality do not exist. The data and information can be as complete and extensive as desired. No data gaps should exist.

DIRECT PRODUCT COMPETITORS

Company	Product/Functional Leadership
Canon	Copiers
DEC	Work Stations

FUNCTIONAL INDUSTRY LEADERS

L. L. Bean	Warehouse Operations
GE	Information Systems
Deere	Service Parts Logistics
Ford	Assembly Automation

GENERIC PROCESSES

Federal Reserve	Bill Scanning
Citicorp	Document Processing

TABLE 4.3. COMPARATIVE COMPANIES IN THE
OFFICE PRODUCTS INDUSTRY

This first step in benchmarking investigations is an excellent basis for not only uncovering differences of interest, but also focusing on the critical issues that will be faced or are of interest for understanding practices from external investigations. The internal investigations may also help define the scope of an external study. It also may in and of itself provide useful information. It may even define an internal operation that is the benchmark.

Competitive Benchmarking

Direct product competitors are the most obvious to benchmark against. They would, or should, meet all the comparability tests that have been described. Ultimately, any benchmarking investigation must show what the comparative advantages and disadvantages are between direct competitors. There are, however, some considerations that may bear significantly on these investigations.

Care should be taken to understand where competitor operations are not truly comparable. The size of operations may have an effect on comparability. Size, measured by throughput, can reflect differences of comparing a function like logistics for a major firm against a logistic operation performed for similar products but for a significantly smaller firm. Size will most likely reveal that the operations are run differently. Large throughput may mean rail shipments compared to truck shipments, or for smaller operations, truckload compared to less than truckload shipment sizes. This will affect the costs. Size also may be reflected in operations being more automated compared to manual, or semiautomated for smaller operations.

An example could be a firm with a large service parts distribution activity determining whether to benchmark against a product competitor. If there is no direct product competitor that has an operation of similar size, it may be more productive to benchmark against the parts aftermarket in the auto industry or Deere in farm machinery or Caterpillar in construction.

While comparability may be a concern, of greater importance is the difficulty of obtaining information about direct product competitors' operations. Information may be impossible to obtain because it is proprietary and is the basis of the firm's competitive advantage.

While obtaining information may be difficult it should still be pursued. What is most productive is choosing the right method and approach. The approach should concentrate on ensuring that both parties understand that the investigations are focused on best practices. Comparing methods, practices, and processes in a structured fashion has created interest for this type of contact. The reason for the success is that the other parties also are interested in understanding best practices that make their operations successful or could further improve them. The method for information exchange can be through a third party such as a consultant guaranteeing confidentiality and anonymity, if desired.

Functional Benchmarking

It is not necessary to concentrate solely on direct product competitors. In fact, there may be serious risk of achieving superior performance if that is the exclusive focus of benchmarking investigations. There is great potential for identifying functional competitors or industry leader firms to benchmark even if in dissimilar industries. This would involve, in the case of logistics, identifying those firms that are recognized as having superior logistics functions wherever they exist.

An example could be the identification of L. L. Bean as a function best industry leader in its order fulfillment and warehousing operations. Comparison to the package goods operation of another firm may reveal practices which, if installed, would provide a superior operation in the package goods industry.

It is not too difficult to determine the leading firms in selected business functions. The firm that has the best inventory control practices or system and the one with the best warehouse handling system can be uncovered in discussions with software and hardware vendors or consultants who specialize in the field. The key to the success of these investigations is determining whether the industry leaders are driven by the same customer requirements, such as high customer satisfaction as mentioned earlier. The operations must be comparable from a logistics viewpoint. That is, if product handling is being investigated, then the operations should have products of similar handling characteristics. Product characteristics that drive handling operations are usually size, shape, weight, and fragility. If these are roughly comparable, the benchmarking of industry leaders, even in dissimilar industries, can be highly productive.

There are further reasons why functional benchmarking is productive. It most often is easier to obtain interest for the investigation and share data. Not only are there fewer problems with confidentiality of information, but there also is a natural interest in understanding practices elsewhere. If operations are approached on the basis of examining industry best practices, there may be interest in understanding how they compare. It has been observed that practices found in dissimilar industries are more readily accepted than those within the same industry. This is because the observation of methods and practices are approached on a more objective basis, not always distracted by the product involved. This fact is considered to outweigh the difficulty of getting observers to truly visualize and accept the practices as operationally feasible when applied to their own operations. There can be the myopia of "if it is not the same product then the methods can't possibly apply." Industry leader benchmarking overcomes the not-invented-here syndrome often encountered when benchmarking within the same industry.

Ultimately what is desired is the best of the practices, because only the innovative application of that combination will lead to superior performance. Observers must be able to visualize adoption of the best practices or adaptation of them to their operations. They must be able to see the possibilities of the assembly of the best of best practices from several sources and from dissimilar operations. An inquisitive, positive interest in uncovering and innovatively applying best practices is a necessary trait for functional industry benchmarking.

Generic Benchmarking

Some business functions or processes are the same regardless of dissimilarities of industries. One such process is the order fulfillment process. It can be described as the order entry, customer service, warehouse order handling, invoicing, and collection functions. A wide cross section of firms must perform these functions to satisfy customers. If such a process were to be benchmarked the product or industry may not be limiting. One could look at the order entry process for electronics, chemicals, and food products as well as for other products or services.

The benefit of this most pure form of benchmarking is that practices and methods may be uncovered that are not implemented in the investigator's own industry. Readily transferable, proven technology may be uncovered, or practices transferable with minor adjustment. The following is an example of generic benchmarking.

A logistics professional was required to visit a major bank to discuss check clearing procedures. The visit was viewed as a waste of time since the professional was in the pharmaceutical industry. During the visit a tour was conducted and a dollar bill sorting operation was viewed. The sorting process involved digitizing the bill and checking the image for a good bill, a mutilated bill, or a counterfeit bill. The operation caught the professional's interest, especially when he was told the procedure sorted at 400 bills per minute. The logistics professional had a similar identification and sorting problem in his warehouse for packages. The highest speed attained so far was 100 packages per minute. The generic process benchmarking revealed a practice that with further development and adaptation is now being used in many major warehouses today.

Generic benchmarking holds the potential of revealing the best of best practices. The greatest need is for objectivity and receptivity on the part of the investigator. What better proof of implementability could be obtained than technology already proven and in use elsewhere. Generic benchmarking requires broad conceptualization but careful understanding of the generic process. It is the most difficult benchmarking concept to gain acceptance and use but probably that with the highest long-term payoff.

Identifying the Best Firms

Once an understanding has been gained of what is to be benchmarked and the desired type of benchmarking to be pursued (or combination of types to be pursued), the best firms must be identified. Initially a skimming operation can be performed based on a preliminary indication of candidate companies. The skimming operation could involve extracting selected key data and developing common business effectiveness ratios such as selling, administrative, and general (SAG) expenses as a percent of revenue, return on assets, and so forth as shown in Table 4.4. These should reveal candidate companies to be investigated further. Since annual report and 10K data are available on public data bases, this step is reasonably straightforward.

The person performing the initial search may want to start within an industry. Industry periodicals often have annual reviews where the Top 100 Electronics Firms or the Top 20 Distributors are identified. The search can be initiated with these lists. Following a review of company summary data, a more focused search should be conducted by company. Annual reports, periodicals, and other information sources should be reviewed for specific "statements of pride" that point to a firm believing it has best practices in a chosen function. Statements such as "we have the most cost-effective processing system in the electronics distributor industry" would obviously merit further investigation. A statement that "SAG costs have steadily declined over the past five years" would also be an indicator of cost-effectiveness and good business practices. Where the investigator goes from these starting points to identify industry leaders is a matter of careful combing and sifting of data and information from a variety of sources.

The fabric of the benchmark process has been started. The next steps can be based on the innovativeness and initiative of the person doing the benchmarking and do not need to be discussed further. What does deserve some review are the potential information sources found to be most productive. These are discussed from the viewpoint of effective data and information gathering for benchmarking purposes, and are purposely not treated exhaustively. That should be done with the assistance of a research librarian.

A somewhat generic category called public information is discussed first because it should be understood at the outset that a great deal of information already is in the public domain. It may not be necessary to have direct or third party contact with benchmarking partners for a considerable amount of the desired data. At a minimum, public information should always be gathered and

Company

	A	B	C	D	E	F	G	H	I	J	K
Gross profit percent	52%	10%	18%	40%	27%	53%	49%	59%	33%	17%	28%
SG&A as percent of revenue	36%	7%	14%	33%	21%	11%	28%	25%	25%	11%	17%
Profit as percent of revenue	10%	3%	4%	7%	6%	14%	13%	25%	9%	6%	11%
Return on equity	9%	19%	15%	15%	26%	23%	21%	28%	17%	7%	16%
Return on assets	4%	7%	6%	3%	9%	14%	11%	16%	10%	4%	11%
Inventory turns	3	8	8	5	6	3	3	4	4	8	3

___ Firms potentially worth benchmarking

TABLE 4.4. KEY FINANCIAL RATIOS

understood first if for no other reason than to keep from being blind sided by data and information already published.

The source of data and information on firms is vast and it would be impossible to describe the pros and cons of each. Potential source categories are shown in Table 5.1 of Chapter 5 and are not meant to be exhaustive. Two specific categories warrant mention: public data bases and professional associations.

Public Data Bases

Automated data bases deserve mention because they are a good starting point, relatively inexpensive, and permit a quick focus on desired information. Data bases contain citations to other sources that are extractable based on the subject matter key words. Data as well as text information are available. The major providers of data are shown in Table 4.5.

Data bases permit rapid, inexpensive assembly of all available public information. Their use is the starting point for weaving the fabric of the complete benchmarking information desired. It is advisable to obtain the services of a research librarian to cover their availability and use adequately.

The difficulty in using data bases is determining the key words from which to extract citations and abstracts. This may be obvious in some cases such as wanting information on selling costs. Often it is a trial-and-error process. An extract on selling costs could include more diverse information than might be useful. So several limiting descriptors will most likely be necessary. Judgment about what is being excluded by use of the qualifying descriptors also is a matter for consideration. One of the more helpful approaches is to find several articles on the topic desired. A librarian can access them to find how those articles were cited and key words used to serve as a further definition of the final descriptors.

There is no guarantee that a data base search will reveal information of use. The extract may be extensive and provide little information, but it is necessary to ensure that no readily available information is left uncovered. Data bases are updated with a defined frequency. Recent articles not coded will have to be researched firsthand at a library. The rest will be left to the ingenuity of the benchmarking investigator.

Professional Associations

Professional and trade associations are probably the second most productive source of information. They can serve to identify industry leaders as well as provide industry data and information. Many

Data Base	Provider	Type	Contents
AB Information	UMI Data Courier	Text	Library citations
Lexis	Mead Data Central	Text	Annual reports
Compustat	Standard & Poor's	Data	Financial
DunsPrint	Dun & Bradstreet	Data	Financial

TABLE 4.5. MAJOR ELECTRONIC DATA BASES

maintain sizable libraries and conduct research on topics of current interest. They can be sources of information from their publication lists, training programs, annual conferences, and seminars as well as specialized library services. The relevant association can be readily identified through the Encyclopedia of Associations.

Most associations are quite helpful. They are sources of good suggestions on how to proceed to find data and information of interest. This might be to identify industry leaders directly or source consultants active in the industry. Often case history examples are maintained in their conference abstracts or encouraged for presentation at conferences. The case histories may discuss industry best practices, methods and processes.

A difficulty with association data is that they are usually aggregated to provide anonymity. Often this is the only way participants agree to share data. There may be very little directly focused on best practices other than that already mentioned. Further difficulties are that data and information may not be current, terminology may not be the same, and conclusions may not be based on extensive data but on opinions.

Other Sources

Other sources of data and information desired to determine practices or to identify industry leaders are only bound by one's resourcefulness. They are extensive and too numerous to cover in a text such as this. There are some pointers for the information search process that are important and will be covered next.

First, a wide cross section of contacts should be maintained. These may be done with consultants, with data base awareness services, or with people considered experts in the subject matter of specific firms of interest. It is only over some time — months, perhaps a year — that the investigator will develop an understanding of what data and information are available and where and how readily accessible they are. It is important that a commitment be made to benchmarking over an extended period. Expect assigned individuals to review source data and maintain files for current as well as future use. A well-woven fabric is not made in a day.

Second, so many industry processes are now electronic- and computer-based that it is wise to stay in touch with this specific field, especially for major business functions like marketing, logistics, service, and other administrative type processes. Contact with hardware and software vendors is encouraged. The functional professional will know who these vendors are. It is productive to visit with vendor reps to discuss what they have observed, where they have observed it, and whether clients are willing to share information or host a visit. If the discussion is focused on uncovering industry best practices, such contacts can yield productive sources of information. While this is true for most business functions, it may not hold true for some — R&D for example. However, the analogy exists somewhere; the key is finding the analogy.

Third, consultants who are experts in their fields are excellent sources to identify benchmark firms. They also are experts in what constitutes industry best practices. They are a source for referrals, client contacts, or their own experience and should be used as such.

Finally, functional professionals within each firm are sources. They may have heard of good practices being used by others. A professional manager or individual contributor will make a practice of staying current with developments in his or her field. He or she will receive trade periodicals and journals and will develop a sense of who has good practices. It always is productive to canvass internal functional professionals as to who and why they believe are industry leaders exhibiting best practices.

The L. L. Bean Experience

When the general problem was identified — the warehousing and materials handling function with special attention on the picking operations — the formal benchmarking activities were started. It was decided early in the evaluation that functional benchmarking of industry leaders would be the benchmarking approach to use. In part this was because the receiving-to-shipping operation process is one that is common to a wide range of products, companies, and industries. The outcome was to define best practices for that process wherever they existed. The exact product being warehoused was of less concern than the product characteristics being reasonably comparable.

One person was assigned part time to the project for a period of six months. Since this was one of the earliest benchmarking investigations, the exact level of resources to conduct the project was not entirely known. So a part-time investigation over an extended period was considered a feasible approach. The extended time allowed the person to investigate the public information more thoroughly before making a recommendation.

Trade journals in the materials handling and logistics fields were reviewed for the three years prior. The principal logistics and materials handling professional associations were contacted to uncover any recent presentations at annual conferences that discussed the efficient design of materials handling for package goods warehouses. Several material-handling consulting firms were contacted for their suggestions on who might have well-designed picking, packing, and shipping operations. Most of these contacts were made by telephone on a professional-to-professional basis.

The goal was to select recent developments in the warehousing and materials handling field as well as to identify companies that had implemented these best practices. As candidate companies were identified, the characteristics of their processes, systems, and products were tabulated. From this approach a list of companies was compiled from the best in the logistics field with generic product characteristics and service levels similar to those desired. Following these investigations an initial report was compiled detailing the information known to date. The report revealed major differences between the internal operations and external candidate benchmarking partners. The report showed enough of an opportunity to warrant making benchmarking a full-time position to pursue the opportunity, especially since this was the logistics organization's initial venture into benchmarking. Other resources were drawn from planning and operations, on an as-needed basis, especially when a team was organized for on-site visits. This marked the formalization of benchmarking as an ongoing commitment.

At about this time an article appeared in a materials-handling periodical citing L. L. Bean's operation and focusing on the fact that it was still a manual operation, carefully planned but intensely directed by computer systems to minimize the labor content. It indicated the operation did not lend itself to automation because of the variety of sizes, shapes, and weight of items ordered by customers. The design relied on basic handling techniques to streamline the materials flow and minimize the picker travel distance. In addition, the design eventually selected was decided on with the full participation of the hourly work force, those who would have to operate the process.

To the layperson, L. L. Bean's warehouse operation would not seem to resemble that of a manufacturer of packaged products. However, to the logistics professional, the analogy was striking: Both companies had to develop warehousing and materials-handling processes and supporting computer-based systems to handle products diverse in size, shape, and weight. This diversity precluded some of the more popular technology being promoted at the time, namely automatic storage and retrieval systems (ASRS).

Therefore, L. L. Bean was identified as having best practices in their warehousing and materials-handling operations worthy of benchmarking. Steps were then taken to set up a benchmarking visit.

CHAPTER 5 DATA COLLECTION METHODS (STEP 3)

Criteria for Information Gathering

Data-Gathering Approach

Internal Information
- Product analysis
- Company sources
- Study piggybacking
- Internal experts and studies

Public Domain Information
- Library search
- Professional and trade association data
- Consultants
- External experts

Original Research and Investigations
- Questionnaires
  - Mail administered
  - Telephone administered surveys

- Direct-site visits
  - Preparation
  - Contacts
    Company representatives
    Professional to professional
    Referrals
  - Visit itinerary
  - Debriefing
  - Attendees
- Focus groups (panels)

Basis for Information Sharing

Development of Evergreen Sources

The L. L. Bean Experience

Quick Reference Guide 5.1. Trade and Professional Association Sources

Quick Reference Guide 5.2. Working with Consultants

Quick Reference Guide 5.3. Preparing a Questionnaire

Quick Reference Guide 5.4. Preparing a Mail Survey

Quick Reference Guide 5.5. Telephone Survey Guidelines

Quick Reference Guide 5.6. Conducting a Personal Interview

Quick Reference Guide 5.7. Site Tour Guidelines

Quick Reference Guide 5.8. Panel Interviews

Quick Reference Guide 5.9. Draft Policy on Information Gathering and Information Sharing

DATA COLLECTION METHODS (STEP 3)

Navigating the Information Resource Maze

Data collection methods are synonymous with and integral to sources of data and information. Several have already been discussed. Their use was covered in sourcing benchmark partners — companies against which to benchmark. Several more important methods will be discussed including a review of their benefits, deficiencies, and pointers for effective use. A list of information sources along with examples is shown in Table 5.1.

It should be evident by now that those performing the benchmarking investigations will want to select the data-gathering approach that best meets the needs of the study. While benchmarking is most often associated with site visits to other companies it is not always necessary to have face-to-face contact. The most productive approach should be used, and the pros and cons of each should be weighed before selecting one approach on which to embark.

It should be up to the investigator to select the best approach based on his or her judgment. It may be appropriate to use one approach for a preliminary survey, then based on the preliminary investigation, decide on a more comprehensive method that will yield the full detail of data and information desired. It may be appropriate to conduct a questionnaire or telephone survey before conducting direct-site visits. As previously mentioned, all public information should be extracted before any approach is used.

Criteria for Information Gathering

Before starting any data-gathering effort some thought should be given to the quality of data desired. There are several data criteria and characteristics that should be given consideration. Among them are the amount and accuracy of the data, the cost of obtaining the data, the time required, and whether specialists need to be used. The time to determine the data specifications and administer the data collection effort also should not be overlooked.

The amount of data gathered may be the result not only of the accuracy desired but how the data will be used. Trend data may require few data points while a single point accurate number may require confirmation from several sources. The accuracy will be a function of the use and importance of the data. A statistic, such as unit cost, multiplied by a large activity requires more precision because it will affect the projection and possibly the justification of the practice.

Source	Example
Internal	
Library data bases	AB information
Internal reviews	Internal experts
Internal publications	Varies by company
External	
Professional associations	American Marketing Association
Industry publications	Electronic Business
Special industry reports	ADL Infotran
Functional trade publications	Materials Handling Engineering
General management	Industry Week
Functional journals	Journal of Business Logistics
Seminars	By professional interest
Industry data firms	Dataquest
Industry experts	K. L. Worthington
Software/hardware vendors	DEC
University sources	By profession
Company watchers	Eugene Glazer, Dean Witter, Reynolds (Xerox)
Advertisements	By product of interest
Newsletters	By subject matter
Original Research	
Customer feedback	Focus groups
Telephone surveys	Specific design
Inquiry service	Specific contract
Networks	Electronic, internal, and external
Consulting firms	McKinsey

TABLE 5.1. INFORMATION SOURCES

Data and information cost money to obtain, analyze, and extrapolate to meaningful comparisons. Care should be taken to assess the best benchmarking method to derive the required data at a reasonable cost. If one thing has been learned about benchmarking investigations it is that they take time. Benchmarking by its nature of searching for and developing data about best practices, requires sifting through extensive material to find the few relevant findings and statistics desired. Also, establishing productive benchmarking partners takes time. In many instances it will be necessary to triangulate on information desired. That is, it will be necessary to confirm the data from several independent sources to ensure valid results. These steps take time. This is one reason why effective benchmarking is continuous over a substantial amount of time to catalog the data until enough are obtained on which to base a valid analysis.

Special skills needed in benchmarking also should be analyzed. While site visits are desirable, it may be more productive to deal directly with equipment manufacturers and their representatives or with consultants. The time and effort required to administer either special studies or site visits should be carefully assessed. These are not insignificant tasks. Since benchmarking investigations often are based on single contacts with others, every effort should be made to create successful first contacts.

One way to assess the requirements for these characteristics is to prepare a matrix analysis of them for the alternative benchmarking methods believed to be the most promising. In this fashion an informed judgment can be made about the quality of the data and gathering efforts required.

Data-Gathering Approach

There are several ways to classify information-gathering techniques and it is helpful to have a scheme for categorizing them into logical groupings. The scheme selected here is based on the logical progression normally used in benchmarking searches. It also progresses from the less difficult to the difficult. It is based on seeking internal information first, then information in the public domain, and finally conducting original investigations and searches. While the last category often is seen as the more interesting and glamorous, it will become obvious that it will be most productive if the first two are rigorously conducted first.

The potential data and information sources are extensive as shown in Table 5.1. While the table appears to be complete it cannot be considered exhaustive. The significant ones are considered here but there are many variations, extensions, and analogies to these approaches available. Some approaches may provide the desired data and information directly. Others may provide leads to the data desired. Still others may only provide leads to the source of the eventual information. A certain level of inquisitiveness, persistence, and calculated exploration is needed on the part of the researcher. In several instances examples will be cited to show the unique experience of the author in the use of several of the approaches. There should be every expectation that similar results, but not necessarily the same results, are available to anyone who conducts benchmarking.

In addition to the basic information sources described, many have quick reference guides provided for their further understanding. These deal not only with the use of the sources, but in many instances deal with the ground rules for the construction of the type of approach used, such as with questionnaires. The guides are meant to cover the principal considerations for their use and are not meant to be all inclusive. Where that is desired the experience of a person who has extensively used the approach or that of a professional, such as a market researcher, should be used. The guides are more than adequate, however, to get the major considerations understood for purposes of selecting among them and to get the benchmarking approach started.

Two extremely important considerations for any benchmarking investigation are also covered. One deals with the basis of the information exchange and the other with the need to remain in continuous contact with sources to become effective in the benchmarking process over time. The basis of information sharing proposed here is one of professionals discussing industry best practices — those practices that are used by leading companies or functional best operations, not only those currently in effect but those planned. This, coupled with staying in touch with principal sources over an extended period of time, will assure that the most productive sources will be uncovered and the best practices found.

This chapter is one of the most extensive. Finding the information on best practices after what to benchmark and who to benchmark are determined is at the heart of the benchmarking process. Once best practices are found, documented, and communicated to management, their acceptance and implementation will be the acid test of not so much a benchmarking process as that of management. The incentive or willingness to implement best practices can be debated. The fact that the benchmarking process has found the industry best practices cannot be debated.

Internal Information

Internal information can come from a wide range of sources; it would be impossible to name them all. The ingenuity of the person conducting the search will be the only limiting factor in obtaining information from throughout the firm. The process of determining all potential sources is exhaustive; the prime sources must be asked for their suggestions on further sources until all productive leads are covered. This usually — but not always — occurs when those recommended turn out to be the original starting set. Again, the potential is only limited by the benchmarker's inquisitiveness and tenacity in pursuing all available internal information.

The three internal sources covered are most likely the more common ones and include product analyses, company sources, and study piggybacking. Product analysis is where benchmarking started, in the manufacturing function. Canvassing all potential internal experts and other knowledgeable individuals, while seemingly time consuming and holding little potential at first, serves to gather all relevant information. It has been shown to be productive if for no other reason than to uncover additional leads to pursue. Since benchmarking can be expensive it is wise to consider joint benchmarking efforts wherever possible. These are covered next.

Product Analysis

It is common practice to have product laboratories of manufacturers obtain competing products for analysis. The products are then operated, disassembled, or otherwise analyzed for features, function, and materials. Beyond this obvious benchmarking method there are other considerations of interest from laboratories. In selected instances they may also be sources of related functional information. On the surface such laboratory type operations do not appear to have relevance to a function like logistics. However, some practices, methods, and processes may be revealed or confirmed from the receipt of products and materials by the laboratory.

A logistics example shows how these are useful. The competing product must be ordered, it must be shipped and received, and in some instances it must be serviced. Information on the method of shipment, including the transportation mode used and origin shipping source, can be obtained from ordering or shipping documents. Observation will reveal the method of installation if that also is required. Packing slips and internal shipping documents may reveal other advanced methods like bar coding for inventory control or an innovative returns policy. In similar fashion product information included with the shipment may document repair service sources. Service practices are included with service documentation. Invoice data may reveal customer assistance information and practices. Order catalogs contain information about ordering methods.

While the logistics example cites data and information available for a business function benchmarking study received from a somewhat obscure source, the principle involved is an important one. Useful information may be available at any point where the firm has contact with the products or services of others. The source of this type information is only limited by the innovativeness and resourcefulness of the investigator. What is needed is to concentrate on where there may be contact with the firm of interest. Useful information can be gleaned from these indirect sources to help put another thread of information into the benchmark fabric.

Company Sources

At first glance it may be seen as a low payback effort to canvass internal organizations about possible information useful to benchmarking a specific organization or function. How could, for example, any other organization have information useful to a logistics function other than those in the logistics function itself? The fact remains that there are many individuals who are keen observers of the external environment or have information that tangentially bears on the subject being investigated, or who have leads to those who do. What is wanted from this effort is to ensure that all known information is cataloged as a starting point in benchmarking.

There are two reasons to conduct an internal search of all possible data and information of interest. One is to gather all the data that have been documented, and the other is to exhaustively cover those individuals who may be productive referrals — people who have seen or heard something of interest. In the first category are those who are by their job responsibility information gatherers of external information. These would include market researchers and those involved in competitive analyses or situation studies. While it is often true that the possibility of these people having functional information of value is slim they should still be canvassed. Usually these individuals do not have specific functional information that would be useful to a function such as logistics. Their scope of investigations is much broader and focuses on whole industries, markets, or companies. Finding specific operational information is more chancy. However, a reasonable effort to cover these information avenues should be pursued. What they have documented in existing and completed reports, studies underway, or studies contemplated for the future should be searched for relevant information. In one such instance, while those canvassed could not give specific information about a logistics network echelon structure, they were instrumental in determining the city location of a facility. A check with the newspaper for that city uncovered several articles about the facility including its scope of operations, a productive piece of the benchmarking information fabric. The value of this peripheral information is what makes the investment to canvassing these sources a worthwhile investment.

In similar fashion functional experts and operational managers should also be canvassed. Many have seen or heard information that can be very useful, although it may have to be verified. Many are active professionally and stay in touch with the principle periodicals of their function. Others have useful contacts that may be worthwhile to pursue. Who these individuals are and what or who they know can easily be determined by explaining the purpose of the investigation and the fact that information that may even peripherally bear on the subject may be useful. There is no easy method for canvassing these types of resources. Their worth rests primarily in the possibility of uncovering information of value or obtaining useful referrals. The effort usually proves moderately productive if for no other reason than to alert these individuals to the fact that this type of benchmarking information is being sought and that they should remember to gather the data and information in the future. This is just one more way of assuring that all information sources are covered in assembling the fabric of benchmarking.

Piggybacking Combination Studies

Benchmarking can be expensive, especially if it is conducted repeatedly over time to ensure that it remains evergreen. The update obviously is necessary because competition and best industry practices, methods, and processes change over time. All efforts should therefore be made to use the existing data of studies conducted by others. More importantly, where benchmarking is being planned it is cost-effective to piggyback on proposed studies. Incremental data and information are much easier to add and much less expensive to obtain. Using such an approach may result in obtaining a valuable piece of information that fills a data gap and thereby completes a benchmarking study.

One of the most productive ways to capitalize on combination studies is to do so through a network. A benchmarking network is a loosely organized set of individuals who are conducting benchmarking studies, are peripherally interested in the topic, or are interested in learning more about benchmarking. Networks have been formed in recent years in part from the ability to communicate electronically. This exceptionally easy method of information exchange lets the individuals stay at their work locations, yet easily send messages back and forth on topics of interest. The network has proven especially helpful to benchmarking since expertise is usually concentrated in selected individuals who are often remote from each other or who find it difficult because of the separate nature of functional organizations to keep up with current benchmarking efforts.

A network can either function informally through the initiative of individuals broadcasting a request for information about benchmarking, or it can function through a bulletin board type clearinghouse of topics established to permit everyone access to the information. These techniques permit study objectives, proposed studies, and experiences from studies in progress to be shared. The early warning of potential studies permits an opportunity for others to request that information be gathered at the same time, at substantially less cost.

It is not always necessary to rely on the electronic communications medium for a benchmarking network. There are many positive benefits to be gained from having those with a common interest in benchmarking meet from time to time to share experiences, discuss possible approaches to difficult benchmarking study situations, and review findings from completed work. In this fashion, techniques for expanding the benchmarking process are highlighted to bring the entire approach to benchmarking to a new level of expertise.

Internal Experts and Studies

Most firms maintain either specific industry awareness organizations or have individuals in business functions who are responsible for keeping up with the outside world. The focus of these individuals is often quite broad — watching markets, products, and prices. They do not always have information about functional business practices in discrete operating units of outside firms. Their focus is not on business practices, methods, and processes at the business unit level. Yet these internal experts often are keen observers or have some data and information that peripherally bear on a benchmarking study. They should be canvassed as well as requested to perform a search of recent documents they have cataloged.

An example from the logistics function is illustrative. It concerns interest in knowing industry levels of customer satisfaction for service parts availability and delivery. A major study had been undertaken to understand the structure of third party dealers. One significant element of a dealer's operation and operating cost often is the service operation. The study tracked parts usage cost along with data on inventory levels and source of parts. A reliable parts availability metric was developed from data which was obtained originally to price out the parts cost of the operation, not the logistics level of service. In similar fashion, other studies have revealed or confirmed the echelon structure for parts movement from source to point of use. The number of levels of inventory is a major contributor to logistics cost structure and therefore overall unit cost.

Public Domain Information

The second category of information sources is that which exists in the public domain. That is, information that exists externally, but which takes concerted and careful attention to find and extract efficiently. The surprising finding about this category is that there is more information there than initial reaction might suggest. In fact it has been the experience of the author that there is extensive information in the public domain. The key is finding it at an affordable cost of time and expense.

External information exists in many forms. There are the traditional sources — periodicals, annual reports, and other hard copy documents which are readily accessed electronically in most instances. There are the less traditional sources — seminar speeches, conference proceedings, newspaper articles, and others. These later must be researched directly or with the assistance of a trained librarian or information researcher.

Those that will be covered here are first the prime sources, namely those accessible through library research. These are most likely the ones that are thought of first. Library research should be seriously considered to ensure that no sources are left uncovered and because it may lead to the correct indexing or key word description to be used, which in many instances is not immediately apparent.

There are the nontraditional information sources also. These include the information and data that professional associations have, which can be obtained through consultants and external experts or company watchers. These may provide original data and information or referrals to other sources and have proven very successful for benchmarking purposes.

Library Search

The use of a business or technical library should be one of the first considerations of a benchmarking investigation. This fact was covered in the prior chapter in discussing the sourcing of companies to benchmark. A library search of relevant materials is considerably enhanced today by the availability of references in electronic data bases. Accessing these with the assistance of a knowledgeable research librarian is the preferred way to ensure that the subject has been covered completely.

The search process can be painfully time-consuming, especially if the topic does not have clear key word index descriptors, or if the descriptors are so all-inclusive that it is difficult to identify the material through them. There may be much search with little yield. Yet finding relevant information is a real added value. There is another reason for conducting a library search: Assuming the benchmarking investigations are conducted over an extended time period as suggested, librarians will watch for information of interest. This is especially helpful for articles and information that are not in data bases because of the update lag. However, familiarity with the subject matter and continuing research usually pays dividends. In addition, a request can be made that a formal watch service be performed. These can be productive when the periodicals or other source documents of interest are known. In one instance the process was very successful in uncovering a speech at a college which detailed quite specifically the logistics network structure of a company. This was a major find which could have been difficult or expensive to develop from other sources.

Professional and Trade Association Data

Professional associations as a source of data and information have already been discussed as being helpful in identifying benchmark partners. They also should not be overlooked as sources for this type of referral. In addition, they may have specific industry reports. While data may be aggregated, they often are useful as background information. Associations sometimes commission special studies. These tend to be oriented toward the future, possibly

Delphi-based, and can serve to define what future practices are anticipated to be. Careful review of publication lists for data and information of interest is a compulsory activity.

One use of professional association programs to conduct benchmarking can be described through the following example. By keeping in touch with a wide variety of sources, a brochure on a joint seminar between two related professional associations was received. On the surface the seminar did not appear to hold much interest. However, on closer investigation two tours were being offered, one to the distribution center of a major competitor. Such field trips along with seminar presentations are common in some professions.

Here was an opportunity to see firsthand a distribution center that the benchmarking person would probably hesitate to set up directly. All that was necessary was to sign up for the seminar and participate in the tour. The tour was run professionally with an introduction to the operation made by the distribution center manager. A brochure explaining key facets of the operation was made available to the attendees. A formal tour with small groups was later conducted throughout the entire operation. The ability to see an operation firsthand through such opportunities should not be missed.

The benefits of associations are derived from the fact that they already know the subject matter. They are useful for referrals and contacts in the functional area. Another benefit is that using associations is reasonably inexpensive. There may be research on the topics of interest, either conducted by association staff members or by contracted professionals.

Factors for successful use of professional associations are outlined in Quick Reference Guide 5.1. The guide shows that professional associations provide a rich source of data and information that may bear directly on the benchmarking investigation. They can serve as excellent leads for where to find information of interest and whom to contact. A source for possible relevant associations is the Encyclopedia of Associations. It should be studied from several different perspectives because association names may not be alphabetized by function. They often have prefixes such as "Association of" which places them in various parts of the encyclopedia.

Most associations have a director or information officer who would be the prime contact. They usually are quite helpful in describing the scope of the association activities beyond that which appears in the abbreviated write up in the encyclopedia. There are two items to discuss with the association officers to assure a productive search for benchmarking information. One is to determine if the association is the principal or predominant one in the function or subject matter of interest. There often will be several associations that cover a particular field. As a case in point there are two principal associations for the logistics field and several more that have partially overlapping scopes. There are at least three in the inventory field. The size of the association membership will provide some clue to the more prominent association, but not always. The second point of interest is whether the association has information potentially relevant to the benchmarking investigation. One can again determine some of the possibilities for source materials by judging from the size of the association. The larger associations will have the resources to conduct research and have the results published; they also will have wider contacts in the field of interest.

Associations often have extensive data and information. They can be initially reviewed by requesting a copy of the association's publications list. In addition, the association's mission and purpose should be reviewed for whether the scope covers the benchmark area being investigated. Beyond the publications list, which may provide direct information of interest for benchmarking, secondary sources provided by associations can be of major importance. Conference proceedings, consultants active in the field, and vendors in the field are all potential sources of information leads. In addition, it would be appropriate to determine if anyone from the benchmarking firm is a member of the association. A visit with such a member can provide quick insight into association activities as well as offer a review of the membership roster. Of course the benchmarker can join the association to obtain the full membership benefits. Even the least productive contact with associations can still hold some potential. Officers of the association can be asked for suggestions on where to find data and information of interest.

Consultants

There are several ways to engage consultants for benchmarking purposes. The most obvious is to have them serve as the intermediaries with well-designed questions, as discussed previously. This is a traditional and valuable role, but others should also be considered.

Request a review of client assignments to uncover best practices. What is involved here is a review of project files (ensuring confidentiality) to determine if during the course of an assignment practices were observed that should be considered. The study is essentially limited to internal files and discussions with other principals of the firm. This may be a good first step to ensure that existing data and information are not overlooked. A questionnaire can be used to document answers and a report can be requested.

An operational design can be requested. Based on the sum of consulting technical and process expertise, a design incorporating best practices can be developed for comparison with current practice. This will bring to bear all consulting experience, whether client observation or technical training. This is especially important where technical understanding of process equipment features may have to be evaluated. Examples include different throughput rates for picking packing operations or various storage rack arrangements and their effect on travel distance.

A third use of consultants is to request comments on benchmark findings already documented through site visits. Where this level of validation is necessary it further brings a level of credibility and may be especially important if few observations are being used to extrapolate effects to a very important or large operation. Some level of confirmation is worthwhile.

Consultant use has advantage over questionnaires alone because a level of interpretation and validation can be obtained. Also, recommendations can be substantiated with justification rationale.

Factors for the successful use of consultants are shown in Quick Reference Guide 5.2. The guide shows that conducting benchmarking studies through consultants can be a productive exercise, especially if participants want to ensure a level of anonymity. The preservation of confidentiality is one of the primary reasons for using consultants. The consultant-client working relationship should be based on sound project management principles as well as an understanding of the benchmarking process. The benchmarking study purpose and output should be clearly defined. Also important is the documentation of industry best practices in adequate detail. Benchmarking metrics should be pursued but as a secondary level of investigation.

The requirements for the benchmarking study should be clearly understood. These would include all outputs to be benchmarked. A realistic way to approach obtaining a clear statement of deliverables is to request that pro forma statement schedules for the data and information analysis and presentation be prepared. This allows for examination of whether the results will meet developing benchmark practice statements and eventually benchmark metrics. The consultant can approach this phase of the study innovatively by bringing new ways to develop the desired data and the data analysis.

Candidate consultants can be obtained from the many sources

already mentioned, such as from associations representing the function. In addition, there are more generic ways to obtain consultant recommendations such as through directories and associations of consultants. For benchmarking purposes, because benchmarking is a relatively new type of investigation, it is probably productive to rely on the experience of consultants who have knowledge of the industry, have performed successful client studies, and are known to the firm. There may be some who have already conducted benchmarking studies.

The consultant should be able to designate who will conduct the benchmarking investigations to permit review of their background. The individuals should be interviewed to assess potential for good results. Similarly the consultant should know who they will be working with internally and have as a continuing contact for the study. It is best to have potential benchmarking study plans reviewed by those internal persons skilled in the benchmarking process to ensure good results. Those are the people ultimately responsible for the study or who act as consultants to the project to see that the benchmarking investigation is conducted according to the 10-step benchmarking process.

External Experts and Studies

External experts exist in almost all subjects. They are associated with consulting firms, brokerage firms, systems development firms, universities, and nonprofit research organizations. Some of these are quite prominent. Perhaps the best known are the company watchers associated with individual brokerages who make a career of knowing one company. They usually are well known in the industry and quoted frequently on the activities of the firms in their realm of expertise. Similarly, certain individuals are consistently sought out by the media to comment on different types of functions or technology. Experts on computer systems and software are typical of these.

These individuals may have information of value to benchmarking activities. Even if they have no direct knowledge, they may serve as valuable references to others who do or to where the data and information can be obtained. They can be selectively used as knowledgeable leads. Some publish industry reports that detail comparative statistics on companies. These reports often are useful in the initial skimming needed to identify potential benchmarking partners. Similarly these experts often conduct seminars on topics relevant to benchmarking. While on the surface it may appear time-consuming to review the seminar brochures, occasionally there will be information or leads useful to benchmarking. Once a person is on the seminar circuit mailing list it is useful to scan the brochures he or she receives.

Original Research and Investigations

Original research must be conducted where it does not exist in internal or external public sources. A major drawback of original research is that it is expensive to obtain. Ensuring that the information desired is correctly sourced requires careful thought, attention to detail, and successful planning.

It is best to approach these investigations in a step-by-step fashion to obtain what is desired. The steps should proceed from the difficult to more difficult. The first approach will be questionnaires, then site visits, and later more advanced techniques, such as panels of benchmarking partners. Direct-site visits are most often associated with benchmarking, and thus will receive the greatest focus. However, as mentioned previously, this step is often only productive after all other approaches have been exhausted.

Questionnaire

Why use a questionnaire rather than direct-site visits for the critical data desired, especially when it will most likely have to be administered through a third party? A questionnaire serves several important purposes. The first has already been discussed. It is a method to ensure that all questions of interest are thoroughly documented. If the questionnaire is pretested within the organization it can be debugged in a receptive environment to further ensure completeness. Beyond serving as a complete listing of data to be benchmarked, a questionnaire permits more extensive data gathering, which may not be readily available during a site visit. It is quite conceivable that data requested may not be kept in the categories or units of measure desired. Operations are too diverse to assume similar records and measurements. The questionnaire outlines data that can be gathered over a period of time, which would otherwise take too long to complete during a site visit.

A chief use of questionnaires, however, is to ensure anonymity. Where confidentiality of the organization's source of information is necessary, questionnaires may be the only method of obtaining cooperative data gathering. They are more comprehensive and provide confidentiality, but invariably there will be questions about interpretation and terminology used. In such instances, it is almost certain a third party will be needed to interpret the questions for the participants and ensure comparability of data and information. In many instances face-to-face visits between the third party and participants are necessary, if for no other reason than to encourage the acceptance of priorities to get the documentation completed.

Questionnaires can be completed in several different ways. They can be filled in by the respondent and mailed when complete, filled out by the benchmarking team, filled out by a third-party consultant, or obtained by telephone. Each has its benefits and drawbacks. The respondent completion is least expensive but lacks the thoroughness of discussion where interpretation of what is wanted is unclear. Only the most unambiguous topics should be considered for this approach.

Questionnaire completion before the benchmarking visit, or perhaps during the visit, provides an opportunity to obtain interpretation of the results and clarification firsthand as well as to obtain documented data and information. It is perhaps the most thorough method. The use of a third party provides the anonymity desired, but can pose serious problems if the third party is not completely conversant with the topic. Finally, telephone questionnaires provide the opportunity to cover a wide cross section of respondents quickly and reasonably efficiently. It should only be used where the topic is clear. It may require advance notification of the call to alert and prepare the respondent for the contact and the subject matter.

The difficulty with questionnaires is that the information will be filtered to a certain extent, especially if a third party is used. In spite of adequate coaching the third party may not know the relative importance of different data. Also, there are no direct-site observations. Creative ideas originated by direct observation or face-to-face discussion will rarely surface, even though the benchmarking questionnaire should contain a category on anticipated future methods and practices. Therefore, questionnaires should be used primarily to gather current or historical information. It should also be kept in mind that questionnaires can be quite expensive.

Factors to consider in the successful preparation of questionnaires are covered in Quick Reference Guide 5.3. The guide shows that questionnaires are quite useful and can serve multiple uses in benchmarking investigations. They often are seen as formidable documents to prepare and are believed to be fraught with pitfalls if not done by professionals to ensure statistical correctness. It is wise to obtain the advice of a professional when preparing a questionnaire. However, the benchmarker is the one person who knows what data and information are desired and relevant to the investigation. It is often most productive for the person knowledgeable in the subject matter to draft a questionnaire and have the professional market researcher check it for completeness. It is helpful for the benchmarker to have some working knowledge of the preparation of questionnaires. They are relatively straightforward to prepare.

There are basically four types of questions: (1) open ended, (2) multiple choice, (3) forced choice, and (4) scaled. Each has its merits and should be reviewed for applicability to the data and information being gathered in the brief examples shown. Most important in the structure of the questions is how they are worded. There should be no leading questions that would prejudice the answer or give meaningless results. Questions should be as neutral as possible to permit respondents to provide true pictures of the situations they are describing.

Preparing a questionnaire may be seen as a chore, but if the benchmarking problem has been cause-and-effect (Ishikawa fishbone) diagrammed, then the casuals for the problem statement are the prime source of questions. This process of preparing questionnaires is derived from the experienced benchmarker or team and possibly supplemented by brainstorming.

Easy questions should be asked first with a progression to the more difficult later in the questionnaire. The questionnaire can close with demographic data and information to document what the respondent firm's business profile is like. The questionnaire should always be pretested. The best way to accomplish that is to administer it to the internal functional organization. This will reveal whether useful data and information can be obtained, and any data and information gaps will be revealed.

A discussion outline can be prepared once the questionnaire is completed. This will be a productive use of the questionnaire even if the questionnaire is not used in its entirety. The discussion outline can then serve as the agenda for any direct-site visits. It may be useful to prepare a questionnaire for the lowest level of detail desired and derive discussion outlines for successively higher levels of management. When questionnaires are used, and then their coded answers are discussed during interviews, their value is greatly extended. This type of interview will yield the maximum information. Not only will the interviewer know how the questions were answered but why. This can only be accomplished if the questionnaire is prescored before the visit. This can be highly desirable but should be balanced with the possibility of being too overwhelming for beginning contacts. It should be reserved for very structured, committed, and mature benchmarking contacts.

Mail Administered Questionnaires

There may be some instances where benchmarking data can be obtained through mail survey questionnaires, such as questionnaires about customer satisfaction with products and services, including those of competitors. Factors to consider in the successful mail questionnaire are covered in Quick Reference Guide 5.4. Because response rates are so low for this type of information-gathering technique, careful consideration needs to be given to the design and incentives to participate.

The questionnaire should only be sent to those targeted as the principal contacts most likely predisposed to answer questions through the mail. This is usually done by securing mailing lists for the targeted population and then by carefully examining the list for those contacts that should logically be discarded. In this way the expense of the mailing is reduced and the probability of returns raised. However, this may still not be enough to get the desired participation level. In many instances a direct incentive must be offered to further raise the probability of a response. These may be incentives of value such as a crisp dollar bill, but often a copy of the results of the study are adequate. If the intended data analysis can be included in the request so that the individual can visualize the outcome, that further adds to the probability of success.

Other ways to ensure success are to preannounce the survey with a mailer or call in advance to obtain verbal commitment to filling out the form and returning it. The latter provides a personalized request for a response as does a well-designed letter. At minimum the questionnaire should be easy to use and attractive as well as have good human factors for the person filling it out. It should be sent first class mail and include a prestamped return envelope. Sometimes a pen or pencil is included so there are no barriers to responding.

Telephone Administered Surveys

Telephone surveys can be used to gather benchmarking information. Factors to consider in the successful telephone questionnaire are covered in Quick Reference Guide 5.5. These usually should be on a professional-to-professional basis for greatest results, but contract telephone surveys can also be used. These surveys are usually specific, highly information targeted, and take only a short time to gather the required data and information. The person being contacted is busy and interruption should be kept to a bare minimum. Benchmarking information gathered through this type of medium is usually information that is needed quickly. Since there will be little opportunity to validate the responses, the technique relies on obtaining many responses to determine the norm.

The greatest difficulty in conducting the survey is locating the right person who has the knowledge and can answer the questions. The benchmarker may need to ask for a referral from the initial contact. There are several ways to ensure a listening ear from the contact. Explain who you are and why you are calling and that you are interested in discussing industry best practices. This should make the conversation interesting to the other party and will help to obtain their attention. Obviously the questions should come from a predesigned and pretested script and should be easy to understand, progressing from the easy questions to the more difficult. Complex questions should be reserved for written response. The cooperation to participate in a written response can be solicited during the telephone contact. Again, the incentive to cooperation may be the opportunity to receive a copy of the results.

Direct-Site Visits

The most interesting and credible benchmarking method is the direct-site visit, where face-to-face exchange of data and information can be conducted. Usually this is coupled with a tour of the operation where one can observe the methods, practices, and processes used firsthand. There will also be an opportunity to discuss the merits and demerits of the practices observed, and to obtain firsthand feedback about the rationale for their implementation and benefits derived.

However, careful planning and preparation are essential to ensure productive use of each party's time, both the visitor's time and those who are interrupting their operations to host the visit. Time should not be wasted on observing and discussing the inconsequential facets of the visit. The visitors will most likely be on site the better part of one day. While there are follow-up approaches to gathering or confirming information after a visit, the time that has been considerately set aside should be used to a maximum. It is essential that the focus of the visit be on the essential, critical data of interest.

It is assumed that the benchmark partners' interests are known from prior investigations (see Chapter 4). With these necessary steps completed, preparation can be made for the visit, including making the contact to set up the visit, determining who should attend, developing the itinerary, conducting the actual visit, and debriefing after the visit. These will each be discussed in turn.

Preparation

Previsit planning should include researching all available public information. At a minimum this includes the review of annual reports and obtaining a Dun & Bradstreet report. The data and information of interest should be well documented and outlined in essential categories. (See Chapter 3, Table 3.4 for an example of areas of interest.) The categories of interest should be compared to the data already available and data gaps should be determined.

The most thorough preparation for a site visit is the preparation of a questionnaire. If planning for the benchmarking project included the development of a cause-and-effect (Ishikawa fishbone) diagram, this is an excellent basis on which to prepare a questionnaire. However, the actual administration of a questionnaire during a site visit is not recommended. Most questionnaires are too time-consuming and cumbersome to use in face-to-face discussions. Furthermore, they are generally too time-consuming for a single day's visit. They also can be threatening and serve to demotivate cooperation. Experience has shown that a detailed questionnaire for site visits should be used as a checklist and preparation for the visit rather than a specific data collection document. It is more useful to extract perhaps 10 to 15 questionnaire categories and use them as an outline for discussion. The categories will serve to open and lead discussion about a topic of interest. With adequate writing space between questions it will allow the documentation of not only the points of interest but also any further information that may be volunteered. The questionnaire categories should be looked on as leading questions that can be pursued further once initial response is received.

Has the preparation of a questionnaire been wasted? The answer is definitely not. If the visit is made by a team, as will be discussed, one member can check the questionnaire while others discuss points of interest. In this fashion thorough preparation and open-ended discussion format with a checklist to ensure all aspects of interest are covered will both be achieved.

In summary, preparation should cover assembling all information that is already available in the public domain, knowing the more important information being sought and identifying the data gaps to be covered at the meeting. Visits also provide a forum for confirming data already in hand if there are questions about the accuracy or interpretation of the data. In fact, reviewing known data from an article, seminar, or annual report is an excellent way to open discussions during visits. There is no better way to obtain cooperation than to comment positively on something about the operation being considered for a visit.

Contact

Making contact with the benchmark partner often is viewed with apprehension. Whether the partner will be receptive to a visit is certainly justification for concern and careful planning. If an improper contact is made there is the distinct possibility of being turned down and that may be the one and only chance for a a very important meeting. There are, however, several productive ways that contacts can be made. What is involved is finding some mutual relationship or interest on which to build.

Company Representatives

First, and perhaps most productive, it should be determined if there is a customer-supplier relationship. Is the firm to be visited a customer? Does it buy your products? If so it can be contacted by your sales rep, or by your national account manager if it is a major firm. Your national account manager can be extremely helpful in arranging for a meeting and should be able to confirm or verify the correct individuals to approach. He or she also may be helpful in identifying the correct organization unit to visit in a divisionalized firm.

The reciprocal relationships can be equally productive. Are you one of the firm's customers? If so, there is a rep from the firm who may assist. Especially in the case of software and hardware, the reps are sources for client companies who use their products and who can be queried for clients who demonstrate best practices. The use of these intermediaries is one of the most successful methods of arranging visits and confirming the correctness of initial findings from reviewing public information.

Professional to Professional

Direct contact between professionals is a worthwhile approach. It is not difficult to determine who your counterpart is in another firm, especially if there is a professional association to which you belong. Canvassing the membership directory is always suggested. If the person is not the correct one he or she can refer you to the correct contact. The objective is to approach a contact on the basis of professional interest in improving operations, understanding current practices, and determining future possible direction. It is most helpful to refer to something recently published about the person's firm indicating innovative practices about which you would like to learn more.

Referrals

Referrals can come from several sources: consultants, professional associations, product reps, and acquaintances. Articles citing practices with statements of pride also provide a direct reason for contact.

Careful thought in exploring these alternative contact sources will in most instances reveal a way to set up a successful visit. Of course the court of last resort would be high-level executive to high-level executive contact. This may be the only feasible basis to set up a get-together. However, experience has shown that a request cascaded down from senior management sets up natural resistance on the part of the operation of interest since the reason for the contact may not be well understood. The interest in industry practices is most readily understood by the operation exhibiting the practices. The pride in having a counterpart show direct interest and firsthand understanding about the operations is usually more successful. The appropriateness of the visit will be checked at the executive level in most circumstances anyway. It is more productive to have the request go up the channel rather than down.

Visit Itinerary

If a questionnaire has been prepared, the outline categories provide an excellent basis on which to establish the visit itinerary and discussion outline. Often it is worthwhile to send the outline ahead so the correct people will be available and can be scheduled to attend the meeting. If there are operations for which a tour is arranged, it is most important to ensure the appropriate operational supervisors are available. The questionnaire outline then, in summary fashion, provides direct definition for areas of interest and should be used to ensure a productive visit.

The actual visit most likely should consist of at least some introduction to the operation, a site or operation tour, if appropriate, and discussions afterward with the appropriate individuals. During the tour, conversations with the supervisors and prior experience in one's own operation should quickly reveal where best practices are being used. While notebooks often are appropriate during tours, discretion is advised. Most data and information can be documented following the tour and during the debriefing cycle. Also discussions away from the operation with designated, knowledgeable people will permit confirmation of observations and discussions of the merits and demerits of the methods observed.

It is also important that discussions explore future planned improvements as well as benefits of current practices. The latter is best conducted in the ubiquitous conference room. At that time the visiting team should also be prepared with what data and information they will be able to share in return.

Factors to consider in the successful personal interview are considered in Quick Reference Guide 5.6. The guidelines should be considered seriously because personal interviews are at the core of benchmarking. They should be approached with care and preparation. It is important to identify the correct person to contact as a benchmarking partner. Several methods have been mentioned previously. Out of courtesy it would be appropriate to determine, preferably internally and beforehand, whether the individual has been contacted before or has participated in benchmarking studies. This will save introducing the topic or covering the same material. It also will smooth the protocol.

An outline statement of purpose and summary of what is desired is paramount. The discussion should be focused on best industry practices. If possible, an outline of the topics for discussion should be sent ahead to permit preparation by the benchmark partners. Before the contact one should be informed as much as possible about the partner firm. The use of a questionnaire with internal answers allows the discussion to be thorough and each question to have a purpose. Each question should be reviewed for absolute need to know and not simply because it would be nice to know. The contact should be based on an exchange of information, not just one-way sharing. During the visit, the rules from the *Information Gathering Guidelines,* Quick Reference Guide 5.9, should be followed. After the visit there should be a letter of appreciation, a debriefing session, and a trip report.

Debriefing

It is imperative that a debriefing session be conducted following or as soon after the visit as possible. It may be on site, at the airport, or back at the office. The important point is that it be done. Since a sizable investment in time has been made, essential facts and observations should be cross-checked.

The debriefing should provide a forum where agreement can be reached about the valuable observations of best practices that were seen and could be implemented.

A trip report is appropriate on return to the work location. It should contain the results of the debriefing with all parties agreeing on what is documented. If items are unclear, follow-up telephone contact may be appropriate. In selected instances where items need to be confirmed, a written confirmation memo can be prepared. This may be especially helpful where data, not readily available at the time of visit, but which need consistent interpretation, are needed. In such circumstance a schedule with definitions for the categories is appropriate. A thank-you letter is common courtesy, both to the participants as well as the intermediary if there was one. If a findings report is prepared, a copy of a summary back to the benchmark partners may also be appropriate. Confidentiality can be maintained by anonymous coding or summary descriptions.

Attendees

The visiting team is usually made up of between one and three people, three considered ideal. Two individuals can document answers and prepare to ask the next question while the third speaks. This process keeps the discussion at optimum use of time. The next preference would be two people. It is almost impossible to conduct face-to-face discussions with one person. Too much precious time is lost documenting answers.

Equally important is who should attend. The team should include the person responsible for benchmarking and someone in an operational capacity who may be responsible for implementing the practices observed. The latter can be critical in obtaining concurrence to what is documented in the trip report. An ideal combination is the benchmark individual, a headquarters planning and analysis individual, and a representative from the comparable field operation.

While mentioned before, it bears emphasis at this point that the mind set of those attending is important. There should be discussion among the three before the visit to confirm the purpose of the visit, the questions needing answers, and the expectations of the visit. If there is ambiguity about the questions they should be pretested with the internal operation to ensure clarity of the desired data and information.

It is necessary to avoid the natural tendency to critically appraise the observed operation compared to the team's own operations. It is human nature to stick up for your own operation as better. However, the concentration should be on what the benchmarking partner does better. What are the best practices being emulated? Why are they better? Which are adaptable if the method is not totally adoptable? An opportunity to see the operation in this light should not be missed for lack of appropriate viewpoint.

Why is such careful attention given to direct-site visits? Aside from the fact that they should be done on a truly professional basis, there is a more important reason. The site visit by knowledgeable professionals is the most credible of all benchmarking methods. The team has had the opportunity to see an operation firsthand, and being able to say they were there cannot be easily dismissed when questioned about observations. It also is the most revealing. For many who have not had the opportunity of a structured external visit it can be quite a rude awakening. It goes against the grain that there are others who have methods, practices, and processes that are different much less better than internal operations. But that is what benchmarking is all about.

Factors to consider in successful site tours are covered in Quick Reference Guide 5.7. Site visits along with personal interviews are one of the primary benchmarking methods. For this reason an entire section has been devoted to their conduct. The guidelines presented here are a brief review of the more important points. They are presented in logical, chronological sequence of a typical visit.

Focus Groups (Panels)

By this time it should be clear that there are many sources of information and they are limited only by one's own ingenuity. (Several more will be discussed.) However, to indicate the range of possibilities, an advanced technique will be introduced for contrast. This technique involves the direct sharing of observations on best practices by inviting benchmarking partners to a panel discussion. Obviously they must recognize the value of the information to be shared and want to participate. Those interests may be revealed through site visits or more likely through a confidential questionnaire administered by a third party where additional information or follow-up studies are requested by the study participants.

A panel discussion may be considered and could be arranged by the third party. It most likely would be well structured and conducted at a neutral site. Often it would be hosted by the third party, especially if careful facilitation is required. Provided that the panel is focused on best business practices and future, a type of advanced benchmarking such as Delphi information gathering (a structured interviewing of experts in the field of interest) this may prove quite productive.

Factors to consider in the successful use of panels are covered in Quick Reference Guide 5.8. Panel interviews used in benchmarking are specific occasions to bring benchmarking partners together to discuss points of mutual interest. Where this has proven to be successful is when the partners have participated in prior benchmarking studies, perhaps through a third party to maintain confidentiality, have had some benchmarking information feedback, and find that there is a continuing interest in further information sharing, but firsthand, on a more direct basis. The panel then takes the form of an interview about prior benchmarking findings. It provides a forum to discuss further why the findings indicated the results they did. It is another way to understand why the practices or metrics are what they are. These forums should be carefully designed. They are obviously targeted to focus on industry best practices both proven and in operation as well as expected future practices. Most useful are the services of a third party to set up the panel and act as facilitator. After care in selecting participants, consideration should be given to the selection of a neutral site. A complete agenda and discussion guide should be prepared before the meeting. Finally, what is to be done with the results in the form of documenting the outcome should be agreed on beforehand.

Basis for Information Sharing

Prior to any benchmarking contacts, consideration should be given to the basis on which information will be shared. What will be the motivation, willingness, and restrictions on the part of others to share information? It has been found from experience that the basic willingness to share — provided the information is not proprietary or confidential — is based on a mutual desire to uncover and understand industry best practices.

A well-thought-out approach to the benchmarking partners should be documented before making contact. The key messages should stress exchanging, on a professional basis, experiences and judgment of best practices in the industry or functional field. Discussions limited to best practices both currently installed and planned for future use are appropriate. The benefits of information sharing far outweigh any initial reluctance to participate.

Specific data to be discussed will be known from the questionnaires already prepared. Data exchange can best be done on the basis of ratios. Ratio data-like unit costs, productivity rates, and inventory turns do not disclose absolute values and can usually be shared. These leave the scale of operation undefined. Ratios can be expressed as a range if the data become sensitive.

Another reason why ratio data are desirable is that their use later will be to quantify the effect of that practice or method on internal operations, if it was installed or adopted for installation. They will be used to project quantitatively how internal operations would change if they acted like external processes.

Often desired data are not in a useable form because the benchmark partner does not maintain records and performance statistics in the units of measure desired. The visit then can serve to discuss the data desired with the agreement that a data sheet will be sent following the meeting. With the categories well understood and documented, the data may be obtained in this fashion providing it is not seen as burdensome. After the fact confirmation may be effective since the data desired do not depend on interpretation of questions because they have been explained in face-to-face discussions.

Factors to consider in successful information gathering are covered in Quick Reference Guide 5.9. Guidelines on information gathering concern what data and information are to be gathered and how to handle sensitivities with the information if there are any. Before any original research or external information gathering is conducted, those involved in benchmarking activities should give careful consideration to what is being gathered and why. It is wise to think through the logic of, approach to, and need for the data and information. For example, why are the data being sought? Why are these data needed in preference to other data? What is the priority of data and information desired? Is there any perceived sensitive nature to what is being requested? The guide is intended to be a general outline; those facets of information gathering that should be considered before a benchmarking study involves original data gathering. It is meant to serve as a starter set of considerations and is not necessarily complete. The person conducting the study can add to and expand the guidelines as the circumstances demand. The guide is presented in two parts: general guidelines and specific. *As a matter of general approach one should never misrepresent himself or herself in any benchmarking contact. One should be open about what and why they are interested in the benchmarking investigation.*

As has been mentioned frequently, the soundest basis for the contact is to gather and share information on industry best practices. It can be pointed out that the benchmarking partner will also benefit. If the purpose of the contact is thought out carefully, it should not pose a problem. Proprietary information in the benchmarker's firm will most obviously also be so in the partner's firm. This is the best way to sort out what is and is not appropriate to discuss.

The more specific guidelines deal with information gathering that may be questionable and how to correctly handle them. Where there is a legal question legal counsel should be contacted — preferably before any visit. In some instances it is possible to share sensitive information but the proper clearances should be obtained.

The use of a third party guaranteeing anonymity may be the appropriate way to gather information. There are, however, general topic areas that are known to be inappropriate. These concern prices and marketplace activities and should be avoided in any discussions.

In general, common sense should prevail. If the data and information are judged sensitive to the benchmarker, then it most likely will also be so to the benchmarking partners. Judging data and information gathering on this basis should forestall any sensitivities, but still allow the maximum benefits to be gained from these mutually beneficial exchanges through benchmarking.

In addition to considering what information is appropriate to gather as covered in Quick Reference Guide 5.9, careful consideration should be given to how information is gathered. Most important is that discussions are limited to industry best practices. These should include those currently implemented in the benchmark partner's operation as well as those planned for implementation. Limiting discussions to this basis will place the data and information gathering on a positive, proactive level.

In similar fashion, information received should be a candidate for sharing on a reciprocal basis. The rule of reciprocal sharing is a sound one. If the data have some level of sensitivity and can be gathered providing confidentiality is maintained, then the use of a third party to act as a clearinghouse is most likely the way the data can be gathered logically.

Development of Evergreen Sources

Benchmarks are not static. They are not created once to remain forever. Processes, methods, and practices change within an industry and in competition. Over time all functions strive to improve their operations or new functions or priorities are created that require new benchmarking initiatives. Benchmarks are constantly tracking a relative position, and updates are needed to keep them current. This is usually referred to as keeping the benchmarks evergreen.

There are several ways to accomplish keeping benchmarks current. One is to replicate the original, landmark studies on the same basis. This approach gives two or more distinct measures and statements at specific points in time. The interval can be selected based on experience but probably should not exceed three years and probably should not be more often than one. The second way is to update over time, as new information becomes available. This is a more gradual approach but one that can be used at desired intervals. Both are viable alternatives. The essential consideration, however, is that a process be installed that will ensure that benchmarks are updated.

In spite of the desire to update benchmark data, one consideration must be understood. There never will be complete benchmark data at any one point in time. There always will be data gaps. Part of the process of conducting benchmarking is to identify the gaps and assess the severity of missing data and make decisions about the value of gathering additional information to complete the benchmarking data fabric. This identification and assessment process is one which must be constantly considered when replicating initial studies or continuous data gathering during the evergreen process.

The L. L. Bean Experience

It was decided early on that the professional to professional contact method would be the approach used with L. L. Bean. The manager in charge of benchmarking had heard a presentation on L. L. Bean's warehouse design and had spoken briefly with L. L. Bean's vice president of distribution in the fall of 1981. In early 1982 when it was evident that a visit to L. L. Bean would be worthwhile, the manager contacted the vice president and discussed the purpose and interest in seeing the L. L. Bean operation firsthand. Substantial preparation preceded the meeting. This included development of a questionnaire and later a discussion outline that became the basis for the agenda. These efforts assumed that effective use would be made of each party's time, for one day. It would also ensure that topics of primary interest would be discussed.

A meeting was arranged in Freeport, Maine, to review the operation. The team going to Freeport consisted of the manager responsible for benchmarking, a headquarters planning manager for the products of primary interest, and a field distribution center manager. The latter two represented the line operations that would ultimately be responsible for implementing any changes.

The site visit included discussions with L. L. Bean's vice president of distribution about the periodical article citing the operation, a discussion of current and planned practices, and a facility tour. During the tour, discussions also were held with supervisors of the individual operations. Adequate time was planned for each step to ensure effective exchange of ideas, data, and information.

Following the visit a debriefing session was held while waiting for the return flight. On return to Rochester the findings from the trip were documented and distributed to interested parties, both field and headquarters. A thank you was extended to L. L. Bean as well as the possibility of a reciprocal visit if deemed of interest.

QUICK REFERENCE GUIDE 5.1

TRADE AND PROFESSIONAL ASSOCIATION SOURCES

- Review relevant trade and professional associations in the Encyclopedia of Associations.

- Contact the association director or information officer.

- Validate that the association represents the function on which information is desired and that it is the single or most prominent association doing so.

- Inquire about sources of information from:
  — Publications and publications lists
  — Research conducted
  — Membership roster
  — Conferences — annual and special event
  — Local chapter agendas
  — Prominent consultants in the field
  — Principal periodical or journals in the field
  — Training courses
  — Equipment or service suppliers prominent in the field

- Review these sources of information for appropriate benchmarking contacts and approaches.

- Discuss the general nature of the information desired with association representatives.

If the above resources are not productive, ask for suggestions on where to find desired information.

QUICK REFERENCE GUIDE 5.2
WORKING WITH CONSULTANTS

- Clearly define and document the purpose and output for the consulting engagement.

- Customer requirements for the consulting engagement should include:
  - Project purpose
  - Question list and data to be collected
  - Targeted survey population or desired benchmarking partners
  - Pro forma survey data presentation, analysis, conclusions, and recommendations
  - Schedule, checkpoint reviews, payment terms, and other policy or procedural requirements

A review of these requirements with the consultant may reveal other opportunities to be pursued and modification of the contract. The ability of the consultant to contribute at this phase should not be overlooked.

- Select the consultant from at least two possible sources. Sources for consultants with desired expertise can be obtained from:
  - Professional associations
  - Consulting associations
  - Directories of consultants
  - Prior experience or the experience of others conducting benchmarking

- Before retaining a consultant determine which staff members will work on the project, including:
  - Their background
  - Samples of prior work
  - A check of prior client references
  - A determination of resources available to the consultant

QUICK REFERENCE GUIDE 5.2 (CONT.)
WORKING WITH CONSULTANTS

- Assess the ability of the consultant to work with internal organizations to achieve the best possible results.

- Follow up on the conduct of the study at regular intervals. Verify that the work is meeting requirements and that there is common understanding of the data and information.

QUICK REFERENCE GUIDE 5.3
PREPARING A QUESTIONNAIRE

- Review the types of questions possible, such as:
  — Open-ended
  — Multiple choice
  — Forced choice
  — Scaled

- Review examples of each type to determine applicability and pros and cons.
  — Open-ended: "How did you choose the order entry process and computer system you have?"
  — Multiple choice: "Why did you select the material handling equipment used for order picking?"
  _____ Vendor reputation
  _____ Cost
  _____ Ongoing maintenance support
  — Forced choice: "Would you buy again from your ASRS vendor?"
  _____ Yes _____ No
  — Scaled: "How important was maintenance support in your choice of ASRS vendor?"
  ____ Very important ____ Somewhat important
  ____ Important   ____ Not important

- Review the phrasing of the question as the wording will influence the reply. Use a balanced wording, such as:
  "How satisfactory is the uptime from your ASRS vendor?" (balanced)
  "What is the best uptime you could expect from your ASRS vendor?" (extreme)

QUICK REFERENCE GUIDE 5.3 (CONT.)
PREPARING A QUESTIONNAIRE

- Write the questions. Review the question list for priority sequence. Open with the easy, straightforward questions. Place more difficult, important questions in the middle. Close with demographic questions (type of business, geographic coverage, organization, etc.).

- Pretest the questionnaire. The most effective testing procedure is to administer it to the applicable internal operation. This process should not only clarify the question wording but also add or delete those which are appropriate. The internal pretest will also prioritize those of highest benchmarking interest.

- Prepare a discussion outline from broad question categories and consider sending that ahead of any visits or other contacts so respondents can prepare themselves.

QUICK REFERENCE GUIDE 5.4
PREPARING A MAIL SURVEY

- Determine the appropriate target population.
- Obtain mailing lists for the appropriate target population. Examples of mailing list sources include:
  - Trade association membership rosters
  - Trade publication lists
  - Mailing list vendors

  It is important to validate the quality of a mailing list before its use.

- Provide an incentive for the contact to answer the questionnnaire. These may include:
  - Cash or a memento
  - Redeemable coupons or a prize
  - A copy of the summary survey results with anonymity maintained

  If the survey is extensive the last incentive may be the only productive approach. A pro forma sample of output will help in obtaining a commitment.

- Consider any of the following approaches to obtain a favorable response rate:
  - For small populations telephone ahead and use the telephone for follow-up.
  - Personalize the request for participation and sign the cover letter.
  - Send the materials by first class mail.
  - Make the questionnaire attractive and easy to complete.
  - Include a preaddressed, stamped return envelope.

QUICK REFERENCE GUIDE 5.5
TELEPHONE SURVEY GUIDELINES

- Obtain telephone numbers for the target population.

- Locate the appropriate respondent to discuss the subject matter desired. If the answerer is not the appropriate person, request a referral after discussing the study objective.

- An incentive may have to be provided to the respondent to gain cooperation or coordinate responses within the firm. A copy of the results may be the primary incentive.

- The following techniques are likely to increase interview participation:
  - Explain who you are and why you are calling.
  - Make opening remarks conversational and interesting.
  - Use questions that have a logical sequence, that proceed from the general to the specific, and move easily from one subject to another.
  - Involved and complex questions should be obtained through written questionnaires or personal interviews.
  - Pretest the questionnaire on the phone.

QUICK REFERENCE GUIDE 5.6
CONDUCTING A PERSONAL INTERVIEW

- Determine the appropriate contact by investigating the following sources:
  - External sources (directories of associations, professional association membership directories, partner company inquiry)
  - Internal sources (sales representatives, account managers, library research)

- Determine if the benchmarking partner has been contacted before to avoid covering the same material.

- Prepare an outline statement summary of what the purpose of the contact is and why the person has been contacted.

- Request a discussion about industry best practices and possibly a meeting.

- To prepare for the discussion send an abbreviated outline of the topics to be covered to allow the partner to prepare.

- Prepare for the discussion and visit:
  - Document the objectives.
  - Review available information about the partner firm.
  - Prepare a questionnaire on the topics that you want discussed.
  - Be prepared to explain why a particular question is being asked.
  - Prepare a set of answers based on your own operation and know what information you are willing to share.
  - Decide what company information you are willing to leave behind.

QUICK REFERENCE GUIDE 5.6 (CONT.)
CONDUCTING A PERSONAL INTERVIEW

- During the visit:
  - Represent yourself correctly.
  - State the objectives of the visit.
  - Use the questionnaire or a checklist on areas of discussion.
  - If appropriate, offer a reciprocal visit.

- After the visit:
  - Send a letter of appreciation for the visit.
  - Debrief the session.
  - Prepare a trip report.

QUICK REFERENCE GUIDE 5.7
SITE TOUR GUIDELINES

- Determine the most appropriate person to contact at the benchmarking partner's firm.

- Have a clear statement of the purpose and objectives for the visit prepared.

- It has been found most productive to stress the interest in uncovering industry best practices. If this is done on a professional-to-professional basis it should create initial interest in sharing information.

- Prepare an outline of the topic areas of interest to act as a guide for the visit.

- Obtain and review all available, relevant data on the company in advance.

- If the company is a customer or a supplier, contact the sales rep or account manager and request assistance in:
  - Identifying the appropriate organization and individuals to contact
  - Acting as an intermediary to set up the visit

- Ensure that the equivalent internal operation is documented and understood from the point of view of the practices involved as well as the applicable performance metrics.

- The best team size is two to three individuals. Roles should be agreed to in advance such as who the leader will be, and who will ask what questions.

- Prepare a list of questions for which answers are desired in two major areas:
  - Best practices — practices currently in use or planned.
  - Metrics — output ratios that support the justification for the best practices.

QUICK REFERENCE GUIDE 5.7 (CONT.)
SITE TOUR GUIDELINES

- Conduct the site visit and gather all relevant data and information.

- During the tour it may not be possible to take notes. Retain key points to be documented as soon after the tour as possible.

- Use time after the tour to obtain clarification of observations and information.

- Be prepared to discuss the equivalent internal data and information.

- Clarify data and information understanding before leaving or provide for follow-up methods to validate information interpretation.

- Offer a reciprocal visit and tour if appropriate.

- Debrief the tour among the team members as quickly as possible following the tour. A productive way to accomplish this and prepare a trip report is to have a recorder present during debriefing to capture the discussion. The discussion should cover observations as well as information received.

- Thank the benchmarking partner for their time and cooperation both informally and formally by letter.

- Document the tour in a written trip report.

- Extend a reciprocal visit if appropriate.

QUICK REFERENCE GUIDE 5.8

PANEL INTERVIEWS

- Determine interest level for panel-type discussion of industry best practices by participants.
- Consider using third party services to set up panel discussion, including:
  - Participants
  - Purpose and objectives of discussion
  - Specific questions to be discussed
  - Agenda for meeting
  - Selection of discussion coordinator or facilitator
  - Documentation procedure for information
  - Neutral site location

QUICK REFERENCE GUIDE 5.9

DRAFT POLICY ON INFORMATION GATHERING AND INFORMATION SHARING

Basis for Information Gathering

General Guidelines

- Represent yourself fully as a member of your firm.

- Ask only for that data and information which you would be willing to share.

- Represent yourself as seeking benchmarking partners who are willing to share information on industry best practices.

- The benefit to the benchmarking partner is that it should improve their understanding of their own practices and ultimately help to satisfy their own customer requirements

- If data and information are confidential or proprietary, they should remain so.

- Use the business test: If this visit were covered by the press in an article written under a byline, would there be any reason for concern?

Specific Requirements

- Where an information-gathering practice appears, questionable contact legal counsel.

- If confidential information is to be shared, obtain all necessary clearances in advance.

- Information on prices, pricing policies, marketing strategies, marketplace activities, and customer information is absolutely inappropriate.

QUICK REFERENCE GUIDE 5.9 (CONT.)

DRAFT POLICY ON INFORMATION GATHERING AND INFORMATION SHARING

Basis for Information Sharing

- Information sharing should be limited to current and future industry best practices.

- Information should be shared on a reciprocal basis.

- Information that is requested should be only that which the organization has prepared for sharing, in return.

- If information is difficult to obtain consider use of a third party where confidentiality is maintained.

- Involve the functionally affected operational management team.

CHAPTER 6 DETERMINING THE CURRENT COMPETITIVE GAP (STEP 4)

Types of Performance Gaps
- Negative gap
- Operations at parity
- Positive gap
  - Analytic superiority
  - Marketplace superiority

Comparative Analysis of the Gap
- Practice opportunity
- Performance metric
  - What is to be quantified
  - Quantification means comparability
  - Quantification precision
  - Alternatives for quantification

Practices Contributing to the Gap
- Process practices
- Business practices
- Operational structure

Recognizing Benchmark Practices
- The practice is clearly superior
- The quantified opportunity is large
- Expert judgment
- The same practice recurs

The L. L. Bean Experience

DETERMINING THE CURRENT COMPETITIVE GAP (STEP 4)

Assessing Industry Leader Strengths and Your Performance

At this point in the benchmarking process, outputs will have been defined, the functional best operations of interest sourced, visits or other data gathering conducted, and the data documented. The next step is to analyze the data and compare the data to internal operations.

What will be revealed by the comparison is a positive or negative competitive or performance gap. The current competitive gap is a measure of the difference between the internal organization's performance and that of the best in the industry. The positive gap should receive appropriate recognition. It is the negative gap that will be primarily discussed in this chapter. First, because it is negative and shows undesirable performance; and second, because it provides the basis for improvement opportunities.

While these are the major considerations for understanding the benchmarking gap covered in this chapter, of equal interest are the two bases for statement of the gap, namely as a practice opportunity and as a performance metric. A scheme for categorizing those practices contributing to the gap is also covered. These result from the process practices themselves — business practices that are applicable to all processes and the operational structure within which the process and business practices are used over a foreseeable period of time.

In addition, this chapter also will describe how a benchmark practice can be judged to be an industry best practice. This is not always a single test. It may be based on several tests including the following: being clearly superior, showing a large opportunity, being based on expert judgment, the fact that the practice recurs in many benchmarking investigations, and that the process would be preferred in a profit-motivated external marketplace — the ultimate test of having found the best.

Types of Performance Gaps

There are three types of performance gaps: positive, negative, and a position where operations are at parity (Table 6.1). What is desired in the gap's analysis is an objective assessment of their magnitude as well as an explanation of why the gap exists.

Differences in practices, especially when external operations are better, are the performance gaps of most interest. They should be analyzed to determine if the practices can be implemented as a whole or if they need to be modified and adapted to obtain the major portion of their benefits.

The basic analysis process is one based on the analysis and understanding of differences; it is a comparative analysis. The basic steps include tabulating both descriptive and numeric data, analyzing the data for understanding and rationale, determining the benchmark, determining the gap by comparison to internal operations data, evaluating and describing the reasons for the existence of the gap, and evaluating the factors that contribute to the best practices' existence. These are standard approaches to analyses of differences found in any qualitative or quantitative analyses text. They will be not covered. What will be covered are those aspects of the analyses relevant to benchmarking.

Negative Gap

Where a negative gap exists it means that external operations are the benchmark. Their best practices are clearly superior. Whether the measure is unit cost, level of customer satisfaction,

TYPE	DESCRIPTION	CONSEQUENCE
Negative	External practices are superior	Benchmark based on external findings
Parity	No significant practice differences	Further analysis justified
Positive	Internal practices are superior	Benchmark based on internal findings

TABLE 6.1. TYPES OF PERFORMANCE GAPS

or inventory turns, the external practices on which these performance measures are based are superior. A major effort is required to change internal practices and methods to meet or exceed the external findings. The major focus of the comparative analysis will be to explain why differences exist and the specific contributing factors which require change. It will be these changed practices that will provide improvement and eventually result in superior performance or a competitive advantage.

Operations at Parity

Where operations are at parity, investigations have been conducted and no significant differences are found. Both operations have similar performance measures. There may be slight differences in methods used but the outcome, or results, are essentially the same.

While these neutral results can be consoling they should not provide comfort for any length of time. The benchmark practices are being examined and documented at a point in time. Meanwhile, industry practices and competitive methods change and a parity position is short-lived.

At the same time the parity position should be evaluated for contributing factors. Analysis of work processes, standards, environmental conditions, and economic or cultural factors should be evaluated for contribution to the practices existence. A critical evaluation of efficiency versus effectiveness may prove worthwhile. Why operations are at parity should be the question. Are operations performing the methods right? Are they using efficient methods? Are the right methods in operation? Are effective methods installed? The analysis will most likely reveal that a level of simplification can be attained to provide further effectiveness and the parity position is truly nonexistent. Although a parity position may be found, the benchmarking activities should be directed continually toward methods that will lead to superiority.

Positive Gap

A positive gap is indicative of internal operations showing a clear superiority over external operations. This may be a surprising finding but one that should not be unexpected if benchmarking is conducted over an extended period of time. The objective is to arrive at a level of superior performance. To the extent that superior performance exists, even in subfunction operations, it should receive its appropriate visibility and recognition.

Benchmarking has both positive and negative outcomes, and should be managed and rewarded accordingly. Emphasizing superior performance will go a long way toward underwriting the continual search for ways to close the negative gaps.

There may be a level of skepticism about operations truly being superior. The burden of proof will be on the benchmarking investigations to prove they are superior. There are several ways to accomplish that task. They should be used to confirm and justify the superior findings. They are derived either analytically or are proofs from the marketplace. An example of logistics operations above, below, and at parity is shown in Table 6.2.

Best Industry Practices

The most significant practices contributing to the benchmark gap are:
- Industry operations have fewer inventory echelons between source and point of use.
- Orders are picked, packed, and shipped from one central source and shipped direct to end users.
- Warehousing activities are computer controlled to plan and direct work flow, on-line in real time.

Operations at Parity

There are some current operations and practices at parity:
- Percent inventory availability level of service at market location is equivalent.
- Local delivery expense within market location zone is equivalent.
- Order entry system for inbound telephone calls is equivalent to others.

Operations Exhibiting Superiority

Several operations exhibit superiority with proven technology:
- Distribution facility ownership costs are lower by virtue of strategic location and historical lease terms.
- Short-term inventory forecasting and ordering system is industry standard because of incorporation of latest proven techniques, based on leading consultant recommendations.

TABLE 6.2.   EXAMPLE DESCRIPTIONS OF OPERATIONS BELOW AND ABOVE BENCHMARK AND AT PARITY

Analytic Superiority

Provided that methods are clearly understood and adequate performance measures are obtained, the performance of internal operations should analytically be able to be proven to be superior. This means the key summary measures of performance will be superior and the operation proven most cost-effective. These may result in efficiencies in labor, facilities, communications, or other factors that directly affect profitability or return on assets. It should not be too difficult to show superiority if adequate, defensible data and information have been documented from the benchmarking investigations. An example is shown in Table 6.3 for the strategic logistics deliverables.

The table shows the summary measure of the size of benchmark gap for the major deliverables of a logistics function derived from initial benchmarking efforts. It is described in quantitative terms as well as summary conclusions. The quantitative comparisons are

	BUSINESS AREA, BETTER/ (WORSE) THAN CURRENT LEVELS PRODUCTIVITY		
DELIVERABLE	A	B	C
UNIT COST	(10-20%)	(15-25%)	(5-15%)
CUSTOMER SATISFACTION	TBD	PARITY	PARITY
INVENTORY, MOS	TBD	(2.0)	PARITY

Summary
- Unit cost disadvantage
  An average 16 percent productivity gap compared to:
     Product competitors
     State-of-the-art operations

- Level of customer satisfaction at parity
  Percent available from local inventory
  Percent delivered next day

- Higher inventory investment
  Due to more material-stocking echelons

TABLE 6.3. BENCHMARK GAP FOR LOGISTICS DELIVERABLES

expressed as a range to indicate that the benchmarking data are preliminary but roughly right. They are more than adequate for determining directionally what has to be done from these initial benchmarking investigations. The data show that there are data gaps as well. There were some data that could not be quantified as of the time of this initial investigation. This is quite acceptable as it is not to be expected that initial efforts will be complete and thorough. That may take some time, possibly months.

The summary, however, is most revealing. As far as unit cost is concerned, the weighted average gap across the three product lines is a 16 percent productivity gap. This measure is a comparison to functionally best operations as well as direct product competitors. Significant effort will have to be made to close such a sizable gap. However, there is some good news. Two measures of customer satisfaction were determined to be at parity. The challenge will be to maintain or improve these levels yet find ways to reduce the costs to deliver them. Finally, the level of assets was found to require improvement. It is interesting to note that one major contributing practice to the higher level of assets already is known. That is, the benchmarking investigations have revealed that there were too many echelon levels of inventory. This is a major detractor to asset levels and to inventory turns. Significant improvement effort will have to be made here also to achieve even a parity position.

Table 6.4 shows benchmark gaps at the detailed level for warehouse operations. This table shows unit cost outputs at a more detailed level that contribute to the gap shown in Table 6.3. They are for warehouse operations. Three companies are compared. Not all companies have complete or even the same metrics quantified at this point in the investigations, but two are significant. Company 1 shows a 24 percent productivity gap based on an often used statistic of orders per man-day. The size of the orders is quite comparable as measured by weight, so there will be serious interest in the practices that contribute to the gap.

Company 2, however, is of most interest because of the sizable gap in lines per man-day picked. The speed of picking is almost three times what internal operations are able to accomplish. This difference cannot be ignored. A complete comparison of internal versus the external practices found here will be the only basis on which the gap will be understood. How that is done will be described in succeeding chapters.

COMPANY & RELATED METRICS	EXTERNAL FIRM	INTERNAL OPERATIONS	INTERNAL BETTER/(WORSE)
Company 1			
Orders/man-day	19.5	14.8	(24%)
Weigh/order, lbs	298	284	equivalent
Truckload shipments/day	37	14	N/A
Company 2			
Lines/man-day			
• Picking only	1440	500	(2.9x)
• Total operation	132	129	equivalent
Capacity utilization			
• Square foot/man[1]	1330	1260	equivalent
Company 3			
Capacity utilization			
• Square foot/stocking unit (SKU)	3.2	5-10	(56%-3x)

[1] Warehouse space only
N/A — not applicable or will not appreciably affect comparative analysis

TABLE 6.4. EXAMPLE PERFORMANCE METRICS SHOWING ANALYTIC BENCHMARK GAPS

Marketplace Superiority

A less considered method of proving superiority is by proof of the operation's services being desired by the marketplace. If the operation's services were objectively made available to willing, interested buyers, would they choose the internal operation's services? The ultimate test of achieving superior performance and industry best practices would be the buying of internal services by a profit-motivated external businessperson to the exclusion of others.

Because many internal operations find they have surplus capacity, it is becoming more commonplace to find business functions offering services for sale. An example of this would be purchasing laboratory testing services from a company that has technologically advanced equipment. Selling services to outsiders is the strongest proof of superiority because an independent businessperson will have evaluated those services among competing alternatives and chosen them.

It is not always necessary to offer services for sale, although filling surplus capacity at fully allocated, profitable prices is highly desirable. Discussions among potential interested parties may be adequate to confirm the desirability of internal operations. However, sale of services is clear proof of achieving industry best practices and having superior operations that are desired by outside independent businesses.

An alternative is to compare practices with a third party provider. In many business functions there are for-hire service bureaus that will perform the given business function for a fee. Transportation and warehousing are examples in the logistics function. The fulfillment activity is becoming a commonly available, complete order entry to delivery service being offered in the catalog business. These vendors of services can often provide proposals for services that will further validate the desirability of the practices to a user.

In summary, investigations may reveal internal operations already at benchmark or superiority. Those operations should receive appropriate credit and recognition for that achievement. Where operations are found below benchmark there should be the challenge to become equal to or exceed a level of those found to be superior. Benchmarking investigations and results should be balanced in their assessment. They should not be focused solely on areas in need of improvement.

Comparative Analysis of the Gap

How are differences in practices to be analyzed and their impact assessed? There are at least two ways: qualitatively (by descriptive analysis of operational opportunity), such as faster order checkout through the use of bar code scanners, and quantitatively (by analytical quantification of the size of the opportunity), such as 100 items per hour.

There is a significant and natural tendency to stress the quantitative before the qualitative. Operations and operations managers who have been provided incentives through objectives, targets, and other quantitative goals have a natural predisposition to want to know what the benchmark number is. They want to know the metric, whether unit cost, level of customer satisfaction, or asset turns, and in turn the effect on profit and loss and return on assets.

Experience has shown that concentrating on the metric for a benchmarking investigation to the exclusion of or even with equal weight to the qualitative can be a serious mistake. The qualitative explains why the metric is what it is. It explains the reason for the difference that the analytical measured gap shows. Ultimately the gap must be quantified and expressed in terms that show the effect on the operations. But it has been the experience of the author that the qualitative should precede the quantitative since one is an outcome or result of the other and not the reverse.

Where possible the benchmarking investigations should concentrate on the clear understanding of practices before attempting to measure the results. For this reason the qualitative will be stressed first.

Practice Opportunity

A qualitative definition of the benchmark practice is necessarily a word description of the practice and statement of opportunity analysis in words. However, it does not stop with simply what is and could be, but goes beyond to describe why and how the opportunity potential exists from the difference or gap. The difference must break down and describe the process to the lowest significant component. The lowest significant component being that which when quantified, based on the judgment of the investigator, will significantly add to productivity and ultimately cost-effectiveness. This probably means those methods that improve a process step by 10 to 15 percent or more.

How does one qualitatively analyze an operation? Most operations are performed in a step-by-step manner. Such a process is shown in Figure 6.1. It is characterized by a supplier with an input, a work process with repeatable practices, and customers who receive its output. It will be this process definition, used throughout the text, that is the focus for investigating industry best practices. There is a beginning, an end, and a process in between that can be broken down into logical sequential steps.

For a logistics function the steps involved in moving products from source to ultimate consumption are the more significant to benchmark. These usually can be described as movement-storage-movement steps and consist of when and how products are transported, inventoried in a distribution center, and transported again from manufacturing to the ultimate customer or consumer. These steps define the echelon network structure through which products move. Each transportation leg and storage location becomes the major cost center to benchmark. These are shown in Figure 6.2. They are the ones that should get the major focus of benchmarking activities.

This figure is quite revealing from a benchmarking point of view. Each echelon level is a major contributor to the cost level and in turn unit cost of the overall logistics deliverable mentioned earlier. The more echelon levels where inventory is stored, the more costs

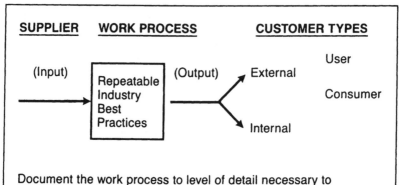

FIGURE 6.1.   ANALYSIS OF A WORK PROCESS AND
              LEVEL OF DETAIL

are incurred. The benchmarking of the echelon structures among these four companies has revealed significant differences for performing essentially the same replenishment function, both regular and emergency, to the final level, the serviceman.

Company 1 shows four echelons: NDC, RDC, BPC, and TR. There are multiple locations at each level, as shown in the parentheses. Company 2 shows only three echelons, given that the region and branch each supply a different type of ESR exclusively. It is quite surprising to find one type ESR has its regular replenishment supplied directly from the manufacturing DC. This is a two-echelon network.

Company 3 is a three-echelon network because the branch level BPC is used for emergency orders only. These usually have a much lower stocking level to support emergency shipments and do not contribute to the inventory investment in any measurable way as does that for Company 1 at the branch level for both regular replenishment as well as emergency-combined. Finally, Company 4 is a three-echelon structure, even with the source origin overseas.

This type of comparison should give serious concern to Company 1, as the practices used by the other three are markedly different and would reflect significant inventory reductions if emulated by

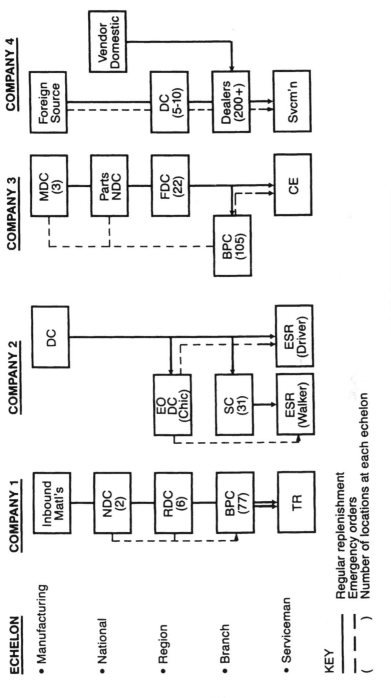

FIGURE 6.2. ALTERNATIVE ECHELON NETWORK STRUCTURES

Company 1 because of the way inventory is deployed. At a minimum there should be serious question for the need for one echelon of inventory. The network could be reduced to three echelons. Beyond the number of echelons there should be further concern for how they operate the echelons, whether full stocking for replenishment or emergency orders only. This further refinement would perhaps reflect itself in a two-and-a-half echelon structure. Therefore, the practices used by comparative companies, as viewed through their echelon structures, have shown a significant opportunity for change and not only reduce unit costs but also reduce inventory levels thus increasing overall inventory turns.

Likewise, an order-processing operation stretching from order receipt to order delivery can be broken down into order entry, customer service and problem resolution, order handling, invoicing, collection, and the handling of returns (Table 6.5). Other operations will have analogous ways to describe their sequential steps.

The best way to analyze these operations is to develop a word description of each step through the use of a word chart as shown in Table 6.6. The word chart would describe the process steps in key terms and for each step the benchmark method would be described. The level of detail is somewhat a matter of judgment but experience and judgment about potential impact will quickly reveal the necessary level. A test can be performed to validate the detail by assessing the completeness of the chart through applying it internally. If adquate for internal descriptive purposes it will be adequate for external.

The word chart should reveal key methods. If not in adequate detail, significant differences may be missed. Perhaps of equal, if not more importance, the opportunity to make slight modifications and find the key differences to successful implementation may be missed. Breakthroughs in methods are rarely accomplished by change in one single contributing factor. More often it is an adaptation of one with a slight modification of another that results in an implementable practice. The ability to ask "what if" from the chart may be critical.

An example may be be helpful. Bar coding documents is becoming commonplace. The bar code permits tracking the location of the document and therefore its status to ensure that none are lost. The practice is in widespread use in hospitals, warehouses, libraries, and other places where data must be captured automatically to track activity.

There are industry standards for the codes. One widely used is three of nine which is an alpha-numeric code. It is a code that is large in size because it encodes both alpha and numeric data. Documents, however, are usually numbered in sequence and are

I. ORDER ENTRY; CUSTOMER INTERFACE

FUNCTION	BEST PRACTICE
• Customer contact	• Full-function WATS • In-out WATS • Mail • Electronic • Calls allocated by ACD • Customer service phone is toll call
• Customer identification	• Easy multiple access methods • Customer information reviewed and maintained • Minimal data capture • Customer structure flexibility • Multiple ship to locations permitted
• Requested transaction	• Inquiries, orders, order modification, quotes, sales tax • Calculation of quantity discounts

II. ORDER ENTRY; ORDER CAPTURE

• Transaction confirmation	• Inventory reservation • Pass/fail credit, full edit, and validation • Order fulfillment options and costs including sales tax and freight
• Order recording	• Execute affected processes and update data bases directly
• Credit approval	• Structured accept or deny • Electronic credit card authorization • Check clearing and approval • Line of credit

TABLE 6.5. ORDER ENTRY BEST PRACTICES DETAIL

133

	COMPANY 1	COMPANY 2	COMPANY 3	COMPANY 4
Source Storage				
• Manufacturing Site	2, NDCs East Coast West Coast	1, DC, East Coast	2 MDCs Mid Continent, West Coast	Foreign
• Central Emerg. Orders		1, DC; Mid Continent, National EOs	1, Mid Continent	
• Type Storage & Handling	Conventional	2, ASRS & Conventional	2, ASRS	Conventional
• Operations	RDC Replenishment	Order Fill to Servicemen	FDC Replenishment	DC Replenishment
Region Storage				
• Number Location	6 RDCs	7 DCs (total) 3 DCs (P/L B)	22 FDCs	5-10 DCs Typical per OEM
• Type S&H	Conventional	1 DC with Mini ASRS	Conventional	Conventional
• Operation	Parts Drop Replenishment	N.A.	Order Fill to Servicemen	Dealer Replenishment
Local Storage				
• Number Location	77 Parts Drops	31 Service Centers	105 Parts Drops	200+ Dealers per OEM
• Type S&H	Conventional	Conventional	Conventional	Conventional
• Operation	Order Fill to Servicemen & Emerg. Order	N.A.	EO Only	Order Fill to Servicemen
Emergency Orders				
• Serviceman's 1st Support Echelon	Parts Drop	SCs-walker, DC-driver	BPC	Dealer
• Serviceman's Last Support Echelon	NDC	DC Mid Continent	MDC	OEM DC, Vendor

TABLE 6.6. WAREHOUSING BEST PRACTICE COMPARISON

space constrained, especially if for an existing document to which the bar code must be added. Analysis shows that this detailed alpha-numeric code could be rejected because of space constraints. However, further analysis reveals that the two of five code, a strictly numeric code, could be used in its place. It is much more compact and insertable on existing documents. The alpha code capability is not necessary for a numeric only sequential order number, especially when scanners can automatically distinguish between three of nine and two of five.

The breakdown of the data capture requirement step into components revealed that further characteristics were numeric only and space constrained for ensuring document control. The latter opportunity could have been missed without the more detailed description. While the detail is somewhat a matter of judgment, ultimately they should be detailed enough to reveal differences necessary to emulate the method, close the gap, and gain a superior advantage.

This method should be described to a level of detail that will eventually permit quantification. It should permit an industrial engineering or financial analyst assessment of its effect. It should permit quantification of what the operation would look like if the operation incorporated the industry best practices. Understanding the methods first is the most important step. Quantifying the effect is the next. An example of practices for a portion of the order-taking cycle is shown in Table 6.7.

Even if an accurate quantified benchmark was obtained, that is, the correct metric was ascertained without the first step of understanding the underlying methods, it would be necessary to backtrack to find them in order to obtain a description of the reasons for the gap in the first place. The description of the gap in quantitative terms will only raise the question, "why the difference?" It is the methods and practices that describe the differences. It will be imperative to be prepared to explain the differences. One cannot adequately determine the differences of the metric without understanding the practices. Therefore, practices and methods should be understood first and quantified second.

Performance Metric

If a qualitative description of industry best practices describes the opportunity for closing the gap, then the quantitative description determines the size of the gap and measures the opportunity. There is a natural tendency to want to know the latter first. Operations want to know what the new target is that must be achieved

COMPANY

	A	B	C	D	E	F	G	H
ORDER METHODS: PHONE								
-Coverage	8AM-8PM EST	8AM-5PM EST	24 hrs/day Every Day	8AM-5PM All Time Zones	8:30AM-8PM EST	8AM-5PM EST	9AM-5PM All Time Zones	8:30AM-6PM EST
-Product Available	Confirmed			Confirmed	Confirmed		Confirmed	Confirmed
-Price					Confirmed		Confirmed	Confirmed
-800#	Yes	Yes	Yes	Yes '44' #'s	Yes	Yes	Yes	Yes
-Shipping Promise	Confirmed		Given by Operator				24 Hours	48 Hours
-Delivery Promise							2-7 Working Days	5+ Working Days
MAIL IN ORDER	Yes-form in catalog	Yes-use own P.O. and 7 digit stock no	Yes-form in catalog	Yes-use own P.O.	Yes-form in catalog	Yes-form in catalog	Yes-must request form	Yes-form in catalog
LOCAL OFFICE PRODUCT CENTER		Yes-Sales Rep		Yes-customer rep	IBM Rep / Yes	Yes	Yes	Yes
OTHER	Telex				Authorized Distributors		PC Authorized Dealers	
TERMS OF SALE, NET 30 DAYS								
Start Invoice Date	Yes	Net 10 Days Past Due 2%/Mo	Required	Yes	Payment due upon receipt	Paid on receipt	Yes	Yes
-Credit Approval		Penalty Minimum $1/Mo.			Required		Required	Required
OTHER METHODS								
-COD		PO System Only		P.O. System Only			Yes	
-Credit Card			AMEX, VISA, MC		AMEX, VISA, MC		AMEX, VISA, MC	VISA, MC
-Check/Cash			Yes $1 Handling charge all orders		Yes	Yes (Check)	Yes-Ship on receipt	Yes-Ship on receipt
MINIMUM ORDER		Must order in minimum quantities as indicated			14 Handling under $40			
-Mail	None	None	None		None	None		
-Phone	None	None	None		None		None	$35/order unless check/ cash
-Local Office			None		None		$20/order	

(Source: Direct marketing catalogs of major companies in the office products industry)

TABLE 6.7. COMPARATIVE ANALYSES OF PRACTICES TO REVEAL INDUSTRY BEST PRACTICES

and how different it is from current targets to judge the degree of difficulty required to achieve it.

A secondary effect of wanting to know the metrics is psychological. While most operations are quantitatively goal driven and targets are a way of operational life, if benchmarking external firms produces performance gaps beyond what may be considered normal and reasonable the shock can be considerable. The facts are that benchmarking industry best practices can and do produce gaps in the 20 to 30 percent or larger range. One reason is that true benchmarking searches for the best of the best, a relatively high standard, yet necessary for true superiority. Such a comparison is shown in Table 6.8.

	EXTERNAL COMPANIES					INTERNAL
	COMPANY				Service Bureaus²	Process Costs
	1	2	3	4¹		
Order Taking	$ 4	$3	$9	NA	NA	$12
Order Processing	4	3	9	NA	NA	9
Warehouse Handling	4	3	10	NA	NA	
Handling						10
Total Order Processing Costs (excluding freight)	$12	$9	$28	$35	$15-20	$31

Conclusion:
• The weighted average cost for external firms was less than $20 per order
• This "benchmark" reflects what internal costs would be if industry best practices were implemented

NA — not available
¹ Estimated
² Price charged to service bureau customers

TABLE 6.8. COST PER ORDER COMPARISON AND BENCHMARK DERIVATION

There is quite a large variance in overall processing cost between the four external companies, although there could be similarities between companies 1 and 2 and 3 and 4 as revealed by similarities in costs. These two sets of comparative companies would have to be more carefully understood in terms of their practices to truly determine the reasons for the differences. Companies 3 and 4 are perhaps more similar to the internal operations. What will be of interest will be what practices contribute to a $9 to $12 range versus a $28 to $31 to $38 range of cost differences.

There must be some significant practice differences because the composite of the service bureaus is in the $15 to $20 range, higher than companies 1 and 2 but lower by a significant amount than the internal operations. The service bureau data are significant because they are the prices that would be charged to perform the equivalent services by contract. It is what a profit-motivated businessperson would charge to perform the operation and still derive a reasonable return. It is one of the most credible ways of establishing a benchmark.

It was on the basis of this comparison and other data that the benchmark unit cost per order was determined to be approximately $20, a considerable challenge for the internal operation. The full benchmarking investigation also documented the practices used. A comparison of those practices to current internal operations showed what would have to be emulated to reach the benchmark cost.

However, once the numbers are known, the reaction varies from rejection to skepticism to anger if a quantitative approach is used first. In fact, the quantitative can be prone to errors, and when coupled with the disbelief, is a strong argument for a qualitative understanding of best practices first. If the qualitative process investigation is thoroughly conducted, it will support the later quantified metrics, add to their credibility, and reduce their openness to argument.

What Is to Be Quantified

What is to be quantified deserves adequate attention. What is desired is a quantification of an operation given that the best practices were incorporated or adapted. The quantification would show what the operation would look like if the best practices were adopted. It is therefore a synthetic number, but a true statement of a benchmark. It most likely will not have a comparable level in any existing budget or performance measurement system. A person will not be able to go to one external firm and find the number in its performance measures. The reason is that no single firm incorporates the best of the best practices. It is first a synthetic, but budgetable number. It is doable. The sum of the best practices support it. It could be built up in a clean sheet or green field fashion for a further proof statement.

An example may be helpful. Following a benchmarking investigation of a function, such as for a logistics operation, there may be no direct, firsthand knowledge or information about a direct product competitor's costs, expense to revenue ratios, or unit costs. First, the information is more than likely proprietary and not released. Second, the effort to ensure the accounting for equivalent operations and costs is not worth the effort.

The logistics function will, however, have knowledge and information about both direct product competitors and leading industry functional best companies structures (such as the number of echelons of inventory) and operational best practices (such as the use of bar coding for automatic data capture). Benchmark metrics can then be constructed based on true data and information.

True benchmarks are based on calculated data that reflect how the internal operation would look if it emulated the best practices. This can be accomplished by either adjusting internal unit costs to reflect the best practices or a clean sheet build-up of all operations based on best practices. Knowledge of the differences in methods can be used to convert or adjust the appropriate elements of unit costs to reflect best practices; or the cost elements can be built up as if the operations were started new. The principle is that the benchmark incorporates competitor or industry best practices for the activities currently being performed. The benchmark does not adjust for activity or unique operations where they must continue to be performed.

A secondary and important extension of benchmarking, that of business simplification, would take the view that activities and operations should be eliminated to obtain a true functional benchmark. That discussion will be left to Chapter 13. The reason for the mention at this juncture is the seriousness of the trap when making comparisons to externally gathered information and used directly to formulate the benchmark metric. Care must be taken to ensure operations that must be performed internally are not arbitrarily eliminated in the build-up or adjustment of practices to industry best. The relationship is shown in Chapter 13, Table 13.2.

Quantification Means Comparability

Operations must be comparable in scope to obtain valid benchmark data. There is a tendency to accept data and information that are believed to be comparable, especially from external visits. This could lead to acceptance of a cost per desired metric (cost per order for instance) as a correct statement of the benchmark. The initial quantification could in fact be a serious mistake. Consider the example of wanting to know the benchmark cost per order for the distribution of a product packaged in cartons.

Such a product can be distributed by a manufacturer's in-house logistics function or marketed by a distributor of many manufacturers' products. There is adequate logic to support that the distributor may have best practices that should be emulated by the manufacturer's logistics organization. Both have to provide warehousing and transportation services; both strive to provide a high level of service and be cost-effective. However, there could be differences that cannot be emulated by the manufacturer.

Most large manufacturers are national organizations and deliver nationwide over large distances to all customers. Many distributors are local to a city, selected counties, or a state. Distances are less and freight costs per unit are less. Comparison of the total cost per unit would be misleading because the delivery territories are different, and delivery distances covered by the manufacturer are longer, which in turn affects freight costs. Acceptance of this perhaps initially attractive, easily obtainable metric would be misleading because the manufacturer cannot arbitrarily shrink back to the delivery territory of the distributor.

What is relevant are the methods used to serve the delivery territory; where and what type of local trucking is used (perhaps covering the metropolitan areas only); and where and what type of contract truck carriers are used for outlying delivery zones. It is the quantification of these practices and methods of the business that are the desired outcome of a quantification of the benchmark metric.

Said differently, what is wanted is an understanding of practices first, then quantification of the effect of the practices to reveal the size of the opportunity. It is desired to ensure that the methods incorporated are the best of the best industry practices.

Quantification Precision

Quantification of what an operation can achieve, the benchmark, is a synthetic, yet achievable number. It is the true benchmark. It is supported by understood best business practices, but such a number cannot be precise. Too many factors make up its basis of calculation — and precision may not be what is desired. What is desired is acceptance of the level and progress toward its achievement. Such a number also will change over time as methods and competition change. Under such circumstances the number may have a mean or average but should be expressed as a range. It should permit overachievement or underachievement depending on the initiative and aggressiveness of operating management.

Alternatives for Quantification

The description until now has suggested that quantification of the benchmark metrics can be accomplished by modifying existing metrics to reflect different practices. This adaptation of current unit cost, level of service, or other performance measure is feasible where relatively few changes are to be made. The approach would be to break down the unit cost into components that represent those to be changed and adjust them based on benchmark findings. The benchmark findings would show relative differences in current and benchmark practices — the latter being used directly as the adjusting factor.

An alternative would be to use a clean sheet, sometimes referred to as a green field approach. In this approach a completely new operation is assumed and all metrics are built up from basic benchmark findings. The approach assumes a much more extensive amount of benchmark data available. The benchmark data would provide all the necessary factors to quantify all facets of the operation completely. While this approach is substantially more comprehensive, it does provide a level of detail for analysis that will allow inspection of a true benchmark operation based on the best of industry practices.

Ultimately, either approach should reveal where benchmark practices are better, how they differ, by how much they are better, and how they can be implemented. The preferred approach is to qualitatively understand the practices first and quantify the effect of a change second.

Practices Contributing to the Gap

It would be helpful to have a scheme for categorizing where major industry practices will occur. The scheme would assist in organizing the investigation as well as preparing for visits and provide a logical statement of what is desired in discussion with external benchmarking partners. There are at least three major components of practices: process practices, business practices, and operational structure.

Process Practices

The most obvious practices of interest are those practices and methods that make up the process itself. If, for example, the process being benchmarked is an order processing operation, then the process practices would be those that make up order entry, customer service, warehouse handling, billing, collection, and returns handling. When these major steps are further divided into their component steps and the methods for each defined, then the practices of interest are those that fully describe the process. There may be methods for the order entry function describing how order entry is performed such as by mail, telephone, or electronic means. These in turn can be broken down further to the level of detail desired. The objective is to describe the business process and associated methods and practices that make the process efficient.

Business Practices

Business practices are practices that apply across the process and generally determine methods for handling resources applied to the process. They are usually operational in nature, employment related, or management practice related. They describe operational practices like the type of facilities used, management of exceptions to the process, job structuring, and related operational use of resources. Employment practices of interest include part-time positions, skill level hired, and so forth. Likewise, management practices such as type of incentives used, the performance measurement system selected, and organization structure also describe business practices that are common across a process. Usually these practices are a matter of business operation approach, standard, policy, or philosophy, but they have major influence on providing resources to run the process and contribute to its efficiency.

Operational Structure

Operational structure is not a practice in and of itself. The structure of the operation remains static over long periods of time, yet it too can be changed, although with greater difficulty. It is important because once selected it is the structure within which the operation must function and by its selection it may impose burdens or provide opportunities.

What structure is important? Two considerations are of interest: geographic location of facilities and operations located at a site.

Whether facilities are centralized or decentralized to be near or far from customers is one consideration. Whether complementary operations are co-located at one site is another structural consideration. In logistic terms, the number of echelons of inventory, their location, and why, are major structural considerations which will add or avoid cost that otherwise cannot be changed by process or business practices.

There are major structural decisions that will affect the type and level of costs incurred. An example of this is a downtown storefront versus a suburban office complex. Location within the country, which will influence facility construction costs such as structural costs for snow loads and heating in northern climates versus lighter construction and insulation for milder climates, is also a factor. These are costs that are a function of decisions on where and why an operation is performed. The availability of labor by skill level and the preference for remote facilities electronically linked rather than co-located also are considerations.

Categorizing and analyzing practices and methods into process, business, and structural areas will ensure that nothing important will be missed. It will allow for a level of completeness in benchmarking important practices and it provides a method for analysis and presentation.

Recognizing Benchmark Practices

Recognizing a practice as being the industry best or benchmark is an important issue. How does one recognize that a practice should be designated the best? There are ways to ensure that what is observed will in fact be recognized and accepted as being the benchmark. Four such standards are available. They are each described using examples from a logistics operation.

Two other methods already have been mentioned in the description of the endpoint maturity phase of benchmarking in Chapter 1 as well as in the section earlier in this chapter dealing with the positive gap. Other ways benchmarking can be recognized are to sell services and to be benchmarked, in turn. Operations often will offer services to the external marketplace where surplus capacity exists or to leverage an already superior process capability. This could involve assembly, warehousing, or document processing operations. External, profit-motivated organizations that are willing to contract for those services rather than provide them internally indicates the process has reached benchmark status; it is preferred by the marketplace. In like fashion, an internal operation may be benchmarked by external firms involved in similar benchmarking investigations. This is indicative assurance that the internal operations are the benchmark themselves. The many visits by outside firms to Xerox to learn about benchmarking most likely makes Xerox the benchmark for benchmarking. Either circumstance is a very positive and pervasive confirmation that a benchmark exists.

The Practice Is Clearly Superior

There will be practices observed on benchmarking visits that will be immediately clear to the observer as being superior based on his or her knowledge. One such operation is a package weighing method that performs to quality standards to assure the correctness of an order. The objective is to have the actual carton and content weight confirm that the order was picked and packed with the exact items requested by the customer. Such an operation usually occurs as packages travel over a weighing station on conveyor. As the carton passes over the scale, the weighing operation will compare the actual weight with the calculated weight developed by the order processing computer consisting of the packed container weight, carton, and contents (the number of items times their individual weights, plus the weight of the carton). The order processing computer has in memory the items ordered and when supplied with a table of the item weights can calculate what the package should weigh. The item weights usually are known in order to calculate the package delivery charges and often are shown in the order catalog.

If the calculated weight does not equal the actual weight within a reasonable tolerance the package is shunted off-line for exception processing. The automatic weighing is clearly superior to manual methods. Furthermore it is able to perform a 100 percent inspection of all cartons rather than only a sample.

The Quantified Opportunity Is Large

Closely following a clear superiority of one method over another is the quantification of the benchmark method showing best practice where the metric of interest is substantially better. A sorting process for packages that must be directed to different transportation carriers such as air, ground, or common carriers, depending on what delivery territory they cover, can be performed manually. Or automatic identification labels can be applied to packages and control sorting equipment once the package passes a scanner.

It may not be obvious whether manual handling or automatic machine sorting is superior. Manual sorting can be quite rapid. Package handlers become adept at recognizing zip or other codes to shunt packages to the correct carrier. The process is made somewhat routine because reorder patterns are quite regular; customers do not change their places of business often. But amortization of all mechanical handling equipment costs over many packages for machine sorting compared to manual processing may show large differences. Only the magnitude of the difference will reveal which method is preferred.

Expert Judgment

There are internal experts or consultants who by extensive observation or analytical experience can and do validate some practices as superior. Usually, since operations differ, some data must be provided to them for analysis. How to locate material within a distribution center may require an analysis of order size, units per order, and complementary items per order. Once the pattern is known, there are several materials handling experts who can recommend a material stocking pattern, usually arranging materials by velocity, that is, arranging fast movers of low bulk closest to the picker to minimize his or her travel distance.

The Same Practice Recurs

Finally, there is evidence of best industry practices when a number of visits are conducted and the same practice is observed several times. The weight of evidence is too overwhelming to be anything but a clear definition of an industry benchmark practice. The practice of investing resources to obtain the weight, dimensions, and critical length of each part or stock-keeping-unit (SKU) when first received into distribution operations in inventory is common practice in several industries. While the time involved and the data maintenance appear to be substantial and of low value, the output of the effort is substantial. First, the dimensions permit automatic and random put-away activities to the closest size bin within which the item fits, thus minimizing travel distance. Predetermined weighing permits picking quality assurance with in-line scales, as mentioned. The dimension and critical length will automatically select the packaging carton. Dimension and weight will permit predetermining freight charges as well as determining the cubic dimension to ensure that the transportation vehicle capacity will not be exceeded.

This industry practice for capture and later use of the data contributes to the effectiveness of the downstream operation so substantially that the practice is found in distribution center after center and is obviously a benchmark practice.

The L. L. Bean Experience

On return to Rochester, New York, from the visit to L. L. Bean's operation in Freeport, Maine, the findings of the trip were documented in a trip report. The trip report was assembled from input of the three attendees and had their collective concurrence on what was observed. The analysis then focused on describing in a comparative fashion how L. L. Bean's practices differed from internal operations and why.

The practices were analyzed first qualitatively to reveal significant differences and potential opportunity. The analysis quickly showed a level of use of computer capability to direct the operational activities that were substantially beyond those used in internal operations. These in turn, with validation from other benchmarking visits and investigations, were developed into a statement of industry best practices as shown in Table 6.9. The specific activities observed at L. L. Bean's distribution center included:

- Incoming materials, usually in carton quantities, were put away into storage rack locations randomly wherever the computer determined there was an empty slot. This practice relieved the operation of having to remember or search for space of adequate size to accept the number of cartons needing storage. The cubic capacity of rack space was more fully utilized and the put-away travel distance minimized.
- Materials were arranged for picking by velocity of movement, that is, by daily order activity. The fast movers were then stocked closest to the beginning of the picking route. With some exceptions bulky items were stocked further away to conserve space for more items closest to the route. The effect was to minimize picker travel distance.
- Once the materials were located by historical velocity, the orders received throughout the day were accumulated for a given period, perhaps hourly, and then sorted and scheduled by computer to ensure efficient picking. This practice, known as short interval scheduling, was used to minimize picker travel distance. It accumulated close-by items into a route and routed the picker the minimum distance to fill a picking cart.

PROCESS STEP

Receiving
- On-line receiving input, reconciliation to purchase order, and status through CRT located at receiving dock

Put-Away
- Predetermined, random put-away location, sequenced to minimize distance traveled
- 100 percent put-away verification through cross-reference of rack location and item bar codes

Picking
- Interactive, on-line pick planning to minimize picker travel distance and maximize shipping container capacity utilization

Stock Relocation
- Automatic relocation of inventory items to coincide with order per day velocity

Pick Area Relenishment
- Automatic replenishment of picking locations from reserve stock based on preassigned thresholds, or on demand by key entry

Shipping
- Automatic package sortation to correct carrier at shipping dock through label scanner
- Automatic shipping document preparation from predetermined weight and label scan

Other Preparation
- Productivity and order fill error rate analysis by area, team, and individual
- Real time, transaction based, inventory update, and control or warehouse operations

TABLE 6.9. KEY WAREHOUSE INDUSTRY BEST PRACTICES

It also accumulated the total quantity of the same items for all orders in that route to require only one trip to a bin location. The items were then sorted into each order's slot on the cart. At the end of the day those orders that fell significantly outside an efficient target travel distance were routed together.

- L. L. Bean, like many warehouse operations with substantial outbound movement by package carriers, documented the weight and dimensions of each item stocked. The weight permitted calculation of UPS delivery charges before the material was shipped. This allowed L. L. Bean to pay transportation charges based on their records, which were accepted by the carrier, and precluded reconciliation and payment after the fact, as is common practice.

- Because of the level of computer routing and scheduling for operational purposes, a secondary benefit was the activity tracking that also was available. L. L. Bean developed and installed an incentive bonus pay system that was based on a merit-demerit scheme. An individual or team would earn credit for the productivity level of actual picks but would receive debits for error rates in picking the items per order. The latter was determined by a sampling and inspection procedure.

The level of computer-directed activities was therefore significantly higher than found in Xerox parts and supplies warehouses and determined a gap that, when combined with other industry best practices, eventually needed to be addressed. In addition to the practices that were directly observed, the benchmarking visit also uncovered several areas where additional, new methods were to be shortly installed. The planned improvement with the greatest potential was the installation of bar coded labels for automatic data capture. The trip therefore revealed both currently existing as well as planned benchmark practices.

CHAPTER 7   PROJECTING FUTURE PERFORMANCE LEVELS (STEP 5)

The "Z" Chart
- Historical productivity
- The benchmark gap
- Future productivity

Understanding the Gap
- Tactical actions
- Strategic actions
- Extent of the gap

Establishing Goals
- Operational terms
- The significant few
- Practice changes

The L. L. Bean Experience

PROJECTING FUTURE PERFORMANCE LEVELS (STEP 5)

Is the Gap Widening or Closing?

Once current performance gaps have been fully defined from benchmark practices, as discussed in Chapter 6, the projection of future performance levels will be necessary. This is the difference between expected future performance and the best in the industry. It is important to project the future gap because industry practices change. And it will be important to understand future trends in the gap. Is the gap expected to widen, narrow, or stay the same? In addition, the projection will define those goals and targets that must be achieved to close the gap and meet or exceed desired or competitive performance. A conceptual understanding is shown in Figure 7.1.

The figure shows the usual findings from a benchmarking investigation. A metric is chosen to quantify the effect of all the best practices. In this case dollars per pound or preferably percent of revenue could be used. Against time, starting at the time of the benchmarking investigations, the differences between the internal logistics functions cost levels and those projected for the industry best practices are shown. This results in a performance gap. Over time the practices will be understood and incorporated into internal operations such that a position of parity will be reached and eventually, a position of superior performance will be attained.

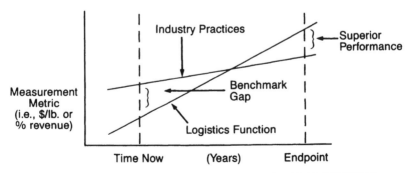

FIGURE 7.1. CONCEPTUAL PROJECTION OF THE BENCHMARK GAP

The analysis phase identified the superior industry practices and determined how they could be applied directly or modified or adapted for implementation. A thorough understanding of what the practices are, why they are superior, and what steps are necessary for implementation is assumed. At this stage the current benchmarks and gaps are established and understood.

The process so far defines the relative position today, but industry practices are not static. Both industry and competitors continue to pursue improvements. Therefore, one must not only analyze the benchmark gap as it exists at the time of measurement, but also project where the benchmark and gap are likely to be in the future. A graphic portrayal is helpful in showing the relative positions and analyzing what is required. The "Z" chart is used for this purpose and is shown in Figure 7.2.

10-YEAR LOGISTICS PRODUCTIVITY TREND

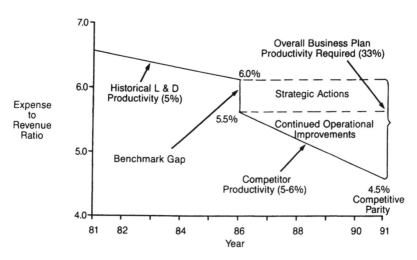

- Unit costs were calculated as if logistics performed similarly to competition and converted to a single summary statistic; expense to revenue ratio.

- The result is an approximate 16% productivity gap compared to state-of-the-art operations or competitors studied thus far.

- During the next year, competitors will also be pursuing productivity, assumed to be 5-6% and equal to distribution's historical productivity.

- The results show distribution must pursue a combination of continuing, historical productivity efforts as well as undertake significant strategic changes.

FIGURE 7.2. THE "Z" CHART

152

The "Z" Chart

The "Z" chart graphically shows the size of the gap. It displays the full extent of the gap currently and in the future. It also permits understanding of the meaning of the gap. For example, understanding the gap in manufacturing unit costs, order-taking cost per order, or billing cost per invoice.

For this purpose it is useful to base the chart on a single summary statistic that portrays the function or business unit's overall performance. The one often used is percent of revenue. That is, the function or business unit's cost base or expenses are expressed as a percent of revenue. Individual subfunction's data and benchmark gap can be converted and summarized to this measure and it is used here. The statistic is readily understood by all management levels. Contributions to the summary measure can be traced to the individual benchmarks and the quantitative metrics.

One benefit from the use of percent of revenue in displaying the benchmarks gap is it can be judged and interpreted for contribution to or detraction from profitability. The sum of all functions percent of revenue benchmark statements compared to current performance will reveal where benchmarks must be achieved to remain profitable or improve profit margin. This is especially necessary as benchmark studies have revealed that the gap can be as large as 50 percent.

The "Z" chart is broken down into three essential components. The historical productivity, or cost reduction, trend is shown. Next the one-time gap size is portrayed, usually as a result of and at the time of completing a comprehensive analysis of the benchmarks for a business unit. Finally, the projected future productivity which must be pursued to achieve superior, or competitive, performance is plotted. Each will be discussed in turn.

Historical Productivity

It is most likely true that no firm has remained completely static but in fact has had some level of productivity over time. In spite of this progress, benchmarking will invariably reveal a performance gap between current methods and industry best practices. It will be assumed that some level of historical productivity has been pursued, that it can be measured, and therefore graphically displayed. In the absence of benchmarking, whether the same level of productivity would continue is an assumption that needs careful analysis. That will have significance for the projection of future performance. The "Z" chart shows the historical trend first. It is plotted as a sloping line up to the time of the gap measurement.

The Benchmark Gap

The benchmark performance gap is plotted next. At the conclusion of the benchmarking studies and investigations the full extent of the gap will be known. It is assumed that this is when the chart is prepared. The gap is portrayed as a one-time step function, which needs to be closed to achieve parity. It is based on and incorporates the sum effect of the difference between current and industry performance. It is shown as a vertical line at the time of the study.

Future Productivity

Finally, future projected productivity is shown. It is shown as a sloping line following the gap measurement. Some level of productivity will be assumed to continue, following closing the benchmark gap. It may be the same, more, or less than the historical pace, but at a minimum it must be equal to the assumed industry or competitive pace to eventually achieve parity, and more to achieve superiority.

This later productivity projection must incorporate the performance of industry productivity achievement. It is a comparative measure between the internal operation and assumed industry productivity. It cannot be assumed that the industry will remain static. It is also pursuing productivity. Full attainment of parity is based on achieving the gap plus continued pursuit of competitive levels of productivity, and not just internal, historical levels. The full gap is composed of the benchmark results or best practice findings plus achievement of competitive or industry best, continuing productivity rates.

The operation's performance is now fully defined by the "Z" chart. It first shows the historical slope of productivity. It next shows the one-time step function gap resulting from investigating industry best practices. And it shows continuing progress into the future. The three segments make up the basic elements of the "Z" shape and thus the chart name. The message shown is graphic and sobering: Not only must performance close the gap but it must also continue productivity at some historical rate equal to that of the external industry.

The realization of the magnitude of the task can be quite unsettling to an operation that had assumed historical productivity levels were adequate. Furthermore, the task required has often been assumed to be the sole achievement of the benchmark gap. The understanding that current levels of productivity must be maintained and perhaps increased as well as achievement of the gap can be unsettling.

Obtaining this level of understanding is why the use of the "Z" chart is so useful and necessary. The "Z" chart correctly portrays the true size of the effort required and provides for complete understanding and analysis.

Understanding the Gap

One way to bring further meaning to the "Z" chart is to segment the reasons for the gap between tactical and strategic actions required to close the gap. While there is not always a direct relationship between these two contributors and segments of the gap, it is often more true than not.

Tactical Actions

In the absence of benchmarking investigations productivity achievement is usually gradual, evolutionary, and achieved at some acceptable level to the organization. Most likely historical productivity was achieved primarily through tactical actions. Change was gradual and driven by internal observations of where internal productivity could be improved and efficiencies were attained. Improvements were based on the experience of the function and knowledge of the operation. This type of productivity is evolutionary in nature and usually not of significant magnitude. Productivity rates ranging from 0 percent to 5 percent, with a 2 percent to 3 percent average are usual. While it is possible that some strategic actions are included, they usually will not incorporate those found through benchmarking focus on the external environment.

Strategic Actions

Major practices differences found from external benchmarking investigations generally will require strategic actions. Industry best practices would not be expected to be found through or be included in the internally focused tactical practice changes. The strategic actions required to close the gap will come from benchmark findings.

The display of the full extent of the gap by way of the "Z" chart and explanations in tactical and strategic terms focuses attention on the extent and severity of the need for change. Both strategic practices changes and continuing tactical actions will be needed to completely close the gap. The explanation and graphic portrayal vividly describe the implications of not pursuing aggressive change. If both tactical and strategic moves are not pursued then the industry and competition will outdistance internal performance. The picture and explanation serve as vehicles to communicate and motivate the organization to accomplish both.

Extent of the Gap

Displaying the full extent of the gap often is revealing and sobering to the organization. It often is not completely understood in its full terms of demand for sizable change and where that change must come from. There will be a tendency to believe that one major practice change can be made — one high hurdle can be overcome, and then everyone involved can settle back into prior levels of productivity and achievement. Benchmarking and the understanding of its implications for change reveals that that level of complacency is not permissible. Benchmarking reinforces that change must constantly be pursued over extended periods of time. Benchmarking reinforces the true importance of the need to search for best practices. Superior performance requires constant attention to structured change toward a well-defined and well-understood benchmark target.

The "Z" chart also reinforces the need to update information. The update and maintenance of industry best practices as current information becomes available as well as assumptions about continuing productivity trends — internal, industry, or competitive — is called recalibration: maintaining information evergreen. Assumptions are made about overall internal progress on productivity, both historical and projected. Assumptions also are made about industry and competitive progress. These assumptions can and do change. There is the need to update information at prescribed levels. Benchmarking best industry practices must include such an update or recalibration approach.

Establishing Goals

There are many texts that adequately cover the goal-setting process and it is not the intent to cover those here. How and when to establish goals and targets may also be ingrained in the corporate process and often are unique to an individual firm. It should be evident by now that benchmarking, in addition to being a standard by which to emulate industry best practices, is very much a goal-setting procedure. The benchmark is a goal or target. This is true whether it is a statement of practice such as bar coded automatic data capture or quantitative metric conversion of the practice such as attaining a 40 percent expense to revenue ratio improvement.

Experience has shown there are several facets of goal setting that are important to benchmarking success. Some may be self-evident but they deserve reinforcement specific to benchmarking. In a search of best practices, the benchmarking effort should result in goals that are stated in operational terms, are limited to the significant few, and are stated as practices changes.

Operational Terms

Goals that are stated in operational terms put the external findings into the language of the function. This greatly helps understanding and gaining acceptance. Benchmarking principally is a search for best practices. Once determined, the best practices need to be quantified for the effect of their installation in the operation. While the focus is on the practice, the eventual worth of the practices needs to be quantified. The benchmarks will result in quantifiable, actionable goals.

Actions such as reducing the number of echelons from four to three or reducing the indirect to direct labor content from two to one are excellent quantifications of goals in operationally understandable terms. As such they give the operation specific identifiable metrics for goals. Coupled with the approach to limiting the goals to a priority few, quantification in these terms focuses the organization on where attention must be focused.

Significant Few

Once the benchmarking investigations and analyses are complete, it is relatively straightforward to determine the more significant benchmarks. Those few that will markedly effect unit cost, level of service, or asset turns will be apparent. They can be ranked. A Pareto analysis, which isolates the most significant problems from the trivial, may be useful in analyzing their importance. Ultimately those that make the largest contribution toward closing the gap will be of greatest interest. Concentration should be on these significant few as they are the result of overall, highest priority, benchmark findings.

Practice Changes

It has been stressed that benchmarking should concentrate on investigating practices. Goal statements should incorporate and be based on the practices found. Those significant practices that contribute most to overall objectives can be cited as specific goals to be achieved. Such statements as computer-directed picking, bar-coded package sorting, or velocity-arranged inventory materials are legitimate goals to be derived from benchmarking. Benchmark findings are excellent, legitimate goal statements and should be used as such.

The L. L. Bean Experience

Following the analysis of the gap between the internal operations and the best practices found at L. L. Bean, a gap substantiated by other benchmarking investigations, it was necessary to project what the effect of incorporating the practices into the operation would be.

Following the analysis of the practices, it was found that the performance measurement metrics were substantially higher at L. L. Bean. They were able to pick almost three times as many lines per man-day as the most efficient warehouse planned at the time. Table 7.1 compares the operational statistics for L. L. Bean and Xerox as of February 1982. The table compares the picking operation by itself and warehouse total for the productivity statistics based on orders, lines, and pieces per man-day. The line per man-day is the statistic most indicative of travel distance since it represents picker trips to a bin location. The number of pieces is the quantity picked. In the Xerox operation that could represent one complete pallet load of 40 cartons (or 40 pieces).

The table reveals that the L. L. Bean picking operation is substantially better than at Xerox. However, the warehouse total does not necessarily indicate the two overall operations are equally efficient. The L. L. Bean warehouse performs functions not done by Xerox, such as a soft goods finishing operation. The latter statistic was documented to emphasize the need for a process comparison that truly reveals differences in comparable functions. It also indicates that the best of best industry practices will not be found at one firm but must be assembled from wherever they exist.

	February 1982	
	L. L. BEAN	**XEROX**
Picking Only		
Orders/man-day	550	117
Lines/man-day	1,440	497
Pieces/man-day	1,440	2,640
Total Warehouse		
Orders/man-day	69	27
Lines/man-day	132	129
Pieces/man-day	132	616

TABLE 7.1. COMPARISON OF PICKING ONLY AND TOTAL WAREHOUSE OPERATIONS FOR L. L. BEAN AND XEROX DISTRIBUTION CENTERS

CHAPTER 8
COMMUNICATING
BENCHMARK FINDINGS
(STEP 6)

Communicating Findings
- The audience
- Methods of communication
- Organization of the analysis

Gaining Acceptance
- Initiative for change
- Operational acceptance
- Validation from multiple sources

The L. L. Bean Experience

COMMUNICATING BENCHMARK FINDINGS (STEP 6)

Obtaining Acceptance from Skeptics

This chapter deals with communicating findings to the organization and gaining its acceptance. This can be a critical step in the benchmarking process since no matter how well the benchmarking has been conducted there is an obvious skepticism for the introduction of new practices. Overcoming the reluctance to accept the findings is an important step toward implementation, and a carefully designed communications campaign should be given serious consideration. It will be wise to give thought to the basis on which the operating personnel — who ultimately have to accept and implement new practices — will be willing to do so. A carefully orchestrated communications approach to the target audiences and reasoned basis for validation of the findings will go a long way toward acceptance.

The opportunities identified by the benchmarking process can lead to the strategic redirection of the specific function and/or the company as a whole. This means that the methodology of the benchmarking study, the results, and the specific opportunities must be communicated both within the function and within the corporate hierarchy.

The benchmarking team needs to communicate its progress both to management and affected field personnel. Simultaneously, functional management must keep top management abreast of developments so that as strategic opportunities are identified, they can be acted on quickly.

Once the function's top management approves the strategies and they are incorporated in the function's long-term targets and business plans, they must be reviewed and approved by corporate management. Meanwhile, the ideas must also be sold to the employees — the people who will implement the new strategies. Representatives on the benchmarking team must sell the new strategies to their colleagues to get them included in operating plan targets, guidelines, and priorities. Without this step, the results of benchmarking have little chance of being implemented.

The goal is to gain acceptance by directly affected management.

Communicating Findings

There are three essential steps to communicating findings to the various affected individuals and organizations. The audience and its needs should be determined. The method of communication should be selected and tailored to the audience, and the benchmark findings should be organized for best presentation and understanding.

The Audience

Communicating specific benchmark visit findings and gaining acceptance are benchmarking process steps of vital importance. All levels of the internal organization may be affected by practice changes to meet industry standards. Upstream and downstream organizations also may be affected. Management will need to know the basis for the new benchmarks in order to buy into their rationale and support the admittedly difficult implementation. Employees should be informed of the new practices and solicited for their support and assistance with implementation since they are closest to the operation.

If the practices uncovered by benchmarking are of a significant nature it is likely that suppliers and customers of the process also may be affected. Suppliers for the organization may be affected by their ability to achieve what is demanded by the practices. Their input to the new process and benchmark practices is vital. Customers who receive output from the process also will be affected very positively. If underlying best practices are uncovered and implemented through benchmarking, then end user customer requirements are truly being met. There is also an opportunity to capitalize on and receive public relations value from installing best practices to meet customer needs more fully.

Methods of Communication

There are several methods of communication that have been found effective for benchmarking findings. They may be used selectively and targeted to a specific audience or a multifaceted approach may sometimes be preferred. The methods include the written report, trip report, newsletter, and a benchmarking network. The use of operating principles also is a very persuasive method to gain full acceptance. It will be described in Chapter 9 since it is integral to establishing goals, but it should also be considered here.

The level of skepticism if not outright disbelief, especially by those who have not had continuous contact with the external environment, will be high. A concerted, multifaceted communications approach will be important to overcome resistance, gain understanding, and eventually gain acceptance.

The basic written report, summarizing the findings in some detail, is one effective means of gaining understanding. The report may be updated and reissued at appropriate intervals to obtain reconsideration and to be a reminder of the practices that must be considered. Trip reports are the main way to communicate specific findings. While their preparation may seem tedious, their information documentation and communication value is exceptional. The ease of preparation can be enhanced if a debriefing session is held immediately following the visit with a tape recorder to capture the observations. The tape can then be transcribed and edited later. The sum of several trip reports on a comparative basis forms the content for a very effective report.

A newsletter has communication value when trying to reach a large audience. It does not necessarily have to be elaborate. If it contains case history examples it not only is interesting but also gets the basic message across in a forceful way. An example mockup with sample contents is shown in Figure 8.1. Maintaining a current awareness or clipping service to accumulate articles about other organization's practices is highly visible and will support the operating principles if tailored correctly. The articles let readers see descriptions by others of how they are implementing change.

Where a benchmarking program is well established and a number of organizations and individuals are involved, a benchmarking network can be productive. The network would be informally organized to provide assistance in benchmarking, exchange case history examples of successful studies, and serve as a forum for those involved in benchmarking to gather and conduct a formal information exchange program. The latter has proven quite successful. A two-day program organized with speakers, roundtables, forums, and tutorials will quickly expand the base of benchmarking knowledge and permit professionals to be more effective. Those involved in casual benchmarking will be more informed and will use the process correctly from the start by attending these sessions.

Finally, a communications campaign to acquaint the organization with the need for benchmarking can be undertaken. Such a campaign would make use of visible reminders of the logic for constantly examining outside practices to stay competitive. One such logic poster that enhances understanding is shown in Figure 8.2.

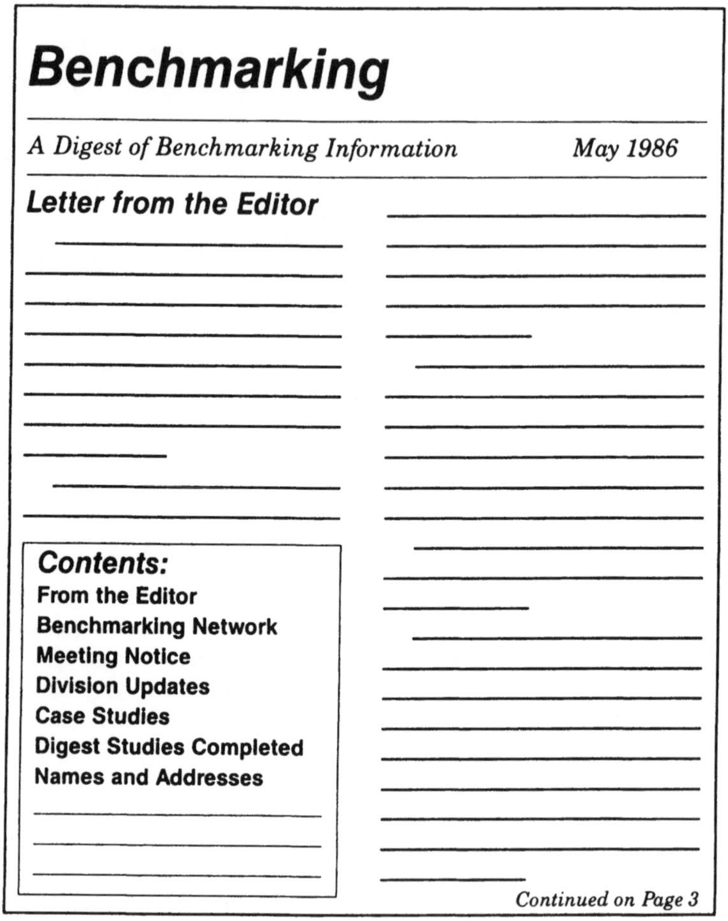

Benchmarking

A Digest of Benchmarking Information   May 1986

Letter from the Editor

Contents:
From the Editor
Benchmarking Network
Meeting Notice
Division Updates
Case Studies
Digest Studies Completed
Names and Addresses

Continued on Page 3

FIGURE 8.1.   BENCHMARKING NEWSLETTER
                   EXAMPLE

BENCHMARKING

PRINCIPLES

PLANS

ACTIONS

BEST
(IN THE INDUSTRY)

FIGURE 8.2.   BENCHMARKING LOGIC POSTER

Ultimately reviews have to be conducted with the affected organizations. If the benchmarking investigations have been conducted using the processes described, there should be a sound, credible basis on which to discuss, understand, and eventually reach agreement on and gain acceptance of the findings. More importantly, a successful implementation of a new practice is the most pervasive. These internal success stories should not be passed up for their communications value.

Organization of the Analysis

The benchmarking study also must be organized for presentation and review. It should include a summary, as well as cover a description of the study process, the presentation of findings, and a discussion of the data and information base that were sourced.

The summary should concentrate on key results, conclusions, and recommendations. It should describe the industry best practices in summary terms and compare them to existing practices. Many of the comparisons in prior chapters are effective styles for the presentation of the findings. The focus will be on the benchmark practices gap and projection of its effect on the operation through summary metrics such as the financial and operating statistics most used. Expense to revenue and return on assets are two that have proven to be those most requested by senior management.

The study process should be described including benchmark partner selection, the data and information gathering method, and the analysis technique. If the benchmark study has been well organized at the outset, this section should be easily completed. The objective of this section is to review why a particular benchmarking approach or approaches were selected rather than others, and why they are most effective for the particular situation.

The findings section is the central focus of the presentation and report. It should include a description of the data gathered, the data and information format, a glossary if needed, and the comparative exhibits themselves. The findings should concentrate on presenting in as clear and concise terms as possible the benchmark practices found. It should project the impact on the organization if adopted, and be stated in descriptive terms as well as the common metrics used within the organization.

Gaining Acceptance

A multifaceted communications strategy will go a long way toward gaining acceptance. The mission statement and operating principles are very effective in that regard as well as an organized communications program. There must be more to obtain change and to motivate initiative for seeking change by individuals throughout the organization.

Initiative for Change

Benchmarking activities have been shown to be a significant motivator to individuals not prone to accepting new practices. People involved in business operations, especially operations with a repetitive nature, often become insulated from external practices and do not know how and in what direction to change. Or there may be an ingrained reluctance to change.

Benchmarking's concentration on industry best practices, however, shows what new practices are and how they will benefit the operation. They are visible, proven methods that guide change. The ability of operational personnel to participate in and eventually conduct benchmarking investigations exposes them to what must be done in relation to their responsibilities and jobs. Most individuals find the prospects exciting and self-motivating. Coupled with a well-designed reward and recognition system, the eventual result is to have individuals seek out benchmarking experiences of their own initiative. This latter step is the full measure of benefit from benchmarking activities.

Operational Acceptance

Benchmark findings must explain not only what the best practices are but how they operate. The two-pronged approach to the descriptive and quantitative statement of benchmark practices is especially pervasive in gaining acceptance. The one describes what and how practices must change. The other describes the size of the opportunity for making the change. They should be convincing, especially when shown to be of value to external firms.

In addition to the descriptive material there are other ways to substantiate the credibility of the findings. The reliability of the benchmark findings can be demonstrated by taking operational people on visits. In fact, their validation of the observations is one specific reason for their inclusion on visits. Seeing the methods

169

firsthand may also encourage initiative for change, suggest adaptations of methods to make them implementable, and serve as a testimonial.

Validation from Multiple Sources

Validation from several different sources also is viable. A visit supported by several articles — not necessarily about the firm visited — will start to contribute to the weight of evidence. If a consultant were to validate the findings from its own client engagements, that becomes a further way to triangulate on the same data. If some internal benchmarking supports the practice's findings, then gaining acceptance is near. Ultimately, the proof of acceptance is embodied by the commitment of the affected organization to develop action plans to implement the findings.

How is acceptance finally validated? There is no precise answer. However, an assessment can be conducted to gain some insight and understanding about the level of acceptance and highlight areas that need attention. Such an assessment is shown in abbreviated fashion in Table 8.1. The objective is to obtain feedback from the implementing organization in a helping/hindering format or analysis of progress toward a known desired state. The analysis conducted through a brainstorming exercise can then be weighted by the participants to show the ranked severity of acceptance. Corrective action can be taken to quickly move to the endpoint or desired state.

The L. L. Bean Experience

The L. L. Bean experience directly contributed to the operating principles and communication of best practices. It was a classic example in gaining acceptance of benchmark findings. Prior to the visit, a questionnaire was prepared which involved obtaining input from line managers as well as their participation in the visits and contribution to a trip report. This process effectively ensured that those affected would be involved intimately, not only in the preparation but in the execution of the investigations — a very important first step in understanding findings and gaining acceptance.

In addition, throughout the benchmarking process the benchmarking team leader continually updated the department vice president and his staff on the project's progress. The periodical article, which was an important description of L. L. Bean's process, was circulated to many managers, including field distribution

Endpoint State Analysis

Present State	Endpoint (Desired) State
Need for benchmarking not recognized.	Acknowledged need for industry best practices.
No benchmarking activity or understanding about the 10-step process.	Benchmarking institutionalized throughout the organization.
No understanding or misunderstanding about industry best practices.	Full understanding of benchmark practices.
Competitive gap unknown.	Understanding of difference in present and benchmark practices in both what they are and how they differ.
No ownership of practices.	Full ownership of practices and practical steps toward implementation.

TABLE 8.1. GAINING BENCHMARKING ACCEPTANCE.
AN ENDPOINT ASSESSMENT APPROACH

center managers who ultimately would be responsible for implementation. The purpose was to acquaint them with the potential new methods early in the investigations. Feedback on application to Xerox operations was solicited and documented for acceptance or modifications necessary to implementation.

The trip report that documented the findings was also widely circulated. It attracted a great deal of interest and attention within the logistics function. Included was a comparison with L. L. Bean's picking operation by itself as well as overall distribution center productivity rate, stated as lines picked per man-day. Debate about the comparison and the measurement metric was indicative of the need for further understanding about the practices, methods, and processes used. Recognizing what L. L. Bean had been able to do with a labor-intensive process supported by a computer system to direct the operations motivated the logistics professionals to find out how the practices learned at L. L. Bean could be creatively adapted to Xerox operations.

A significant contribution to benchmarking industry best practices and the understanding of the purpose for functional benchmarking was obtained in reviews with upper management. Annual benchmarking reviews were made part of the business plan presentations. The L. L. Bean experience was cited in these briefings to demonstrate the ability of benchmarking to uncover best industry practices, regardless of where they existed. L. L. Bean was the first of these examples and was instrumental in broadening the focus of benchmarking to ensure obtaining superior performance. The L. L. Bean experience, in fact, became synonymous with functional, noncompetitive benchmarking to obtain competitive superiority.

L. L. Bean is a well-known firm; many had had personal ordering experience with L. L. Bean. L. L. Bean was widely known for its exceptional customer satisfaction practices which were legion in the annals of the mail order industry, and sporting goods in particular. Whenever a point about functional benchmarking was made, the L. L. Bean experience was cited. Many references were made both in internal presentations and documents as well as in the press.

CHAPTER 9 ESTABLISHING FUNCTIONAL GOALS (STEP 7)

Functional Goals and Benchmarking
- Process
- Rationale

Operating Principles

The L. L. Bean Experience

ESTABLISHING FUNCTIONAL GOALS (STEP 7)

Planned Performance versus Benchmark

This chapter covers the relationship of benchmarking to goals and the effective ways the goals, based on benchmark findings, can be stated for acceptance by the organization. Goals are a statement of planned performance. In the context of benchmarking, goals are derived from benchmarks. Benchmarks, by their nature, are statements of industry best practices. Therefore, functional goals as described here are based on a conscious and concerted view and search of the external world.

Once goals have been established there needs to be a way to translate the benchmark findings into statements of how the organization will change in a nonorganization, business unit, or positions-specific manner. The most effective approach found has been to convert the more important benchmark findings into statements of operating principles. The principles, directly derived from benchmarking, serve to place the organization on notice about what will be considered when decisions for change are made, how the organization will be expected to change over time, and ultimately how the organization will look when it arrives at a position of maturity derived from benchmarking.

Functional Goals and Benchmarking

Each firm has its own approach to goal setting and it is not the purpose to cover that standard business process here. What will be covered is the goal-setting process and the rationale in relation to benchmarking.

Process

Benchmarking by its nature requires examination of goals and the goal-setting process. Procedurally, the list of current goals is reexamined as a result of benchmarking efforts. This starts with an examination of the existing goals. They may exist in several forms and should be cataloged as a start. Goals are incorporated in annual objective statements. They exist in the annual budget and in the strategic or long-range plans of the firm. They also exist in the operational performance measurement systems of each function, often in the form of standards. Benchmark findings force reexamination of these goals in light of industry best practices. The metrics and units of measure used in current goals, however, may be retained. It is not necessary to develop new metrics as a result of benchmarking. In fact, it is preferable to incorporate benchmark findings into existing, commonly understood operating statistics for reasons of acceptance.

The benchmark findings will, however, require changes in current goals. The changes that should be made are determined next. There are several ways that benchmarks can change goals. Benchmarks confirm that goals are directionally correct. That is, that unit costs over time must decline, or inventory turns over time should increase. Benchmarks may drive a change in emphasis on which goals are most important. A prioritization may be revealed that was not perceived before, such as product quality. Finally, the most thorough use of benchmarks would change the absolute value of the goals' metric. This often is the most widely made use of benchmark findings.

While it is true that the ultimate use of benchmark findings is in changing the metric, it should be done with some care. The benchmark data and information cannot be precise without extensive data having been gathered. It is probably best to recognize some range about the mean value of the goal. And, as mentioned previously, while the metric is important, it is the underlying best practices that require the most understanding.

In the process of changing goals to incorporate benchmark information, the effect on other upstream and downstream organizations should be clearly understood. The cost to implement the change is likewise of importance. These two in relation to both acceptance by management and effect on customers must be grasped. Managers will need to project the degree of competitiveness and level of performance superiority achieved. The extent to which changed goals will meet customer requirements will need to be assessed.

The final step in the process is to determine the new performance gap and obtain commitment to change. Both have been covered in prior chapters.

Rationale

Each firm has its own approach to goal setting. For benchmarking purposes, the hierarchical cascade of mission, operating principles, performance goals, strategies, and tactics is an effective scheme for goal setting and is shown in Figure 9.1. The organization's mission statement already has been covered. The benchmarking program should support the mission and be derived from it. Planning principles are an effective way of communicating the benchmarking practices that the organization supports. It will be discussed more fully in later chapters. Planning principles are important qualitative statements of the benchmarks while performance goals and metrics are important quantitative statements of the benchmarks. Strategies and tactics cover the benchmark industry best practices at two levels of detail.

It is the specific thesis of this text that no worthwhile goals can be established without being based on benchmark findings. Benchmarking should precede and be an integral part of goal definition. Benchmarking incorporates the reality of satisfying customer requirements and ensuring those requirements are based on the best industry practices. Thorough and complete benchmarking will ensure not only a definition of the benchmark but will also describe how the best practices will be achieved. Goals cannot be set based on extrapolation of the past into the future, nor can they be based on assumptions about productivity, inflation, and market growth. Goals can only be set effectively based on the factual data of the external world — industry best practices.

Two considerations are important in the relationship of benchmarks to goals development. Experience shows that the conversion of benchmarks to planning principles markedly adds understanding and acceptance. Communicating specific benchmark visit findings and gaining acceptance of the findings are of equal importance as was discussed in the previous chapter.

Operating Principles

Benchmark findings invariably will show a performance gap that needs to be closed. Methods and practices must be changed. The benchmark statements also will describe how the operation must change. With this information it is relatively straightforward to project how each individual, position, or organization will be affected if benchmark practices were emulated. The benchmark findings may be quite traumatic. After reviewing the findings, the natural reaction is to question what organization or position will

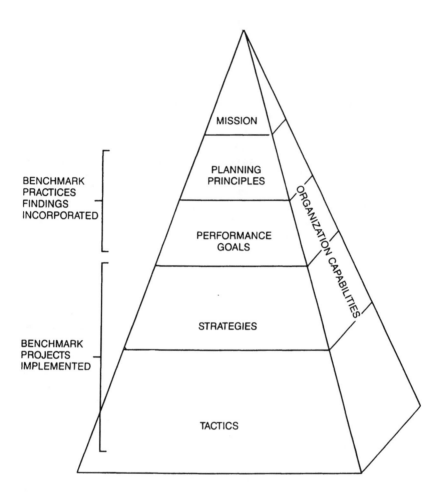

FIGURE 9.1. GOAL SETTING AND ACTION PLANNING PROCESS

no longer be needed. If operations are changed to meet the benchmark, then benchmarking findings will show detailed effects on budgets, organizations, and positions.

If discussions are initially allowed to reach this level of detail, there will be an emotional debate about the worth of benchmarking. What is wanted is an acceptance of any concentration on the more important topic, namely the need for change. More importantly, a description of an achievable endpoint — a future state incorporating best practices — is what is needed. How is an objective, unemotional statement achieved? How can such a statement foster understanding and acceptance?

The method found most successful is to convert the benchmark findings into statements of planning or operating principles. Operating or planning principles can be derived from the more important, fundamental benchmarking practices. Table 9.1 shows a statement of principles for a logistics function. They state in generic, yet functional terms what will be pursued as an overall guiding set of principles by the organization.

The benefit of the principles is that they are not specific to any organization, position, or individual. They do not attack anyone's turf as such. Only the application of the principles to specific circumstances will do that. Thus, the principles can be discussed openly, and discussed and understood at almost all organizational levels. They should be the basis of discussion, understanding, and acceptance by a wide cross-section of individuals. They serve to delineate clearly how the organization will change when specific opportunities arise. They serve notice on how the organization will change and why.

The statement of principles is a powerful, positive statement for change. And it is solidly grounded because the principles are a direct result of benchmark findings. It is difficult to argue against customer requirements and industry best practices found from firsthand benchmarking visits. The statement that "this is what we must do to meet or exceed industry or competitive practices" is a highly credible position. The operating principles statement derived from benchmarking investigations is therefore an important bridge to acceptance of external findings. Lack of principles would only result in short-term decisions and no direction or plan.

The L. L. Bean Experience

The L. L. Bean experience was only one of many benchmarking investigations that, in total, resulted in an overall set of comprehensive goals and statements of operational best practices. But it

- Provide competitive levels of customer satisfaction by market segment

- Reduce unit costs

- Increase inventory turns

- Fewer echelons
  — Shortest path from source to use or consumption
  — Material handled least number of times

- Fewer locations (distribution centers) at an echelon

- Centralize slow moving and scheduled delivery materials

- Modernize facilities to state-of-the-art
  — Materials handling equipment
  — Control systems based on bar code and scanning data capture

- Capitalize on opportunities presented by deregulated transportation
  — Use volume to negotiate favorable discounts
  — Route contract carriers to maximize full truckload mileage

- Examine where and how much packaging and labeling is essential to move material without damage

- Delivery to customers unconstrained by arbitrary geographic- or systems-dictated boundaries

TABLE 9.1. LOGISTICS PLANNING PRINCIPLES

was an important one. It was one of the earliest benchmarking visits and it was instrumental in showing that major practice changes were necessary. The practices uncovered were fundamental to showing how a major operation should change warehouse materials handling.

The approach to analyzing improvement in warehouse materials handling was one that broke the problem into two logical components. The first was material flow simplification. This exercise was essentially an operations layout design, but a design whose objective was to minimize the steps in the process and the distance traveled from receiving inbound products to shipment of customer orders. The second component was one that dealt with how the operation should be managed once the design was complete. This latter component was a bit more intangible, but important because its objective was to maximize the amount of orders flowing through the facility for the lowest use of resources, principally labor. Said differently, once the design was set it had to be operated efficiently. Of course the operating practices to some extent did dictate materials handling equipment design.

Both components incorporated best industry practices. In this case many of them were found at L. L. Bean. The benefits from the streamlined flow by itself were very worthwhile. But the methods of operating the new design were not well defined. The L. L. Bean visit confirmed that the opportunity was significant and exceeded that of the streamlined flow phase, and more definition and benchmarking visits fully confirmed the magnitude of the potential.

The practices found at L. L. Bean for the computer-directed picking activity were made part of the logistics goals statement, with each named practice a goal for achievement. The industry best practices became goals in and of themselves.

CHAPTER 10 DEVELOPING ACTION PLANS (STEP 8)

Action Planning
- Task considerations
- Behavioral considerations

Relationship of Benchmarking to Business Planning

Enablers Are Not Practices

Action Plan Process Capability
- Analysis for implementability
- Analysis of activities

Effectiveness and Efficiency

The L. L. Bean Experience

DEVELOPING ACTION PLANS (STEP 8)

What Changes Are Necessary to Achieve Benchmark Findings?

This chapter deals with the development of action plans to implement the benchmark findings. Basic action planning considerations are covered as they apply to benchmarking, but not in detail. Each organization has its own established ways for effectively implementing new practices. What is discussed here are a number of important considerations for the development of action plans to permit more effective implementation of benchmark findings. One such consideration is to embed benchmarking in the planning process up front to plan for benchmarking and to expect results from benchmarking on which to base operating and longer term plans.

In developing action plans for the implementation of benchmarking practices there often is interchangeable use of the terms enablers and practices. This confusion may be misleading and result in poor implementation. The distinction is more clearly delineated in this chapter. Also covered are two additional ways to maximize the implementability of benchmarking. One is to rigorously examine the transactions moving through the new benchmarked process to ensure there are minimum exceptions to the use of the new process. The second is to examine benchmark practices from the viewpoint of their contribution to efficiency and effectiveness and the resulting actions required.

Once best industry practices have been defined by benchmarking, operational action plans showing specific events must be pursued to implement them to achieve superior performance. The basic action planning process, shown in Chapter 9, Figure 9.1, is a cascading process, now supported by benchmark findings and industry best practices. Benchmark practices became a basis for the development of operating principles statements. They are incorporated in performance goals. Strategies and tactics are then developed to implement changing practices through specific projects. In this way benchmark project targets are incorporated into the operating unit's plans, targets, and goals. It is only through this later step that success can be ensured.

Action Planning

During action planning of benchmarking findings one should consider the two facets of implementation that are part of the standard action planning process followed by most businesses. The first deals with the activity or task that must be accomplished. This involves the definition of who, what, when, and how for the task. It will be discussed in some detail shortly. The second part deals with the people and behavioral aspects of implementing change. This involves the consideration of how the support of the organization will be obtained for the implementation of the new best practices. Each of these two facets of implementation should be considered in any action planning. It is the experience of the author that no amount of superb planning in one area will make up for lack in the other.

While there may be many ways to approach the action planning phase and there is a wealth of reference material on these topics, some of the key steps will be reviewed here because of the critical nature of converting benchmarking findings to action. The review is not meant to be exhaustive. Reference to appropriate topics to investigate further will be cited and it will be up to those most concerned to pursue them further. But the relationship to benchmarking and other material in the text will be referenced.

It is assumed that most firms already have some approach to this type planning in place. To the extent that it is different than that described here, its application should be readily apparent from this discussion.

Task Considerations

Task considerations in action planning involve asking the standard question of who, what, when, and how. More specifically they involve the following steps:

- **Task specification.** The task should be fully specified and clarified for those who will be responsible for implementing the benchmarking findings. This may involve a more complete description of the benchmarking practice than that described in the findings.

- **Task sequencing.** The steps to accomplish the task should be described and put into logical sequential order. The step-by-step approach considered most successful to implement the benchmark practice should be broken down into its components and placed in priority sequence.

- **Resource needs assignment.** Resource needs to accomplish the practice implementation should be determined. These will include the resources for the transition as well as any investments required to implement the benchmark practices.

- **Schedule establishment.** The schedule for the individual tasks should be defined. This can involve the typical Gant chart display of the tasks for the practices.

- **Responsibilities assessment.** The responsibility and accountability for each task should be defined. Since implementation of many benchmark practices are cross-functional in nature, the responsibility may be shared and should be so specified.

- **Expected results.** The deliverables expected from implementation of the benchmark practice should be described. This is a description of how the practice is supposed to work.

- **Monitoring.** The measurement of the results should be specified. This is the conversion of the practice into its resulting output metric or measurement. It is the result of the adaptation of the benchmark practice into the work process and the resulting change in output expected.

Action plans developed from benchmark findings would be expected to support the organization's mission and goals because the initial benchmarking steps to determine what to benchmark was, in most cases, based on these. It will be helpful to show the relation of the implementation actions to the support of the overall mission. One way to show this relationship is to display it by level as shown in Figure 10.1. The restatement of the effect of the benchmark practice shown to support the goals of the organization focuses attention and gains commitment of the organization on the accomplishment of the action plan. Supported by a graphical display and appropriate reinforcement, the entire organization's efforts will be driven toward accomplishment of the action plan and therefore the benchmark.

A further step to ensure maximum opportunity from the action planning for the benchmark practice is to determine the impediments that may have to be overcome by the organization to permit successful implementation. Impediments can be documented through a force field analysis shown in Figure 10.2. The analysis graphically details the helping and hindering forces that will affect the implementation of best practices. Helping factors may be

COMMUNICATING OBJECTIVES

ORGANIZATIONAL	OBJECTIVE	GRAPHICAL COMMUNICATOR
Vice President	Expense/ Revenue	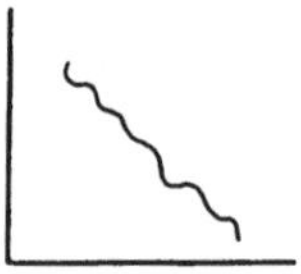
Distribution Center Manager	Productivity	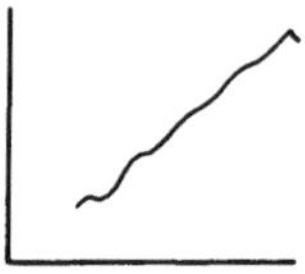
Hourly Work Group	Absenteeism (Benchmark Practice Finding)	

CONCLUSIONS

There is no better way of communicating desired performance than graphically displaying objectives to the individuals who can fulfill them and then positively reinforcing achievement and progress.

FIGURE 10.1. GOAL CASCADING SCHEME

stressed or further strengthened for acceptance. Hindering factors can be minimized or avoided and methods found to overcome them. The size of the effort involved is shown by the gap between the two forces.

In similar fashion weighted analysis can be used to analyze practices for greatest payback. The analysis would consider how important the benchmark practice is, how much time is required to gain the benefits, what resources are required for implementation, what the probability of success is estimated to be, and what degree of control is necessary to have the practice operating successfully. With weighting allocated to each category, a score can be derived to obtain a guide to the action planning for benchmark practices. A format is shown in Figure 10.3.

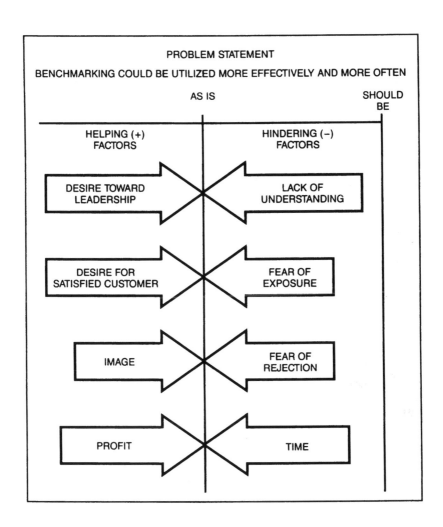

FIGURE 10.2. FORCE FIELD DIAGRAM OF IMPLEMENTATION — HELPING AND HINDERING FORCES

List the benchmark practices being considered. Rate the practices by working across each row.

CONSIDERATION   BENCHMARK PRACTICE

How Important

1	2	3	4	5
Little				Great

Time Required

1	2	3	4	5
Little				Great

Reasons Requested

1	2	3	4	5
Little				Great

Probability of Success

1	2	3	4	5
Little				Great

Control Needed

1	2	3	4	5
Little				Great

TOTAL POINTS

FIGURE 10.3. WEIGHTED SELECTION WORKSHEET

Next the action plan should be organized. The plan should include what the action or industry practice is, the time frame, responsibility, resources, and a description of the effect the action will have on closing the gap. The latter can be supported by key statements from the force field and weighting analysis. The plan would now be complete and serve as the document against which periodic tracking can be performed.

Needless to say Gantt- and PERT-type analysis and tracking, especially through some of the computer-based project management programs now available, would be appropriate for a comprehensive benchmark practices implementation plan. The project management plan would serve to be the most complete conversion of the action plan into a tracking program.

Behavioral Considerations

People's behavior when major change is planned should be given equal attention as the task considerations of planning for benchmark practices implementation. The primary purpose in this effort is to gain the organization's support and commitment for the changes. There are several ways to accomplish this important step and many have already been discussed in other sections of the text.

Chapter 8 is entirely devoted to communications and gaining acceptance. A section of Chapter 12 covers management behaviors crucial to successful benchmarking. Ultimately benchmarking must be embedded into the vital processes to ensure it becomes institutionalized and an accepted way of life that sensitizes the organization to the fact that change will happen in a constructive and desired way. Chapter 11 covers the considerations for the embedding of benchmarking into the four major business processes. The inspection process for the use of the benchmarking process as well as the outcome of benchmark practices are covered there as well. Finally, Chapter 2 covers success factors for benchmarking. Each of these sections should be referred to in developing a plan for successfully incorporating the people considerations of benchmark practice implementation.

From a more generic viewpoint there are topical areas that can be researched to add to the list of success factors to consider in any change. These involve the topical keywords of change management, project management, and performance management. What is wanted are success factors to consider when making changes in productivity or perhaps quality. It will be left to those interested to research these topics further and gain the desired insight.

Gaining acceptance, concurrence, and commitment for benchmarking practices is, needless to say, a vital step in action planning. While the benchmark practices themselves may have been accepted, the acid test of acceptance is shown in the willingness to change. Obviously changes based on industry best practices and the need for superior performance are large motivators in and of themselves. However, acceptance should not be left to that motivation alone. Action planning, considering both task and behavioral considerations, along with attention by senior management, will be the primary ingredients.

Relationship of Benchmarking to Business Planning

Each firm, at some juncture, performs two levels of planning: the annual budgeting and a longer horizon, usually multi-year planning. Benchmarking is an essential part of each. Benchmarking determines those practices that must be changed over time to become competitive or achieve superior performance. Benchmarking becomes, both from a practice statement as well as metric viewpoint, the basis for long-range planning for change as shown in Figure 10.4.

It is appropriate therefore to have benchmarking as a key ingredient in the long-range planning process and document. There are at least two places where benchmarking should be covered in a long-range plan. First, there should be a section devoted solely to benchmarking. This section reviews past results, current activities, and future plans for benchmarking. It is a key section that commits the organization to benchmarking as the basis of its plans in that vital view of the external environment. It also should be a place where the organization can mention its accomplishments in benchmarking and receive appropriate recognition. Second, each section of the plan should reference the appropriate benchmarks that are the basis for resource changes or requests. The benchmark practices and metrics should be the basis for justification of these requests. There can be no other more concrete basis for resource justification than basing the request on industry best practices. The benchmarking steps and their relationship to business planning are outlined in Table 10.1.

Once the pattern of committed benchmark practices have been established in the long-range plan these, in turn, feed the annual budget and are converted into specific functional action plans. The actions may arise from several sources and categorizing some of them may assist in their understanding. Table 10.2 is a chart of possible source of gaps and actions required.

Another important relationship of benchmarking to the planning exercise is the planning for benchmarking. A part of the planning process is to ensure that benchmarking remains evergreen. Milestones should be built into plans that will trigger a new round of benchmarking. Usually following an initial benchmarking investigation the concentration for future benchmarking

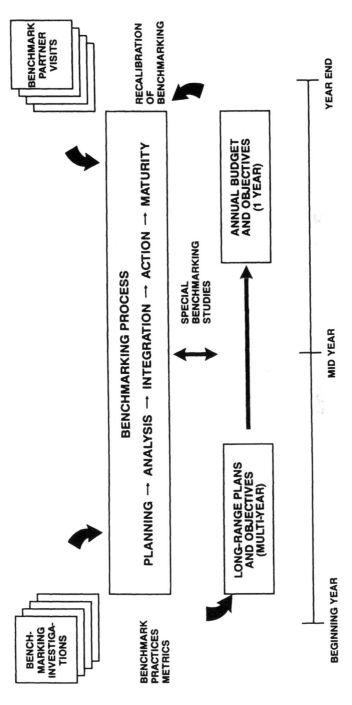

FIGURE 10.4. PLANNING RELATIONSHIP TO BENCHMARKING PROCESS

- Goals of the organization are based on benchmark findings.

- Goals established as a result of benchmarking are accepted by functional management, are derived from the mission, and cascade to objectives and operating principles.

- The mission, goals, objectives, and operating principles are communicated to the organization for understanding and commitment.

- Goals are documented in the business plan.

- Strategies and action plans are developed, based on industry practices to meet approved goals.

- The business plan is reviewed with and approved by senior management.

- Operating unit plans based on best industry practices are reviewed and approved by senior management.

- Operating budget submissions and reviews describe progress toward benchmark goals.

- Operating plan approvals include commitments to benchmark.

- Plans and target performance are built into the performance appraisal and recognition and reward processes.

- Benchmarks are recalibrated as part of the annual business plan update.

- Progress toward benchmarks is discussed with employees at regular communications meetings.

TABLE 10.1. BENCHMARKING STEPS AND RELATION TO BUSINESS PLANNING

SOURCE OF BENCHMARK GAPS	ACTION/SOLUTION REQUIRED
• Benchmark relationship to planning assumptions and targets not understood	• Communicate the interrelationship between benchmarks and overall planning goals
• Benchmarks are not visible during planning process	• Benchmarks are specifically reviewed as part of planning process. Progress toward benchmarks achievement are displayed/discussed
• It is not clear how individual practice benchmarks build to an overall summary benchmark statistic, such as % of revenue	• Review the critical business functions to be benchmarked. Structure a roll up, weighted averaging process to obtain meaningful summary
• Relationship of cost benchmarks do not relate to customer satisfaction benchmarks	• Tie appropriate customer satisfaction provided to practices
• Benchmarks, established from several studies/firms may be difficult to show as coherent whole	• Benchmarking program should be designed to deliver results by appropriate business function
• Insufficient constructive discussion exists between benchmarking team and affected unit	• Better up-front preplanning and incorporation of functional individuals on benchmarking team

TABLE 10.2. FUNCTIONAL BENCHMARKING ACTION PLANNING

activities will be on information gaps, especially those that are deemed important. Thus, the second wave of benchmarking may result in a set of special, highly targeted investigations to fill those gaps. However, specific plans should be formulated to require the update for changed industry practices as an evergreen process itself.

Enablers Are Not Practices

There often is a tendency to use the term enabler for a benchmark practice. This is a natural tendency since a variety of means are usually examined to make the benchmark findings useable.

But it is a mistake to work with them interchangeably. In the context of benchmarking best practices of the typical work process, as used in this text, there should be a clear distinction between practice and enabler. A practice is a method used in the work process. It and only it can be changed to emulate an external practice, and it and only it provides the opportunity for closing the gap. Concentration on enablers will not.

Webster defines enablers as "the supply of means, knowledge, or opportunity to be or do something. To make feasible or possible." Enablers are helpful in the implementation of benchmark practices, but they should not be confused with the practices themselves. The benchmark practices are specific new methods or practices that require a change to meet a stated goal. Enablers are a broad set of activities that enhance implementability. In sequence of priority they may be as shown in Table 10.3.

The table makes the point that there is a hierarchy to the progression from enabler to benchmark practice and finally to the overall goal being achieved through a practice change. The process that must be changed is the data capture process. The benchmark practice found that reflects the best in the industry is the use of the bar code and scanning device to accomplish the data capture automatically. Neither the practice nor the process can be confused with any enabler. It is a simple fact that the practice must change to obtain the benefits of the benchmark findings. Enablers may assist, and they may assist greatly. In this instance training is seen as a significant enabler. It permits effective use of the scanner. But it does not replace it. It is important to keep the definitions of practices and enablers clear and not permit them to be used interchangeably.

HIERARCHY	OBJECTIVE
Goal	Reduced clerical documentation workload
Benchmark practice	Use of bar coding for automatic data capture
Enabler	Training in use of scanners

TABLE 10.3. COMPARISON AND DISTINCTION BETWEEN BENCHMARK PRACTICE AND ENABLER

Enablers should be considered along with benchmark practice changes to not only facilitate their implementation but to empower those making changes. A partial list of enablers is shown in Table 10.4. Lists of these supporting activities may readily be generated and prioritized by brainstorming the objections for benchmark practices being considered. Ultimately, a practice change must be implemented. Enablers cannot be substituted for the benchmark practice itself.

- Practices that are based on sound, simple processes.

- Practices that are based on proven technology.

- Communication of clear objectives which govern outcomes from benchmark practices.

- Process practices that have good operator feedback.

- Provide problem-solving skills to process operators.

- Utilize quality circle teams to implement practices.

- Utilize a program management process and a computerized program management system during implementation.

- Implement based on experience of other successful programs or projects.

- Develop approaches for early identification of problems.

- Implement through multifunction skilled teams.

- Concentrate on problem avoidance rather than problem reduction.

TABLE 10.4. LIST OF ENABLERS

Action Plan Process Capability

The capability of the action plan to deliver the required benchmark practice should be assessed, that is, to ensure that the full benefits of the best practices are achieved. There are two considerations that should be given careful thought. The first is an analysis for implementability. This is an examination of the practices themselves directed to uncover all potential obstacles. The second is an analysis of the activity that moves through the process. This is an analysis to ensure all possible activity or transactions can be handled by the process and minimizes exceptions to gain maximum benefit from the streamlined, more efficient industry practices.

Analysis for Implementability

Beyond the firm's broad annual and multi-year planning, the benchmark practices must be implemented in the organization. Recognizing that that change, especially the most likely significant change revealed by benchmarking, may be traumatic, the process for change must be managed to gain acceptance and ownership. One of the more effective means for accomplishing this step is to convert the practices into a statement of decisions that will be necessary for implementation. Since any change is expected to have some effect on more than one individual, function, operation, or business unit, it is imperative that these effects be approached in a structured fashion.

It is reasonably straightforward to convert a best practice into a statement that shows what has to be changed and who or what organization is responsible. The responsible organization can then investigate the upstream and downstream effects and document any hindrances that might prevent implementation. For each significant hindrance, alternative solutions may be developed to permit acceptance. In this structured fashion, the objective is to clearly understand what potentially might prevent implementation and have hedges developed for acceptance. The severity of the risks involved, in an impact statement form, can be extremely useful to the acceptance of the type change derived by benchmark findings.

This phase of implementation planning therefore should not be minimized. While it is true that many changes may have only minor effects and can be implemented based on judgment and experience, benchmarking findings usually are of a greater magnitude and will require this implementation analysis phase. All affected parties will have a chance to input their relevant impacts.

The practice change will be clearly understood, and the organization or individual responsible will be clearly identified. Thus, an informed decision can be made.

The development of functional plans often requires an additional, different kind of analysis from benchmarking itself. The analysis is focused on implementability. It is primarily an analysis of fostering and inhibiting forces. Both are important. While hindrances need to be overcome, it is often the sometimes slight, but critical modifications based on understanding by the affected organizations that make the new practices successful. The benchmark method or practice is not being changed. Other, affected practices are being changed to permit the full benefit of what has been found from benchmarking. Success factors found important to action planning are shown in Table 10.5.

ACCEPTANCE	How can the acceptance of the benchmark practices be gained from others? What benefits can be shown for the industry best practices? How can these benefits be demonstrated?
ANTICIPATION	What objections to the best practices being proposed can be anticipated? What should be the most effective response?
ASSISTANCE	How can other organizations or groups assist with the implementation of the best practices?
LOCATION	What place or location would be best suited for putting the initial application of the best practices into operation?
TIMING	How can special timing, days, or date provide advantage in the implementation? What dates should be avoided?
PRECAUTIONS	How can the implementation be piloted, pretested, or simulated to ensure an effective solution?

TABLE 10.5.   ACTION PLAN SUCCESS FACTOR ANALYSIS

Analysis of Activities

The concentration of benchmarking investigations has been on practices for a business process. Such processes as order entry, fulfillment, and billing are typical. Each process has practices or methods. In addition, each process has activities or transactions that move through the process. The transactions or activities should receive as much attention during implementation as the process practices themselves.

Once the benchmark practices are understood, the activities that lend themselves to the practice need to be considered and analyzed. There are at least three distinct types of activities for any process or practice: (1) those that are readily implementable, (2) those that clearly are not implementable and that cannot for good reasons use the practices, and (3) those that are implementable with change in the activity that moves through the process and uses the benchmark practices, a gray area. This latter group may be substantial and provide a major portion of the benefit. There should be a structured approach for dealing with these exception transactions. An example such as an order taking, fulfillment, and invoicing process will most likely be helpful.

It is difficult to maintain a simple, straightforward, cost-effective ordering process. Demands are placed on the process externally by customers for meeting their basic information requirements, and internally by the marketing function to encourage further purchases by a variety of pricing options. The complexity of the pricing plans are inhibitors to quick order placement and add to cost. The level of complexity adds to potential billing errors and also adds to exception costs.

The most straightforward pricing scheme would be one based on a fixed list price. Simple quantity discounts and discounts off-list would be further enhancements adding some level of complexity, but not much. At the other extreme would be prices that could vary by promotion, customer volume of purchase, ability to obtain premiums, and repetitive billing such as that required for a service contract. Some of these transactions may be supported by a simple order taking process. Others will significantly detract from its cost-effectiveness, either in the length of time to take the order initially or in administering the order to successful completion and later payment. The transactions need to be analyzed as to which most readily lend themselves to the process and which need to be modified to use the process.

The approach often taken is to not consider those transactions in the gray area as candidates for a benchmark process because of their complexity. The view taken here is that, in addition to practice changes of a process, the transaction types moving through the process should also be candidates for modification. The transactions may need to be changed also to fit the new process practices. Pursuit of changed transactions is equally as important to changing practices to obtain the maximum benefits. What should be explored are alternatives for the transaction changes in a similar fashion to the implementation planning already discussed.

Effectiveness and Efficiency

Another consideration for implementation that may assist in gaining understanding, not only of the practice but also what must be changed to obtain implementability, is the segregation of practices into those practices that contribute to efficiency and those that contribute to effectiveness.

Efficiency often is termed doing the job the right way; effectiveness often is termed doing the right job. One can, and often does, have a level of implementation effort substantially higher than the other. In most circumstances, practices that contribute to efficiency are wholly within the decision-making authority of the operation, such as a logistics function. No external operations are affected by the change and the change can be implemented entirely with local management commitment.

Benchmark practices that contribute to effectiveness, however, generally involve other parties. Negotiations have to be conducted with upstream suppliers of input and downstream customers of the operation's output. This level of effort is obviously more substantial because it will require changes by these external operations to gain the full benefit of the internal benchmark practices. Table 10.6 shows an example of efficiency and effectiveness practices in a logistics setting. It permits those involved with implementation to consider the magnitude of implementation effort and prepare for it to gain acceptance and the full benefit of the actions.

The L. L. Bean Experience

The combination of many benchmarking investigations, confirmed by the L. L. Bean visit, was crucial in handling the increased volumes projected. The outgrowth of the L. L. Bean visit was the establishment of a full-time project team to tackle delivery of the new way of operation, which capitalized on the streamlined flow design. The former resulted in justifying computer support for

---

EFFICIENCY
- Deliver specific programs uncovered by benchmarking
  - Bar coding
  - Velocity material location
  - Item weight capture for packing quality assurance
- Capitalize on possible trade-offs, such as inventory reduction for systems with more timely information
- Economies of scale, such as filling underutilized capacity

EFFECTIVENESS
- Eliminate nonproductive practices not performed by industry leaders
- Segregated customer satisfaction levels offered for choice by customer at a cost or designed to complement specific geographic or customer market segment
- Consider implementing P & L based reporting to incent the organization on a profitability measurement
- Consider full charge-out of services to users to ensure meeting customer requirements
- Sell services to outsiders to confirm benchmark (If outsiders buy, why not insiders?)

TABLE 10.6. EFFICIENCY VERSUS EFFECTIVENESS PRACTICES IN A LOGISTICS FUNCTION

order processing not originally contemplated in the flow streamlining phase.

A warehouse modernization program had been launched at the time benchmarking activities were started. The modernization program primarily focused on achieving a streamlined material flow with the fewest steps possible. During the design of the modernized warehouses some of the best practices of L. L. Bean were incorporated. These included material locations arranged by velocity to speed material flows and minimized picker travel distance. The other practices, collectively described as "computer-directed picking," were not incorporated in the design. They became the set of practices benchmarked at L. L. Bean, along with other benchmarking investigation defining industry best practices, that could be pursued and provide further efficiencies to the streamlined design. They were the principle basis for definition and justification of this second phase of the warehouse design.

CHAPTER 11
IMPLEMENTING SPECIFIC ACTIONS AND MONITORING PROGRESS (STEP 9)

IMPLEMENTING SPECIFIC ACTIONS AND MONITORING PROGRESS (STEP 9)

Change: The Ultimate Objective of Benchmarking

This chapter covers several items important to successfully implementing and monitoring benchmarking action plans, and in installing industry best practices. Benchmarking has the potential for redirecting resources of the organization, and how this is accomplished may be significant to success. There are standard processes by which to implement. These are usually done directly through line management or through the use of a dedicated program team. There also are some nontraditional ways found effective, especially for work process related practices. One is implementation through performance teams, or those closest to and responsible for the operation of the process. Another, found especially effective for process implementations that are cross-functional, is the appointment of a senior management level "process czar." Such an appointed individual would become responsible for the implementation of the benchmark findings and the further improvement of the process.

This chapter also covers monitoring progress through the management and financial processes as well as ensuring program success. Since monitoring means inspection by management during implementation, guidelines for inspection are provided. The latter ensures that two important aspects of benchmarking are inspected: 1) the effective use of the 10-step benchmarking process, and 2) the results expected from benchmarking to ensure success.

Introduction

Once the benchmark findings have been developed, committed to, and converted to accepted action plans, the final acts of implementation and monitoring are critical to success. Implementing specific actions depends on understanding the new practices and the ways the benefits will be captured. Roles, responsibilities, and rewards also must be understood. The monitoring of progress includes the standard approaches followed in industry: comparing progress against predefined milestones, determining the causes for variances, taking corrective action where variances are significant, and reviewing results with management.

There are many ways to accomplish these standard management practices that have been used successfully for some time. There is literature rich in advice on what is important; it is not proposed to review these here. What will be reviewed are those aspects of taking action and monitoring that are improved or changed by successful use of benchmarking. Needless to say, the topics of change management, project management (including project management computer software tools), and performance management also deserve review for further insight into taking action and monitoring.

From a benchmarking perspective, action taking and monitoring may significantly affect the strategic redirection of resources. There are proven successful alternatives for implementation. It will be important to success that benchmarks be incorporated in the management and financial processes to obtain commitment. And project success may depend on several key factors. These and their successful relationship to benchmarking will be reviewed next.

Strategic Resource Redirection

The real value of benchmarking occurs when an organization acts to implement industry best practices. The action may result in a new strategic direction for an operation and thereby ensure superior performance. In addition, the real value of benchmarking is derived when the benchmarking process is institutionalized throughout the organization. (This will be discussed later.) It is through new, continuously benchmarked directions, that maintaining competitive or industry superiority can be guaranteed by using best practices.

For a business unit internal to a large firm there is no direct profit incentive. At best, most operating units are cost centers. The incentives to drive efficiency and effectiveness are primarily focused on the size of the budget. They rarely consider industry best practices as the fundamental basis for developing resource plans and budgets. The budgeting discussions are reduced to exercises on debating the size of the allowable expense and the extent of responsibility or turf, not what should be the correct level if subjected to the external marketplace of supply and demand.

Benchmarking is the mechanism for bringing the competitiveness of the marketplace as incorporated by the industry best practices into the budgeting process and action plans. It forces the operation to consider how it would act if its services were to be sold in a completely free environment — were its customers to have a choice of internal versus external support. In this sense benchmarking is the next best approach to placing the operation on a charge-back or full profit and loss (P & L) basis in its approach to meeting customer requirements.

Alternatives for Implementation

Ultimately functional management must be made responsible for planning and executing the installation of benchmark practices. It must organize for this activity and most often carry it out within the existing functional structure. There are several ways to accomplish this activity. Two methods are straightforward and traditional — the implementation through line managers and the use of project or program teams. Two methods are nontraditional or new — the use of a "process czar" and the use of performance teams. Each has its strong points and deficiencies. The latter two will be the main focus since the others are common approaches to successful implementation.

Line Management Implementation

Given that the best practices, action plans, and responsibilities are well understood, there is little reason why line managers could not implement the changes themselves. There often is a level of operational detail best understood by line management that increases the probability of success and timely implementation. The commitment level should be high. The drawbacks include the lack of time and time taken away from supervising the operation. However, the sheer size of change may argue for a different approach.

Project or Program Management Implementation

The alternative often used for large complex projects involving change is the traditional project or program team approach. A team effort is established separate from the operation's line management to oversee the implementation. This approach permits line managers to continue concentrating on daily operations, yet they must have expertise in the new practices nearby to carry out the actual changes. The approach often is successful where there are important inter-project and inter-functional considerations and dependencies. The project team provides the idea transfer from the benchmarking effort to line operations.

Both alternatives have merit. Where benchmark practices of an efficiency nature are involved, the line management route may be preferred. That is, where practices are entirely within the control of the function, line managers can often be most effective at change. Where effectiveness practices are involved, the program or project team often is preferred. They generally have upstream and downstream effects that need special expertise and time to resolve — and line managers cannot afford to direct their attention to work this through. There are, however, two other approaches that should be given serious consideration.

The Use of a Process Czar

Benchmarking focuses on the basic business processes and practices of a company. By basing those processes on industry best practices, it is expected that internal processes would become simplified, contain only essential steps, be documented and understood, and meet customer requirements. Critical hand-offs and consequences of activity swings and complex input should be expected to be known so that required resources can be justified. Unfortunately this is rarely the case.

The situation facing the implementation of new, changed benchmarking practices often is completely different. There sometimes is little interest in process study, process detail, or process optimization by management at a senior level to marshal the cross-functional resources and bring focus to the need for change. Few could relate the essential steps of many business processes like order entry, delivery, and billing. Therefore, a substantial potential for automating manually intensive processes, reducing multiple hand-offs and error rates, as well as correcting poor computer applications goes unnoticed.

One reason is that many business processes are cross-functional in nature. There is no focal point or empowered accountability at high enough management levels to see the benchmark practices implemented and the processes simplified. The usual organization focus is on product and function, but efforts to simplify, through benchmark practices, have to cross those boundaries. There needs to be some way to gain acceptance of best practices that are for the collective benefit, but are outside the traditional compartmentalized functional organization structure.

There is a need for an accountable individual who can concisely describe all the essential process characteristics and who is empowered and responsible for the effective operation of a business process. That individual would have understanding and interest in process bottlenecks and process capacity limitations. When new processes or new uses of existing processes are proposed, the individual would be able to have a full understanding of the effect on existing processes. Such an individual would reward simplified thinking that results from installing industry best practices. Recognition would be given to simplified solutions that save steps and meet customer requirements.

A successful approach has been to appoint a process czar. The process czar would be a senior manager designated as the responsible process manager for each key business process. The process czar would be responsible for accepting ownership of the process. He or she would acquire and direct cross-functional resources to see that the best industry benchmark practices are implemented. The process czar would be responsible for driving simplification and proven automation technology. He or she would see that the benchmark practices changes would be implemented and would inspect the implementation and ongoing process operation.

To accomplish this activity, the process czar invariably needs a project or program plan. The elements of the plan would be the direct outcome of the benchmarking effort. These elements would include selection of the critical business processes that are to be benchmarked, development of the best industry practices, documentation of the current process steps, definitions of outputs and hand-offs, guarantee that the process meets customer requirements, definition of the endpoint process design and targets, and development of the practices to be implemented and schedules to be followed.

With this detail, derived from benchmarking activities, a recommended senior manager can be designated the process czar and have a specific proposal on which to act. The benchmarking of industry best practices implemented through a designated senior management process czar is an effective way of overcoming the often difficult steps of making change.

Those key critical business processes that deserve this level of management attention can be determined by each organization. However, those processes affecting customers would be prime candidates, such as order entry, delivery, billing, collection, service, problem resolution, and pricing.

Performance Teams

Another highly effective way to implement benchmark practices is through performance teams. Performance teams, also known as quality circles, can be used effectively to implement best practices. The unique benefit of performance teams is that they are involved in the work process directly. What better group would there be to install a change than those performing the task already.

The establishment of performance teams is widely known and their effectiveness and limitations are well documented elsewhere. That will not be covered here. What should be stressed is their use to refine and adapt benchmark practices, and to carry out the actual implementation. There is no reason why a performance team cannot be directed to concentrate on a predefined industry best practice. They would be instructed to determine the most effective way to incorporate the best practice into their process.

It is essential to gain their active participation and support. Emphasizing that the practices being proposed were developed from a concentrated investigation of best industry practices should help. They can have assurance that the practices are being used by others, and many of these others are the best.

The performance team can often make the installation a success. Their input early in the benchmarking investigation will help, and their insight in making minor modification to the basic industry practice to adapt it will often ensure successful implementation and avoidance of problems.

Monitor and Report Progress

There are several monitoring and reporting approaches that can enhance benchmarking success. Those few, high visibility metrics that indicate the progress toward efficiency should be monitored. They should be reviewed at appropriate intervals along with a view of specific benchmark project milestones. The metrics should be few, but should show a direct link to actions and change generated from benchmarking.

Each firm and function has its own readily understood metrics and they should continue to be used. The expense to revenue ratio metric also is one that is productive for benchmarking purposes. Because it indicates the contribution or detraction to profit margin by a cost center or business function, it is a most useful statistic. It not only incorporates what expense reductions are possible from benchmarking by examination of the denominator (expense), but it also shows what efficiencies must be pursued to increase the activity in order to remain profitable over the long term based on the numerator (revenue).

It therefore is essential to tie benchmarking directly into the existing financial and performance measurement processes and systems. Since the benchmarks are goals toward which the organization is directing its efforts, the benchmarks can be shown as goals as in Figure 11.1. In this regard it is useful to show the benchmark goals not only as a mean but also as a range. The range indicates the existence of some flexibility in achieving the benchmark goals as well as the fact that the goal itself will change due to changes in future industry or competitive practices.

Integrate Benchmarking into Vital Business Processes

To further ensure benchmarking investigations are conducted and provide a standard means to monitor progress, benchmarking should be integrated into the vital processes through which the organization performs work. While there may be many areas where benchmarking can be embedded, at least four are critical: the planning process, the management process, the quality process, and the financial process.

The planning process, which sets strategic direction, is a primary place where benchmarking is crucial. Goals and objectives derived from the organization mission will generate benchmarking investigations and the findings from benchmarking will influence and possibly change those goals. The decision-making process of the organization is the management process. Management will want to know that benchmarking has been performed to substantiate recommendations brought to it for decision. The increasing quest for quality and productivity has led many firms to establish a formal quality and problem-solving process. Embedding benchmarking into these processes ensures that the external environment and customer requirements are considered when relevant data are gathered. The financial process should require benchmarking when resource changes are being justified.

Integrating benchmarking into these and other processes at key points will ultimately institutionalize benchmarking and assure that it is practiced at the key points desired by management.

DISTRIBUTION QUARTERLY UNIT COST TRENDS

$/CUSTOMER DELIVERY

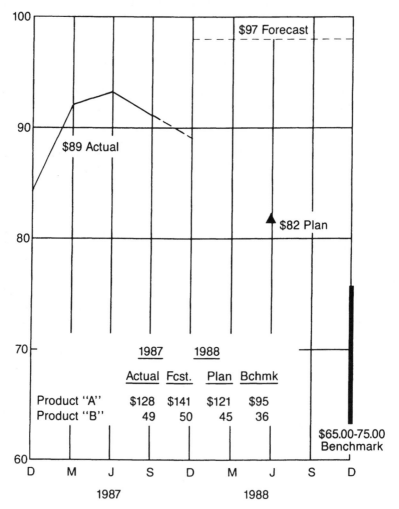

SUMMARY
1988 PLANS SHOW PROGRESS TOWARD BENCHMARK

FIGURE 11.1. EXAMPLE MONITORING OF PROGRESS TOWARD BENCHMARKING METRICS

The Planning Process

It is in the planning process that goals and objectives, success factors, and measurement metrics are defined, having been derived from the mission of the organization. An external focus is vital during this effort as it will establish the direction of the organization and marshal scarce resources. Benchmark findings about practices and customer requirements are critical input to these direction-setting activities. The results of these efforts will establish resources, budgets, and customer satisfaction levels. The planning process also will generate action items to be investigated. These most likely will require benchmarking. These items are in addition to showing the relationship of benchmarking findings to the establishment of strategic direction. Benchmarking should be a requirement in all planning efforts. A secondary outcome of benchmarking at this point is to create a felt need for change based on defensible, credible reasons — namely the external focus on best practices.

Both long-range plans and annual operating budgets should incorporate goals and objectives based on benchmarking. The planning process can incorporate benchmarking in at least two formal places: in a description of the progress to date and in the justification of proposed changes. A stand-alone section of each plan submission should include a section on the progress to date in conducting benchmarking. It is assumed that benchmarking will be conducted over some extended time period and management will require an update of progress. This should include a description of the process being followed by the business unit or function in past efforts, current progress, and future action plans for benchmarking. It should include an update on any goals and objectives changed by recent benchmarking findings. It should include descriptions of specific benchmarking projects completed and planned. Any success factor or measurement metric changes as a result of benchmarking investigations should be updated.

Following the general discussion of the progress in benchmarking, each succeeding section of the plan should support its request for practice changes and customer satisfaction levels justified by specific reference to benchmarking findings. The conversion of the benchmarking industry best practice findings to measurement metrics therefore will be the data to support this section of the plan. The results selected to become the forthcoming year's targets toward achievement of the benchmarks will feed the annual operating plan or budget.

The Management Process

The management process is the basic process used by the management team to make decisions. Each organization establishes its own set of practices for the management process. These could include establishment of meeting types, calendars and meeting process guidelines through which decisions are made, and the eventual communication of those decisions to the organization. It will be important that benchmarking become an integral part of this process, first to ensure that benchmarking is performed when critical management decisions are required, and second to send a strong signal to the organization on management's expectations for benchmarking. These could take the form of a specification that benchmarking will be performed for certain types of requests for funds or capital. Or there can be the more direct questioning during the discussion of recommendations where it can be asked whether the recommendations are based on benchmarking findings. Even the subtle question,"how do you know?" which by implication means "have you benchmarked?" can be pervasive in the establishment of benchmarking as an accepted requirement of management in its desire for quality decisions. The only valid response is information, knowledge, and insight gained from an objective assessment of the external business environment — namely, benchmarking.

Management reviews of operations, organization performance to plan, and individual performance are all very legitimate places for discussion of benchmarking. Benchmarking discussions about functional goals, objectives, and action plans should be based on a conscious understanding of how they are grounded in industry best practices. Performance to plan should also include a discussion of performance to benchmarks as well as how the benchmarks have changed due to the external environment. Individual performance can include a general discussion of the use of benchmarking as it relates to the specific requirement that there be the investigation of at least one industry best practice or outside visit as part of an individual's annual performance appraisal. Individual manager's recognition and reward can be made contingent on reducing specific benchmark gaps covered in the quality section of the performance appraisal. Each of these opportunities to question recommendations based on benchmarking or specifically request benchmarking findings to support decisions should clearly establish management's desire for benchmarking.

The natural outgrowth of the decision process will be the need to now communicate the results of those decisions to the organization. In formal communication sessions, management correspondence, internal publications, and individual conversations about the purpose and use of benchmarking can be mentioned, as well as benchmarking's contributions to the decisions made or strategy being pursued. The communications process can include an awareness of the external marketplace and "what others are doing that may affect our work" as a basis of sensitizing the organization to the fact that an external focus is important and desired by management. It also might include the performance of the organization to accepted benchmarks for its critical success factors. Specific reference to benchmarking success stories in internal publications will add further credibility to the benchmarking process itself.

The Quality Process

With the increasing interest and demand for quality most organizations have established a quality program or process. The basic objective of the process is to ensure that customer requirements are being met. The process can be described in many ways, but determining the output, customer for the output, requirements for the output, specifications for the requirements, the work process, appropriate measurements, process capability, and evaluation is one accepted description.

The process most often requires the gathering of data on which to base, at a minimum, the requirements phase. It is at this step that benchmarking should be considered. It may be that internal benchmarking is all that is required to develop the necessary definition of requirements. But the competitive, functional, and generic benchmarking approaches also should be considered. The use of benchmarking in the quality process is not limited to just the requirements phase. If the objective of the process is to meet customer requirements then nearly all steps could have some aspects of benchmarking. Why shouldn't the output, customer identification, and other steps be benchmarked if the desire is to have data-based approaches to customer satisfaction?

As part of the quality process, tools for analysis and problem solving often are provided. These require the gathering of data on which to base decisions. The obvious question is "what data?" Should the data gathering consider the external environment? And is this appropriate to benchmark? At least the appropriateness of benchmarking to the problem being solved should be considered and questioned. One way is to specifically make benchmarking a part of the formally defined process: It becomes one of the steps. Another way is to require benchmarking as part of a quality improvement project investigation as a demonstration of the benefits of benchmarking. Ultimately what is wanted is a consideration of benchmarking where it is most appropriate in the effort to improve quality in products and processes.

The audit of a quality improvement project, often called the inspection process, is the other area in the overall quality program where the need for benchmarking can be reinforced. The improvement team can be queried about the usefulness of benchmarking to their results. The responsibility for the overall growth and maturation of benchmarking should most likely be that of the chief quality officer of the organization.

The Financial Process

The natural outgrowth of the planning process is the feed to the financial control and performance management process of the organization. Benchmarking should be put in every operating plan review and annual targets should be based on a considered judgment of what progress can realistically be made toward the benchmark. In this way benchmarking becomes embedded in the very operation of the organization. Operations managers and senior management must develop a mutual trust about understanding the size of the gap. The size will become a reminder of the overall task and it is therefore an appropriate topic of discussion at financial reviews. But performance will be based on the progress toward the achievement of the benchmark. Benchmarking should be strongly supported by the financial officer.

Benchmarking should be seen as the basis for the correct justification of resources. Project and business proposal justification will most credibly be supported by well-executed benchmarking investigations. Requests for capital also should be based on industry best practices. While initially benchmarking studies will be seen as large, time-consuming, and expensive, their continued use will prove that they are routine, simple, and inexpensive. The payback will make the justification process substantially more credible.

Functional management will be responsible for the consolidation and summarization of the benchmarking investigation project findings to summarize metrics and operational statistics that portray their commitments to senior management. It will be important that the financial organization understand and concur in the benchmarking findings and conversion to budgets. The actual measurements should be developed with the following considerations. First, they should be developed based on satisfying customer requirements. Best industry practices are a reflection of meeting customer requirements, otherwise they would not prevail in the external marketplace. Second, the measures should include the elements describing the processes' specification, the cost of providing it, and the schedule for implementation. These three facets complete the metric's parameters. Finally, process checks should be developed.

Ensuring Program/Project Success

Periodic review of progress, no less than quarterly, would be based on the now-established management and financial processes. The focus of attention, beyond actual accomplishment of the benchmark metrics and specific business practices, should be on early detection of deviations from the benchmarking study action plan or the implementation plan.

Where new practices are to be implemented through a program team and eventually spread to multiple sites, it is essential that commitment be gained at the first site. Its status as a test site should be clearly established. It should be understood that new practices are to be tried, modified, and eventually incorporated in the process. This activity will be a disruptive, missionary one. At this site, extra effort will have to be made to prove the worth and implementability of the practices. The attention of those who implement the practices and extra resources required should be established at the outset. The site should be selected with care to ensure success.

Furthermore, the extra effort will necessarily detract from management and supervisory attention to ongoing daily details. Where a current process at an existing site is to be changed, as opposed to a new site startup based on benchmark practices, the level of difficulty in making that type of change often is most severe. Provision for recognition and reward to complete the implementation successfully will be essential. This type of extraordinary effort will require that a plan for recognition be part of any implementation planning itself.

Inspection Process

To ensure benchmarking effectiveness, there must be inspection by management. There are two kinds of inspection of interest. The results of benchmarking must be inspected to ensure the findings are implemented. That is the subject of this chapter on monitoring and reporting progress. It is a method of formally inspecting the output of benchmarking.

Of equal importance is the inspection of the conduct of benchmarking: Were all the steps followed? Were alternative approaches investigated? Where is the organization on the path to being proficient in benchmarking? Is benchmarking institutionalized in the organization such that individuals proactively search out benchmarking projects that will improve their operation of their own initiative?

To provide a basis on which to conduct an inspection of the process Quick Reference Guide 11.1 has been devoted to inspecting the benchmarking process. It details the elements of the 10 essential process steps that must be followed. The guide can be used as an inspection tool by managers to ensure benchmarking is being conducted in the most effective way. The steps are stated in generic process terms. The specifics, examples, and alternatives for conducting them will have to be gained by referring to the relevant chapter text.

Inspection of the 10-step benchmarking process can be performed by management as an audit to ensure compliance or it can be a self-administered check to see that all the best practices of benchmarking have been followed. The guide provided is one that mimics the process at its basic elements. By referring to the questions, a manager can quickly determine if the steps were followed. The knowledgeable manager can project the questions into the relevant mini-steps which must be followed to complete inspection.

There is little need to cover the steps here. They are part of the body of this text. The questions are generic enough to allow each manager to interpret them in light of his or her own situation. In addition to serving as a post or process audit, the guide can also serve as a quick reference to the kinds of steps required to exercise the 10-step benchmarking process on a pro forma basis.

The L. L. Bean Experience

Since the extent and complexity of best practices was substantial it was decided to use the program team approach for implementation. A comprehensive development project was organized. A requirements document was prepared incorporating the best practices observed at L. L. Bean as well as those observed at the other benchmarking partner firms. Potential hardware and software vendors were qualified. Proposals were requested from vendors to satisfy the benchmark requirements. A sizable, multi-year contract was negotiated for development and installation. For Xerox this involved a commitment of considerable development and implementation resources over a two-year period.

Monitoring and reporting were implemented at two levels based on the benchmarking program as well as on the specific findings at L. L. Bean. Departmental targets were established based on the metrics shown in Table 3.4, Chapter 3. These were reviewed quarterly along with the individual productivity programs developed to install the best practices and achieve the targets.

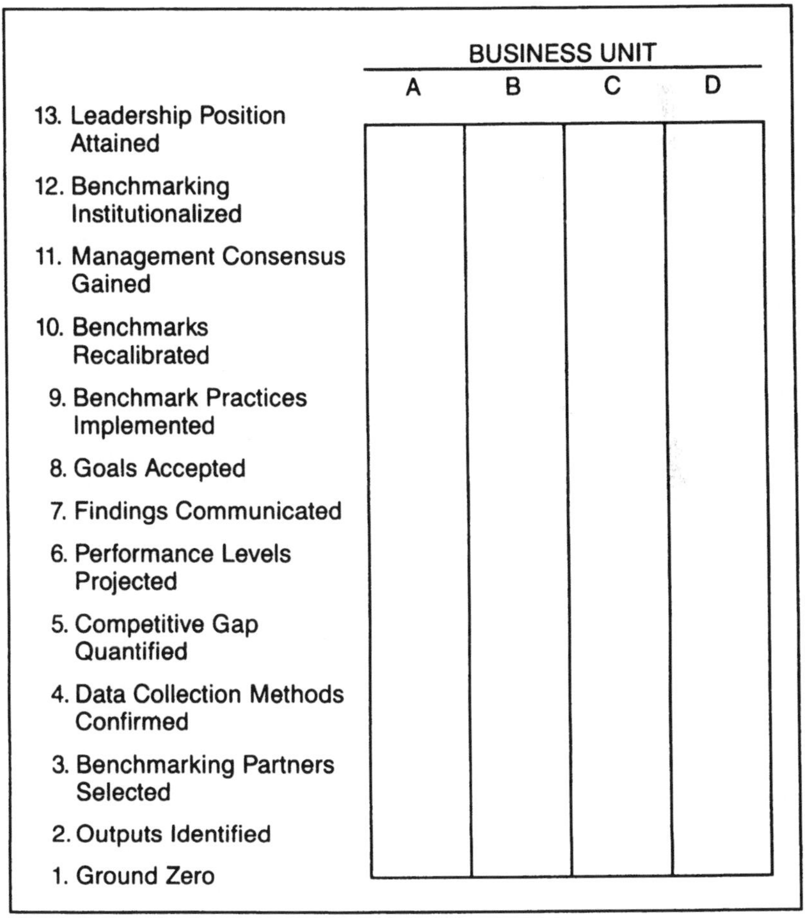

FIGURE 11.2.   MONITORING BENCHMARK PROGRESS
ACROSS BUSINESS UNITS

The chart reflects the progress by various business units or departments toward eventual leadership position. The scale is made up of the more significant benchmark milestones that must be covered successfully to get there. The chart obviously masks the difficulty of each step and the time required that could be significantly different. It is a quick visual means to portray progress by individual business unit to senior management.

In addition, to track progress by department or business unit for senior management, a summary monitoring chart as shown in Figure 11.2 was developed to permit quick indication of overall progress in benchmarking. While some judgment must obviously be used in determining the relative position of differing units, the chart serves as a quick reference to which departments are following the benchmarking steps best and achieving benefits from a comprehensive benchmarking program.

Both long-range and operating budget submissions had statements about benchmarking progress indicating not only the benchmark but the date of achievement. These were typically part of the annual long range reviews for the logistics plans that were presented to upper management. They also were reviewed at communications meetings within the department as well.

The specific project on "computer-directed activities" was established as a stand-alone project with project management process and supporting software that allowed progress measurement. It was reviewed within the department and with affected organizations at agreed-on intervals. The benchmark findings from the L. L. Bean visit were a significant portion of all these reviews. The findings at L. L. Bean were a point of interest and focus for benchmarking that caught individuals' imagination of the possible and, therefore, the doable.

QUICK REFERENCE GUIDE 11.1

10-STEP BENCHMARKING PROCESS INSPECTION CHECKLIST

STEP 1. IDENTIFY BENCHMARK OUTPUT

- Was the benchmarking study topic an outgrowth of the function's mission and deliverables?
- Was the subject selected critical to the success of the operation?
- Were practices benchmarked as well as key performance measurements?
- Was the subject and purpose of the benchmarking study reviewed with functional management and customers for their concurrence?

STEP 2. IDENTIFY COMPARATIVE COMPANIES

- Were the comparative companies selected the best competitors or functional industry leaders?
- Were all types of benchmarking considered in identifying functional, industry best leaders?

STEP 3. DETERMINE DATA COLLECTION METHODS

- Was a questionnaire prepared prior to gathering the data?
- Were the questions pretested by answering them for the internal operation?
- Were internal sources researched for data and information?
- Were existing public data and information sources researched?
- Were original sources and investigations, including direct-site visits, considered?

QUICK REFERENCE GUIDE 11.1 (CONT.)
10-STEP BENCHMARKING PROCESS INSPECTION CHECKLIST

- Were all research methods reviewed before the benchmarking investigations were conducted?
- Was the basis for information sharing reviewed before the research was conducted?

STEP 4. DETERMINING THE CORRECT COMPETITIVE GAP

- Did the benchmark findings identify the differences in practices?
- Did the practices show for what reasons the differences resulted?
- Was a gap identified? Negative? Parity? Positive?

STEP 5. PROJECTING FUTURE PERFORMANCE LEVELS

- Did the projection of the gap consider the best industry knowledge of trends?
- Was the gap understood in terms of tactical and strategic actions required?

STEP 6. ESTABLISHING FUNCTIONAL GOALS

- Were the findings communicated to the affected organizations?
- Were all methods for gaining acceptance considered?
- Was there concurrence and commitment to the findings from the affected organization or customer?

QUICK REFERENCE GUIDE 11.1 (CONT.)
10-STEP BENCHMARKING PROCESS INSPECTION CHECKLIST

STEP 7. DEVELOPING FUNCTIONAL ACTION PLANS

- Were functional goals reviewed to incorporate benchmark findings?
- Were the benchmark practices clearly delineated to show how the industry best accomplished their results?

STEP 8. IMPLEMENT SPECIFIC ACTION STEPS

- Did the action plans clearly show how the gap would be closed?
- Was the action plan implemented?

STEP 9. MONITOR AND REPORT PROGRESS

- Were benchmarks incorporated with the management and financial process?
- Was an inspection process implemented?

STEP 10. RECALIBRATION AND MATURITY

- Is there a plan for recalibration?
- Has benchmarking become institutionalized?
- Has a leadership position been attained?

CHAPTER 12
RECALIBRATING (STEP 10)

How Not to Get Blind Sided Again

Recalibration Assessment
- Understanding benchmarking
- Attitude toward benchmarking
- Management behaviors

A Plan for Recalibration
- How often
- How extensive
- Critical benchmarks

The Recalibration Process

Benchmarking Institutionalized

The L. L. Bean Experience

Quick Reference Guide 12.1. Management Behaviors
  Important to Benchmarking

RECALIBRATING (STEP 10)

How Not to Get Blind Sided Again

This chapter covers the recalibration process so necessary to stay current with changing conditions and the process for reaching a mature benchmarking position that yields superior performance. The objective of recalibration is to maintain current benchmarks. Competitive and industry practices are constantly changing. A recalibration process must be installed to ensure that benchmarks are reevaluated and updated to ensure that they are based on the latest methods and practices. Benchmarks need to be examined to see if they are still valid in light of external changes and modified accordingly.

It has been found effective to perform a recalibration assessment before conducting further confirmation of benchmarks. The assessment that can be conducted through a questionnaire will reveal not only what gaps exist in the benchmark information but also the attitudes and predispositions about benchmarking held by the organization. Changing attitudes and understanding about benchmarking along with gathering new data will maintain a dynamic benchmarking program throughout the organization.

Also covered in this chapter is how benchmarking eventually becomes institutionalized. In early stages of benchmarking it is probably wise to have a trained professional start the benchmarking activities. However, as the organization matures in its benchmarking knowledge and begins to exercise the 10-step benchmarking process, it can be pushed down to operational managers to conduct their own benchmarking investigations with the advice and guidance of the internal professional. Ultimately, what is desired is to encourage the initiative of responsible managers to proactively conduct benchmarking and search out industry best practices on which to base their plans and objectives. This latter stage is the true institutionalization of benchmarking.

Recalibration Assessment

Before assuming that recalibration is necessary an internal assessment often is worthwhile. The results of the assessment can guide the recalibration process and determine where emphasis must be placed. The assessment is recommended because it will allow the careful allocation of scarce benchmarking resources to those areas of perceived greatest payback or information gap.

Recalibration reassessment areas deserving investigation and feedback are shown in Table 12.1.

• Understanding the benchmarking process

• Understanding industry best practices

• Benchmarking importance and value

• Benchmark appropriateness to target setting

• Benchmarking communication

TABLE 12.1. RECALIBRATION ASSESSMENT AREAS

An internal questionnaire is the most straightforward way of obtaining internal feedback. The questionnaire should, at a minimum, obtain internal data from those involved and affected by benchmarking in at least the areas of understanding about benchmarking and attitude toward the benchmarking process so far.

Understanding Benchmarking

Many critical questions comprise the degree and detail of understanding benchmarks and the benchmarking process: Are the unit's goals established based on quantitative benchmarks? Are benchmark findings about new practices and methods a part of the unit's goals as well as part of the action plans for change? Are benchmark practices understood? Is how the benchmark partners conduct their businesses clearly understood? Have action plans been put in place to close the gap? Is recalibration performed at regular intervals?

Questions such as these indicate the degree to which there is understanding about the quantitative metrics of benchmarking and also about how well the practices have been sourced and adopted, and are in the process of being implemented. They indicate the degree to which benchmarking has been understood, accepted, and institutionalized within the business unit. A sample assessment survey is shown in Figure 12.1.

BENCHMARKING ASSESSMENT SURVEY

	Strongly Agree	Agree	Neutral	Disagree	Strongly Disagree

Understanding the Benchmark Process

1. The 10-step benchmarking process is understood.

2. I understand how the benchmarks for my function were developed.

Understanding Best Practices

3. There is full understanding of how benchmark partners operate.
   - Their practices are better and we should emulate them.
   - We can do it differently and accomplish the same/better results.

Benchmarking Value

4. Benchmarking is important.
5. Benchmarked new practices are included in action plans.
6. The value of benchmarking for setting goals is recognized.

Benchmark Appropriateness to Target Setting

7. Targets derived from benchmarking are, in my view, realistic.
8. We must meet benchmark targets to attain superior performance.

Benchmark Communication

9. Our planning/operating principles are based on benchmark findings.
   - They are reviewed throughout the organization.
   - They are understood to be based on external industry practices which we must achieve.

General Comments About Benchmarking

10. Benchmarking can be improved by:

11. I would like to know more about (benchmarking):

12. My specific suggestions for benchmarking are:

Title and Organization

My title is_____ My organization is_____

FIGURE 12.1. RECALIBRATION SURVEY

Attitude Toward Benchmarking

Benchmarking, when first introduced and initially practiced, can be confusing and threatening to some. The reason is that a new process for establishing fundamental operations of the business unit is being utilized. This is the basis on which goals, targets, and plans are being redirected to base them proactively not on traditional approaches, but on a concerted view of external findings and partnership firms. It is necessary to deal with the perceptions and attitudes of those internally who may be involved in or affected by benchmarking. In this manner the perceptions can be dealt with as part of the recalibration. Specific steps can be emphasized, clarified, or benchmarked again as part of the recalibration process to overcome misperceptions and gain acceptance.

Critical questions that address attitude could include the following: Is benchmarking important? Is the 10-step process understood? Is there value to be seen in benchmarking? Are targets based on benchmark investigations realistic?

Other pertinent questions can be derived from an inspection of the relevant chapters of this text. A questionnaire should also be supplemented with some open-ended questions: Where and how can benchmarking be improved? What more would you like to learn about benchmarking? Along with gathering a nominal amount of demographics, the feedback should be of exceptional value in directing recalibration efforts.

The questionnaire provides an additional opportunity to obtain relevant feedback for benchmarking recalibration. The respondents can be interviewed to determine the reasons for their scoring the numerically scaled questions. In this fashion not only is the score obtained indicating the severity of the response, but the reason why the question was scored is also obtained. This is an opportunity to obtain quantitative and explanatory information helpful for setting a direction for recalibration.

In addition, the questionnaire can be used at several intervals to determine progress toward establishing a positive benchmarking program. One logical stage would be after initial benchmarking efforts have been initiated and initial understanding about the use of benchmarking findings have been understood. This first measurement would establish a baseline from which to measure progress in benchmarking. Following the initial survey, it can be administered at key times, possibly following dissemination of major findings or incorporation of practices into the operating or business plans. These additional measurements will permit seeing if perceptions and opinions have changed. Thereafter the use of the survey, expanded to a more comprehensive format, can serve to show progress toward the institutionalization of benchmarking.

Management Behaviors

Closely aligned with success factors are those management behaviors that, when emulated by managers, will contribute to successful benchmarking. Those considered critical to the practice of successful benchmarking are covered in Quick Reference Guide 12.1. Management behaviors cover a wide set of possibilities. Those that have been found successful are covered here. Among the more important is the support for benchmarking during its infancy in any organization. Management support is needed for the process during the planning and organization phase. Visible support by management will help the investigations over the initial set of hurdles.

Included in these initial efforts are agreement on benefits to be derived, approaches for the investigations, role definition for the team members conducting benchmarking, and a pro forma discussion and analysis of barriers to benchmarking. The latter would include how the barriers could be overcome to permit effective benchmarking. It is during these initial phases that expectations will be set for benchmarking activities. The behaviors of support by managers will quickly be interpreted by the organization as the way more effective work — not just extra work — is done.

Beyond support for initial efforts, management should inspect the work at various stages to assure good progress. However, the next major focus of management attention is on the end of the process, when findings have to be accepted and implemented. This includes ensuring that benchmarking findings are adequately understood and accepted, and that they are converted into achievable plans. Performance measurement metrics and systems need to be updated to include the findings and strategies pursued to implement them. In addition to current performance, future performance must be projected and periodically recalibrated.

A significant role is played by management to communicate the reasons for benchmarking and the results to the organization. A monitoring and reporting process should be supported. The ultimate level of support is having benchmarking become an integral part of an individual's performance appraisal. The communications process can be greatly enhanced if it is supported by case history examples that show the "how tos" of benchmarking.

A Plan for Recalibration

Benchmarking recalibration will not just happen — it must be planned. Given that an initial effort at benchmarking was planned and committed to, it is necessary to recalibrate to assure success and effectiveness. There are no hard and fast rules on the frequency and method for recalibration.

There are several approaches that can be pursued in recalibration. Specific, targeted studies can be undertaken to fill known information gaps. A complete reassessment of all critical benchmark metric targets and best practices findings can be undertaken. Or a new productive direction for investigation, revealed by findings to date, can be further pursued. All are viable approaches to ensuring that a completed picture is obtained and opportunities not missed. At some juncture, however, a complete reassessment must be made to ensure timeliness of information.

One approach would be to recalibrate the critical benchmarks annually. A shorter time frame is not worthwhile since practices do not change that fast. Recalibration beyond three years becomes a massive exercise. A level of insightful maintenance is probably most productive. Each business unit needs to determine the frequency based on the characteristics of their industry and the external environment. Rapid external change would argue for faster benchmarking updates. Those involved in benchmarking, assuming they continue to receive awareness data about their industry, will be able to determine when and how to recalibrate.

The Recalibration Process

How is recalibration performed? It is a matter of reexercising the 10-point benchmark process. Each of the 10 steps should be reviewed in preparing a recalibration plan. With the aid of the internal feedback it should be straightforward to determine what deficiencies need to be covered and what areas of new information are needed. In reapplying the benchmarking process steps it is imperative that all steps are reexamined. No step should be skipped or assumed not necessary to repeat. The assumption that nothing has changed can be a dangerous approach. It is important to not only review the process steps for what was done in the past, but also to incorporate approaches taken by other benchmarking investigations elsewhere in the firm. Many new insights will be obtained and efficiencies and refinements in the process will be revealed. The full value of the recalibration is not only in refining the output of the benchmarking process, but also making the process more efficient and responsive to benchmark needs.

At some point the benchmarking process becomes continuous, but there are always guiding principles in the process. These are shown in Table 12.2.

In addition to the guiding principles there are a number of myths about benchmarking that need to be dispelled. These are shown in Table 12.3 and read like the 1,001 reasons why "it won't work here." It will be obvious to the reader that the direct opposite of nearly all of these is the truth and that they have each been dispelled by the material in this text. They do provide a lighter touch to the subject of benchmarking, which is sometimes needed.

Benchmarking Institutionalized

Ultimately an organization will institutionalize benchmarking throughout its operation and ensure its continued success. Individuals at all levels will, of their own initiative, seek out those best practices that will enhance their operations. They will be assured commensurate recognition and reward for their efforts.

There are many indicators of how benchmarking becomes institutionalized. It can be programmed into the organization. Milestones can be established in business plans which will trigger another round of benchmarking activities or activities to fill specific information gaps. Part of this may be necessary because of the steep learning curve associated with benchmarking. Once started with individuals skilled in benchmarking it is expensive to lose those skills and restart with new teams.

Managers can be required to include as part of their annual objectives a plan for their individual unit's benchmarking activities. These may involve specific trips or investigations. Employee involvement teams may be used to either perform specific investigations, but more likely to develop implementation action plans for already defined best practices. It would be appropriate to ask an employee involvement team to tackle the further definition, assessment of implementability, and opportunity or risks of a benchmark practice. The close linkage of employee involvement to benchmarking as the vehicle to implementation is pervasive.

- A high degree of ownership exists for the benchmarking process and findings

  — Management directed
  — Function supported

- The benchmarking effort is continuous

  — A competency center exists to provide benchmarking consulting expertise
  — All information potentially relevant is examined and cataloged, on an ongoing basis, for possible future reference

- Benchmarking is eventually performed by those who will be responsible for implementing the findings

  — Benchmarking is the responsibility of the line operations managers
  — Benchmarking expertise is available to assist in effective use of the process

- The organization is encouraged to have pride in benchmarking because it makes the work easier

  — The operation wants to be the best at each task
  — It sees benchmarking as the means to achieve the best of the best

- Operations reviews inspect for and include a compulsory discussion of progress toward attainment of benchmarking findings

TABLE 12.2. GUIDING PRINCIPLES FOR THE BENCHMARKING PROCESS

- Benchmark targets should be established first and practices investigated later.

- There is only one way to benchmark, against direct product competitors.

- Benchmarks are only quantitative, financially based statistics.

- Benchmarking investigations are focused solely on operations showing a performance gap.

- Benchmarking is something that needs to be done occasionally and can be accomplished quickly.

- There is a single company, somewhere, most like my firm, only much better, that is "the benchmark."

- Staff organizations cannot be benchmarked.

- Benchmarking is a target-setting stretch exercise.

- Benchmarking can most effectively be accomplished through third party consultants.

- It is not obvious what should be benchmarked for each business unit.

- Processes don't need to be benchmarked.

- Internal benchmarking between departments and divisions has only minimal benefits.

- There is no benefit in qualitative benchmarking.

- Benchmarking is comparing to the dominant industry firm and emulating them six months later.

- Benchmark practices are the same as enablers.

TABLE 12.3. BENCHMARKING MYTHS

The L. L. Bean Experience

The L. L. Bean experience was instrumental in starting the benchmarking activities on a positive note within the logistics function. It captured the attention of both management and employees because it was a firm they recognized. The experience taught an important lesson using unexpected circumstances — namely that much can be learned from functional benchmarking, even outside one's own industry.

Beyond the internal and competitive benchmarking, once the process was understood functional and generic benchmarking became much easier to perform. The approach was used time and again in dissimilar industries and providing the characteristics of the process throughput activities were similar, the comparisons were valid. The results were pervasive. Table 12.4 shows some of the practices that were uncovered and hold potential for adoption gained from benchmarking visits outside the office products industry. The basic functional, noncompetitor approach was copied many times to ensure best methods were uncovered which will lead to superior performance. The example derived from the L. L. Bean experience was indicative of having reached true maturity in the application of the benchmarking process.

TYPE FIRM	BEST PRACTICE
Drug Wholesaler	Electronic ordering between store and distribution center
Appliance Manufacturer	Forklift handling of up to six unpalletized units (appliances) at one time
Electrical Components Manufacturer	Automatic in-line weighing, bar code labelling, and scanning of packages
Photographic Film Manufacturer	Self-directed warehouse work teams
Catalog Fulfillment Service Bureau	Item dimension and weight recording to permit order filling quality assurance based on calculated weight compared to actual

TABLE 12.4. BEST PRACTICES APPLICABLE TO WAREHOUSE OPERATIONS FROM DISSIMILAR INDUSTRY FIRMS

QUICK REFERENCE GUIDE 12.1

MANAGEMENT BEHAVIORS IMPORTANT TO BENCHMARKING

- Provide supportive leadership in planning and organizing the benchmarking effort.

- Gain agreement on the benefits to be achieved, the partnership companies, the approach to be used in the investigations, the roles of each member of the benchmarking team, and determining the barriers to effective benchmarking.

- Foster the viewpoint that benchmarking is the way more effective work is done, not extra work.

- Ensure that the benchmark findings are adequately understood and accepted.

- Ensure that performance levels needed and strategies pursued are based on benchmark practices.

- Ensure that performance is projected and periodically recalibrated based on benchmark findings.

- Ensure that a communications process is agreed on that will inform the organization of its progress toward benchmark targets and goals.

- Integrate benchmarking findings with the organization's objective setting, performance appraisals, and operating plan processes.

- Seek out successful case history examples which can be used to show how the process is used and how the "how tos" of benchmarking are applied.

CHAPTER 13 BEYOND BENCHMARKING

Management's Influence and Benchmarking

Business Simplification

Benchmarking and Change Initiative

BEYOND BENCHMARKING

Superiority Achieved

There are implications from benchmarking that transcend the process itself and the benefits to be derived. These have to do with implications for management, the pursuit of business simplification, and benchmarking's influence on change initiative. The benchmarking process needs continued management attention to achieve optimum results — in particular for the interpretation and application of the findings. The fully exercised use of the benchmarking process combined with other considerations goes beyond the basics of benchmarking and results in a standard by which to judge the effective simplification of any business. The focus on non-competitive or functional benchmarking provides the opportunity for strategic breakthroughs as well as potential for acceptance of new practices to provide superior performance.

Management's Influence and Benchmarking

The many examples covered in this text provide a vivid portrayal of the benefits of benchmarking. Every function of every business should be considered a candidate for this type of comparative investigation and drive for operational improvements. Because of the enormous potential for improvement that benchmarking can provide, there is a critical need for senior management's orchestration of this effort. Functional management, left to its own devices, may be highly reluctant to identify productivity opportunities that, they believe, could be construed as profits forgone or otherwise be a reflection on their past performance.

Benchmarking should ultimately be conducted by the people who will use it, whenever feasible. This practice would complete the institutionalization of benchmarking, but arriving at this state will require senior management support. The attention will be worthwhile because the unit doing its own benchmarking will take ownership of the goals derived from uncovering industry practices. They also will be those best able to develop approaches to achieving the goals since they have the operational insight. They know the most productive timing for use of benchmarking data and information. Finally, knowledge of the workplace, with management interest in their action plans, will motivate them to implement in a creative and innovative way. The benchmarking process itself may even be improved.

Another reason that benchmarking needs to be directed by top management is that the subfunctions performed by an organization like logistics may vary significantly from firm to firm. Adherence to strict functional comparisons may not yield the optimum outcome because gains from changing the organizational boundaries within the firm might be passed up. Thus, top-level oversight is essential for the benchmarking process to succeed and to ensure that opportunities that might reduce the size or scope of empires are not unreported or poorly interpreted. Whether it be internal, competitor, or noncompetitor, benchmarking should be corporate-wide, comprehensive, controlled, continuous, and an integral part of the planning process.

Business Simplification

What lies beyond benchmarking? If benchmarking uncovers proven industry best practices that meet, but do not exceed customer requirements, then benchmarking provides the standard against which to judge the cost-effectiveness of operations. It becomes the vehicle for business simplification. A comparison of the characteristics of benchmarking and business simplification is shown in Table 13.1.

	BENCHMARKING	EXTENDED BENCHMARKING
Objective	Efficiency	Effectiveness
Requirements Met	Internally Defined	End User Defined
Process	Current	Industry Standard
Practices & Technology	Best	Best
Cost of Nonconformance	Partially Reduced	Eliminated
Results	Productivity	Business Simplification

TABLE 13.1. USES OF BENCHMARKING FOR BUSINESS SIMPLIFICATION

Business simplification through benchmarking is an adaptation of the same process where activities necessary to meet customer requirements are identified and those that are not necessary are eliminated.

The characteristics of simplified business processes would include the following: meets true customer requirements, is easy to learn and use, makes the firm easy to do business with, is affordable and cost-effective, has the fewest steps possible, minimizes all possible redundancies with other processes, stresses process control (that is, the process is repeatable and predictable), and is sensitive to changing customer requirements.

Achievement of these business simplification benefits derived from industry best practices contributes to improved customer satisfaction and business results. The full scope of benchmarking that ensures superior performance is shown in Table 13.2.

| | | | ADJUSTMENTS TO YIELD | |
UNIT COST ELEMENTS	CURRENT OPERATIONS	BENCHMARKS	BUSINESS SIMPLIFICATION
Activities or Throughput	Current Levels	Current Levels	Changed Levels
Practices	Current	Best Industry Practices	Best or Possibly Eliminated

TABLE 13.2. ADJUSTMENTS TO CURRENT OPERATIONS TO CREATE BENCHMARKS AND PURSUE BUSINESS SIMPLIFICATION

Benchmarking and Change Initiative

There was an additional by-product of the L. L. Bean experience. The change of focus from strict comparisons within one's narrow competitive industry to the search for functional best practices often broke down the reluctance of managers to actively consider and adapt the ideas of others. When professionals consider competitive comparisons there is a tendency to inspect for differences and put plans in place to achieve parity. The results of this are obvious and potentially disastrous. First, the firm always is playing catch-up since competition is also improving productivity. Second, change is gradual since the perception is that all that is needed is to meet competitive practices and the requirements of benchmarking will be satisfied. No strategic view of best practices will be obtained from the approach that would give the firm a technical break-through to achieve superiority rather than simply meeting competition.

Key considerations that must receive focus to attain superior performance through benchmarking are shown in Table 13.3. The 10-step benchmarking process must be brought to bear on business simplification. This means not only practice simplification but process simplification, that is, what can be eliminated and still satisfy end user customers. The focus will still be on industry best practices and, where possible, reliance on proven technology — one which most likely will be found in another industry.

KEY CONSIDERATIONS

- Focus on meeting end user customer requirements

- Focus on best practices

- Include proven technology

- Focus on business simplification
  — Process simplification
  — Business practice simplification

- Concentrate on major contributors to the cost base

- Define long-term endpoint and migration strategy

- Use of quality improvement tools

TABLE 13.3. SCOPE OF BENCHMARKING THAT ENSURES SUPERIOR PERFORMANCE

The focus should be on meeting the end users of consumers' requirements. These would be the set that meets but does not exceed those requirements. With these there must be a vision of what the operation will look like once it is converted to emulate industry best practices. That endpoint definition is easily constructed from the benchmark findings since they incorporate the changes to be made.

While there are many practices that can and should be changed, they should be prioritized by those that concentrate on affecting the cost base, customer satisfaction, or assets to the greatest degree. The quality process tools of cause-and-effect diagramming, force field analysis, and weighted prioritization will greatly aid in sorting out those practices to concentrate on.

The approach to functional benchmarking as a search for industry best practices in many instances overcame the not-invented-here syndrome of focusing solely on the competition. If practices could be shown to be superior in diverse industries, there was a more active and ready consideration and acceptance. The weight of evidence outside the industry can be pervasive for getting individuals to leave parochial viewpoints behind. Coupled with a personal attraction such as many had with L. L. Bean, the ability for individuals to more openly consider change was substantial.

APPENDICES

A. MANAGEMENT PRESENTATION CHARTS

B. CASE STUDIES

Case Study — The Sale Order Process

How to Measure Yourself Against the Best, *Harvard Business Review*, January-February 1987

BENCHMARKING DEFINITION

FORMAL DEFINITION

Benchmarking is the continuous process of measuring our products, services, and practices against the toughest competitors or those companies recognized as industry leaders.

WEBSTER'S DEFINITION

A surveyor's mark...of previously determined position... and used as a reference point....

A standard by which something can be measured or judged.

WORKING DEFINITION

Benchmarking is the search for best industry practices that will lead to superior performance.

BENCHMARKING DEFINITIONS

BENCHMARK<u>ING</u>: A PROCESS OR ACTIVITY

Xerox Definition

Leadership Through Quality Definition

Webster's Definition

A Generic Definition

The 10-Step Process

BENCHMARK<u>S</u>: AN INDUSTRY STANDARD

Descriptive Benchmarks or *Practices*

Quantitative Benchmarks or *Performance Measurements*

BENCHMARKING DEFINITIONS

BENCHMARKING: A PROCESS OR ACTIVITY

There are several definitions of benchmarking that are relevant and provide varying insight.

XEROX DEFINITION

The continuous process of measuring our products, services, and business practices against the toughest competitors or those companies recognized as industry leaders.

LEADERSHIP THROUGH QUALITY DEFINITION

A standard process used to evaluate success in meeting customer requirements.

WEBSTER'S DEFINITION

A standard against which something can be measured. A survey mark of previously determined position used as a reference point.

A GENERIC DEFINITION

A basis of establishing rational performance goals through the search for industry best practices that will lead to superior performance.

THE 10-STEP PROCESS

A structured way of looking outside to identify, analyze, and adopt the best in the industry or function.

BENCHMARKS: AN INDUSTRY STANDARD

Benchmarks may be descriptive, as in the description of a best industry practice, or they may be converted to a performance metric which shows the effect of incorporating the practice. The challenge is to close the gap between the current practice and benchmark.

DESCRIPTIVE BENCHMARKS OR PRACTICES

Any work process is made up of an input, repeatable process based on a method or practice and an output. The practices deliver the output. If the practices are the best in the industry they will most fully satisfy customers.

QUANTITATIVE BENCHMARKS OR PERFORMANCE MEASUREMENTS

Benchmark metrics are the conversion of benchmark practices to operational measures. There can be benchmarks for all goals or objectives such as the four selected for Customer Satisfaction, Employee Satisfaction, Business Results, and Quality.

BENCHMARKING DEFINITIONS

Work Process Focus

BENCHMARKING

- A continuous, systematic process for evaluating companies recognized as industry leaders.

- To develop business and work processes that incorporate " best practices" and establish rational performance goals.

BEST PRACTICES

- The methods used in work processes whose outputs best meet customer requirements.

BENCHMARKS

- Performance measurement standards derived from definition or quantification of best practices.

BENCHMARKING ORIGINS

SUN TZU (THE ART OF WAR, 500 B.C.)

"If you know your enemy and know yourself, you need not fear the result of a hundred battles."

JAPANESE SAYING (SOURCE AND DATE UNKNOWN)

"Dantotsu; striving for the best of the best."

TYPES OF BENCHMARKING

INTERNAL BENCHMARKING

A comparison of internal operations

COMPETITIVE BENCHMARKING

Specific competitor-to-competitor comparisons for the product or function of interest

FUNCTIONAL BENCHMARKING

Comparisons to similar functions within the same broad industry or to industry leaders

GENERIC BENCHMARKING

Comparison of business functions or processes that are the same regardless of industry

THE QUALITY PROCESS AND BENCHMARKING

QUALITY PROCESS

Meeting external and internal customer requirements

BENCHMARKING

Establishing objectives based on industry best practices

PERFORMANCE TEAMS

Involving employees in solutions to work practices

PERFORMANCE MANAGEMENT

Communicating objectives and recognizing employees for performance

BENCHMARKING AND CHANGE MANAGEMENT

KEY FACTORS FOR SUCCESSFUL CHANGE

• Belief that there is a need for change

• A determination of what you want to change

• Development of a picture of what you want to look like after the change

HOW BENCHMARKING MAKES CHANGE SUCCESSFUL

• The gap between internal and external practices creates the need for change

• Understanding industry best practices identifies what you must change

• Externally benchmarked practices developed from others give a picture of the endpoint after change

BENCHMARKING CONCEPTUALIZED

- Comparing ourselves to the toughest competitors

- Comparing ourselves to the applicable best practices for our function, regardless of industry

- Developing strategic plans to adopt the best practices found

- Meeting customer requirements

- Acting like a competition-fearing businessperson

GENERIC BENCHMARKING PROCESS

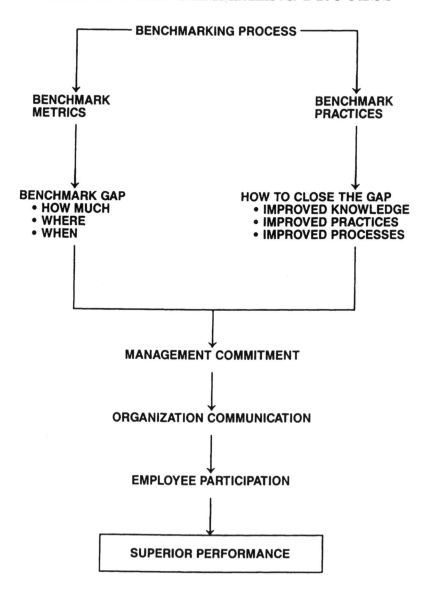

BENCHMARKING PROCESS STEPS

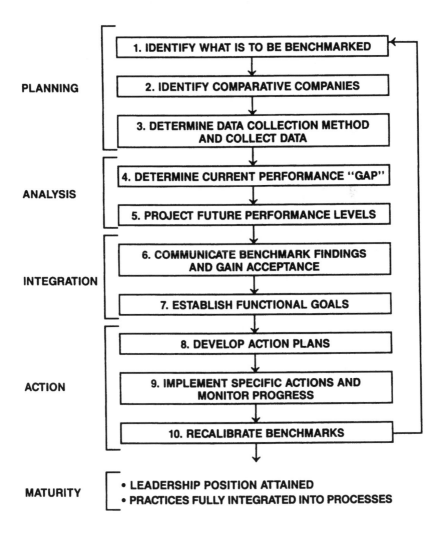

PLANNING
- 1. IDENTIFY WHAT IS TO BE BENCHMARKED
- 2. IDENTIFY COMPARATIVE COMPANIES
- 3. DETERMINE DATA COLLECTION METHOD AND COLLECT DATA

ANALYSIS
- 4. DETERMINE CURRENT PERFORMANCE "GAP"
- 5. PROJECT FUTURE PERFORMANCE LEVELS

INTEGRATION
- 6. COMMUNICATE BENCHMARK FINDINGS AND GAIN ACCEPTANCE
- 7. ESTABLISH FUNCTIONAL GOALS

ACTION
- 8. DEVELOP ACTION PLANS
- 9. IMPLEMENT SPECIFIC ACTIONS AND MONITOR PROGRESS
- 10. RECALIBRATE BENCHMARKS

MATURITY
- • LEADERSHIP POSITION ATTAINED
- • PRACTICES FULLY INTEGRATED INTO PROCESSES

REASONS FOR BENCHMARKING

WITHOUT BENCHMARKING	WITH BENCHMARKING

BECOMING COMPETITIVE

Internally focused	Concrete understanding of competition
Evolutionary change	New ideas of proven practices and technology
Low commitment	High commitment

INDUSTRY BEST PRACTICES

Not invented here	Proactive search for change
Few solutions	Many options
Average of industry progress	Business practice breakthrough
Frantic catch up activity	Superior performance

REASONS FOR BENCHMARKING

WITHOUT BENCHMARKING	WITH BENCHMARKING

DEFINING CUSTOMER REQUIREMENTS

Based on history or gut feel	Market reality
Perception	Objective evaluation
Low fit	High conformance

ESTABLISHING EFFECTIVE GOALS AND OBJECTIVES

Lacking external focus	Credible, unarguable
Reactive	Proactive
Lagging industry	Industry leading

DEVELOPING TRUE MEASURES OF PRODUCTIVITY

Pursuing pet projects	Solving real problems
Strengths and weaknesses not understood	Understanding outputs
Route of least resistance	Based on best industry practices

CANDIDATES FOR BENCHMARKING

**CUSTOMER
REQUIREMENTS**
  Products
  Services

**PRODUCTS
MANUFACTURED**
  Copiers
  Repair parts

SERVICES PROVIDED
  Repair services
  Financing

**CRITICAL SUCCESS
FACTORS**
  Customer satisfaction
    level
  Delivery service
  Unit costs
  Asset utilization

PRODUCTS PURCHASED
  Components
  Material handling
    equipment

PROCESSES USED
  Order entry
  Customer inquiry/problem
    resolution
  Warehouse fulfillment
  Billing
  Collection

ROBERT C. CAMP

KEY BENCHMARKING CHARACTERISTICS

BENCHMARKING OPERATION	RELEVANCE	DATA COLLECTION EASE	INNOVATIVE PRACTICES
Internal Operations	X	X	
Direct Product Competitors	X		
Industry Leaders		X	X
Generic Processes		X	X

COMPARATIVE COMPANIES IN THE OFFICE PRODUCTS INDUSTRY

DIRECT PRODUCT COMPETITORS

Company	Product/Functional Leadership
Canon	Copiers
DEC	Work Stations

FUNCTIONAL INDUSTRY LEADERS

L. L. Bean	Warehouse Operations
GE	Information Systems
Deere	Service Parts Logistics
Ford	Assembly Automation

GENERIC PROCESSES

Federal Reserve	Bill Scanning
City Corp	Document Processing

INFORMATION SOURCES

SOURCE	EXAMPLE
Internal	
Library data bases	AB information
Internal reviews	Internal experts
Internal publications	Varies by company
External	
Professional associations	American Marketing Association
Industry publications	Electronic Business
Special industry reports	ADL Infotran
Functional trade publications	Materials Handling Engineering
General management	Industry Week
Functional journals	Journal of Business Logistics
Seminars	By professional interest
Industry data firms	Dataquest
Industry experts	K. L. Worthington
Software/hardware vendors	DEC
University sources	By profession
Company watchers	Eugene Glazer, Dean Witter, Reynolds (Xerox)
Advertisements	By product of interest
Newsletters	By subject matter
Original Research	
Customer feedback	Focus groups
Telephone surveys	Specific design
Inquiry service	Specific contract
Networks	Electronic, internal, and external
Consulting firms	McKinsey

LOGISTICS BENCHMARKING GAP EXAMPLE

10-YEAR LOGISTICS PRODUCTIVITY TREND

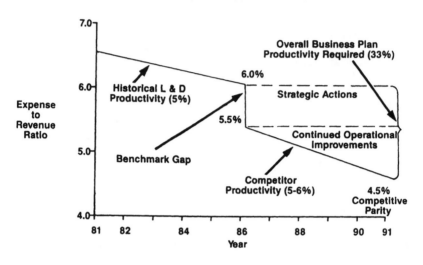

GOAL SETTING, ACTION PLANNING PROCESS, AND RELATIONSHIP TO BENCHMARKING

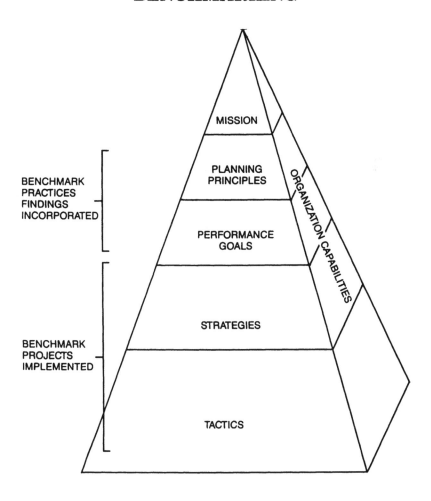

LOGISTICS PLANNING PRINCIPLES

- Provide competitive levels of customer satisfaction by market segment

- Reduce unit costs

- Increase inventory turns

- Fewer echelons
  - Shortest path from source to use or consumption
  - Material handled least number of times

- Fewer locations (distribution centers) at an echelon

- Centralize slow moving and scheduled delivery materials

- Modernize facilities to state-of-the-art
  - Materials handling equipment
  - Control systems based on bar code and scanning data capture

- Capitalize on opportunities presented by deregulated transportation
  - Use volume to negotiate favorable discounts
  - Route contract carriers to maximize full truckload mileage

- Examine where and how much packaging and labeling is essential to move material without damage

- Delivery to customers unconstrained by arbitrary geographic- or systems-dictated boundaries

MANAGEMENT BEHAVIORS IMPORTANT TO BENCHMARKING

- Provide supportive leadership in planning and organizing the benchmarking effort

- Gain agreement on the benefits to be achieved, the partnership companies, the approach to be used in the investigations, the roles of each member of the benchmarking team, and determining the barriers to effective benchmarking

- Foster the viewpoint that benchmarking is the way more effective work is done, not extra work

- Ensure that the benchmark findings are adequately understood and accepted

- Ensure that performance levels needed and strategies pursued are based on benchmark practices

- Ensure that performance is projected and periodically recalibrated based on benchmark findings

- Ensure that a communications process is agreed on that will inform the organization of its progress toward benchmark targets and goals

- Integrate benchmarking findings with the organization's objective setting, performance appraisals, and operating plan processes

- Seek out successful case history examples which can be used to show how the process is used and how the "how tos" of benchmarking are applied

SCOPE OF BENCHMARKING THAT ENSURES SUPERIOR PERFORMANCE

KEY CONSIDERATIONS

• Focus on meeting end-user customer requirements

• Focus on best practices

• Include proven technology

• Focus on business simplification
  — Process simplification
  — Business practice simplification

• Concentrate on major contributors to the cost base

• Define long-term endpoint and migration strategy

• Use of quality improvement tools

USES OF BENCHMARKING FOR BUSINESS SIMPLIFICATION

	BENCHMARKING	EXTENDED BENCHMARKING
Objective	Efficiency	Effectiveness
Requirements Met	Internally Defined	End User Defined
Process	Current	Industry Standard
Practices and Technology	Best	Best
Cost of Nonconformance	Partially Reduced	Eliminated
Results	Productivity	Business Simplification

SUMMARY DIFFERENCES BETWEEN APPROACHES FOR MARKET RESEARCH, COMPETITIVE ANALYSIS, AND BENCHMARKING

Item	Market Research	Competitive Analysis	Benchmarking
Generic purpose	Analyze industry markets, customer segments or product acceptance	Analyze competitive strategies	Analyze what, why, and how well competition or leading companies are doing
Usual focus	Customer needs	Competitive strategies	Business practices which satisfy customer needs
Application	Products and services	Marketplace and products	Business practices as well as products
Usually limited to	How customer needs are met	Marketplace activities	Not limited, competitive, functional, and internal benchmarking are used
Information sources	Customers	Industry analysts, etc.	Industry leaders as well as competitors

CHINESE PROVERB

IF WE DON'T CHANGE OUR DIRECTION,

WE MIGHT END UP WHERE WE'RE HEADED.

I NEED YOU
TO "BENCHMARK"

Case Study
The Sale Order Process

A Practices Benchmarking Investigation

Introduction

The origin for this benchmarking study was the perceived need to reduce the cost of the order entry, fulfillment, and administrative operations for a complimentary class of products. A cross-functional team evaluated the practices employed by other companies, compared those practices to current and planned practices, identified opportunity areas for implementation, and made recommendations on how the opportunities could be captured. The specific focus of these benchmarking investigations was on practices. Once the opportunities were identified several approaches were used to quantify the effect of the practices and convert them to benchmark costs per order.

The scope of benchmarking investigations covered five areas: external customer requirements, external business practices, emerging process capabilities, current practices, and supporting external research results. The description covered here will concentrate primarily on the external business practices investigations. These involved visits to 16 companies believed to have order and fulfillment processes handling products of comparable characteristics.

Benchmarking Objectives

The objectives of the benchmarking investigations were further defined as follows:

To define, design, develop, and implement a streamlined, low cost endpoint process and delivery system for high volume products.

The process scope included all after sale support activities. These were defined as:

- Order processing
- Warehousing and delivery
- Invoicing and collection
- Customer service

Method of Investigation

At the outset of the project it was evident that a principal focus of the investigations would be based on external company methods of operation. What was needed was a functional best practice benchmarking effort as a basis to establish the viability of delivering a streamlined sale order and fulfillment process. The comparison to internal processes would highlight method and technical differences. These differences would reveal sources of potential opportunity to reduce costs, improve customer satisfaction levels, and increase return on assets.

The team operation involved the following detailed steps:

Organization. Background material on the purpose and scope was reviewed and further defined. Team working methods were established. Working methods were considered especially important for this unique, ad hoc team involved in innovation.

Conduct internal reviews. Extensive internal reviews were conducted to document the current process and gather any relevant benchmarking information already obtained or studies completed.

Investigate internal and external information. All important public information available was gathered through a search of the key external on-line data bases. Important professional associations were contacted for special studies or ongoing information about seminars and conferences of interest. These groups were also asked to provide references to experts in the field. The data were used selectively to supplement the findings.

Source candidate companies for visits. Experts in the field were canvassed for operations which, in their opinion, represented best practices. This approach, in addition to sourcing candidate companies, also was instrumental in identifying third party contract firms offering order entry and fulfillment services. Since the business process under investigation would, most likely, be heavily computerized, off-the-shelf software products from major vendors were reviewed. Each application vendor was asked to provide a candidate list of installations that would demonstrate best practices as well as actual operating conditions.

Conduct internal and external visits. An extensive questionnaire was prepared to assist in the collection of data from external companies. The itinerary for each visit included a tour of the operation and discussions with operations supervisors and end users of the process. Copies of relevant documents of interest were obtained, the visits were debriefed, a trip report prepared on each, and acknowledgment of appreciation sent to each firm.

Documentation and data summaries. Extensive summary comparisons were documented from the trip reports and observations. These were assembled by significant process function to describe external operating practices. The comparisons yielded a composite description of practices.

Document customer requirements. Statements of external customer requirements were developed to assess the customer satisfaction levels desired by the users of the process. The requirements were those of the external end-user customers. In addition, the minimum requirements for the process necessitated by legal, accounting, and audit practices were documented.

Develop industry best practices. Review of the external visit information, findings from other expert sources, and customer requirement observations enabled the team to define a set of industry "best practices" for the order processing and fulfillment cycle.

Contrast industry and internal practices. The internal practices were contrasted with the industry best practices. This led to an understanding of areas of opportunity for improvements in order processing and costs of operation.

Conclusions. The areas of opportunity were evaluated for their contribution to cost-effectiveness and customer satisfaction. The conclusions were documented. A follow-on effort converted the findings into implementation alternatives for consideration by senior management. An evolutionary approach to implementing the findings was selected following an exhaustive justification process.

Benchmarking Findings

What follows is a description of the findings from the external visits. The team concluded that it was most important to visit the operations of the benchmarking partners firsthand. In this fashion the operations could be observed and provide the most credible information. Usually at least two members of the team participated in the vists.

The following findings cover the more significant and are presented in logical process step progression:

A. Business Overview — The business overviews documented the organization structure, employment practices, and systems that significantly contributed to cost-effectiveness
    1. Organization — A wide range of companies were visited with geographical coverage ranging from regional to national. The organizations were found to be relatively flat, with three management levels evident in most companies. Sales,

warehousing, and administrative functions tended to be co-located.

2. Business Profile — Inbound phone ordering was found to be centralized for national order taking. The companies visited felt strongly that the geographic proximity of the sales, administrative, and warehouse functions enhanced efficiency and facilitated quick problem resolution.

   Low labor rates predominated because of the common practice of using a high proportion of part-time company employees in order taking, administrative, and warehousing operations. Remote warehouses were used to provide responsive order delivery and reduce freight penalties.

3. Systems — The one consistent feature of all data processing systems was the utilization of interactive and integrated systems applications. Combined with the co-location these systems solutions virtually eliminated redundant processing and paperwork.

B. Order Entry — Order entry functions could accommodate phone, mail, and electronic modes of order submission. A mix of full- and part-time personnel performed order entry. The order entry function was supported by a customer service staff to handle technical inquiries, nonstandard orders, and customer problem resolution.

1. Order Acceptance — Order entry in all operations was designed for use of on-line and interactive systems.

2. Order Editing — Computer data entry fully validated all data elements during order entry. This resulted in very few downstream errors which needed resolution subsequent to order entry.

3. Customer Data — The primary methods for retrieving customer records for repeat customers were phone number, customer number, or name. Data for tax application was obtained from zip code tables.

4. Inventory Status — Current inventory status data were available to the order entry personnel at time of order.

5. Pricing — Pricing at all companies was determined at time of order entry. In all cases product prices were derived from price tables and contained the list price, quantity, and customer type discounts.

6. Credit Checking — For existing customers credit approval was based on an established line of credit and current payment history. Purchases and payments were immediately reflected in the customer's line of credit.

   New customers' credit establishment required bank or trade

references or Dun & Bradstreet data. These references were validated to determine credit worthiness before shipment of goods. New customers received a line of credit based on a standard algorithm after reference check or D & B confirmation.

7. Reserved Inventory — Most companies reserved inventory at time of order entry.

8. Emergency or Rush Orders — Emergency or rush orders were treated as an exception process through color coding schemes and manual support.

9. Returns — Returns were consistently processed as a negative order, that is as a negative quantity, reducing the need for redundant return processes and systems.

C. Warehousing and Delivery — Warehousing and delivery is often referred to as the fulfillment operation and includes the essential steps of inventory control, warehouse order filling, and shipment to customers. An important requirement is for easy methods of making returns. Therefore efficient handling of reverse orders is necessary.

1. Network Structure — The network structure has a direct effect on complexity and more importantly cost and was therefore documented for the companies visited.

   • Number and Locations of Facilities — It was almost uniform practice to have one centrally located warehouse operation delivering nationwide, especially if the products shipped tended to be UPS size and weight. Where bulk or heavy products must be shipped from closer locations for freight economics they were drop-shipped from vendors or limited line warehouses.

   • Order Filling — Orders were filled on a first-in-first-out (FIFO) basis and only when the order was complete. However, with customer approval, shipment from multiple locations to arrive on or near the same date was used.

   • Shipping — Products not shipped from a central warehouse were shipped from the most logical location with stock available. Split shipments could occur, but the customer was advised at the time of order taking.

2. Receiving and Inventory Control

   • Receiving — Automated warehouse locator systems were implemented to determine the logical put-away location based on available cubic space.

   • Data Capture — The practice of weighing incoming material to determine an item weight was common. The data became part of the SKU descriptive information and was used later in the process to (1) check for order filling errors by comparing actual weight to a calculated weight, and (2) to precalculate either UPS freight or USPS postage.

- Warehouse Layout — Warehouse storage was almost exclusively conventional where there was a variety of product size and weight. Material was arranged by velocity by aisle.
- SKU Designation — Vendor SKU numbers and descriptions were used to maintain customer recognizable terms and to avoid cumbersome cross-reference catalogs and chance for error.

3. Order Processing and Picking
   - Order Scheduling — Orders received in time sequence throughout the day were sorted to group them by logical picking order sequence to minimize picker travel distance. The sorting to coincide with the velocity location of material in the warehouse would group orders for fast movers or batch pick items for a group of orders.
   - Order Picking — Picking was based on conventional materials handling. A zone for quick-picking fast movers was common. Picking was generally done directly into the packing carton. The second most common method was into a tote or batch picking to a cart.

4. Packing — Several methods are used to verify order completeness. One method is to compare the actual weight, from an in-line scale, to precalculated weight. Orders exceeding a given tolerance were checked. However, sample audits were also common.

5. Delivery — Orders entered before 2:00 pm were picked up that evening by the carrier and delivered next day where the warehouse was located in the same city. Remote delivery was estimated for the customer and stated as a range at time of order taking.

6. Systems — Reporting systems, tailored to the individual's or team's productivity and handling error rates were observed and increased in sophistication. The objective was to provide incentive pay for productivity, but decremented by error rates.

D. Invoicing and Collection
   1. Method of Payment — The predominant method of payment was "bill on account." Where internal credit was granted, many firms established a credit line for their customers. Since on-line, interactive systems were the rule the credit line was an integral part of the order process.

2. Invoicing
   - Frequency — All companies were billed daily. Invoices were mailed to the customer the day after the products were shipped.
   - Invoice Accuracy — Because all edits and validations for customer data and pricing were performed during the order entry process as well as the calculation for sales tax calculation, these practices resulted in an extremely high invoice accuracy.
   - Invoice Data — The invoice itself contained the customer name, bill-to and ship-to addresses, customer number, and details of the specific order. Serial numbers, where applicable, were placed on the invoice for information only.
   - Invoice Inquiries — Inquiries from customers regarding their invoice were directed to the customer service section. There was no separate billing department since the process was essentially complete at time of order entry.
   - Payment Terms — Firms had payment terms ranging from net 10 to net 30. The majority were net 30.
   - Collections — Aging on the accounts receivable file was based on the invoice date. Those companies with low DSO tended to have aggressive collection policies and shorter payment terms. Telephone collections were used by most companies based on dollar amount and invoice due date. Invoice collection commenced 15 to 60 days after start of aging.
   - Bad Debt Write-Off — Write-off varied from company to company, although most firms turned over their accounts to a third-party collection agency in the 45 to 90-day range. When an account was deemed a bad debt, credit agencies were notified.

Financial Implications

Most of the benchmarking partners visited did not express their operating costs on a per order basis. Those that did tended to be the lower cost operations. There was a distinct relationship of profit margin to cost per order. Companies with lower profit margins were able to achieve lower order processing costs on an absolute, as well as percent of revenue (or gross profit) basis.

The range of processing costs expressed on a cost per order basis ranged from $6 to $35 excluding freight. The median cost per order was $20 and was concluded to be the benchmark for the process if the best practices had been implemented. The benchmark process offered a significant cost opportunity. In summary, substantial cost savings could potentially be realized if the benchmark process described by the best practices was implemented.

How to Measure Yourself Against the Best

Frances Gaither Tucker, Seymour M. Zivan, and Robert C. Camp

(Reprinted with permission from *Harvard Business Review,* January-February 1987.)

Frances Tucker is assistant professor of marketing and logistics at the School of Management, Syracuse University. Seymour Zivan is vice president for logistics and distribution in the Business Systems Group of Xerox Corporation. Robert Camp is manager of business analysis in the business planning organization in that group. He was closely connected with the benchmarking activities described in this article.

The preparation of this article was prompted by readers' inquiries into benchmarking when Tucker and Zivan mentioned the practice in their May-June 1985 HBR article "A Xerox Cost Center Imitates a Profit Center."

One way to judge the performance of an organization is, of course, to compare it with other units within the company. But these measurements often merely reinforce complacency or generate "not invented here" excuses. Comparisons with outsiders, however, can highlight the best industry practices and promote their adoption. This technique is commonly called "benchmarking," a term taken from the land-surveying practice of comparing elevations.

When Xerox started using benchmarking in 1979, management's aim was to analyze unit production costs in manufacturing operations. Uncomfortably aware of the extremely low prices of Japanese plain-paper copiers, the manufacturing staff at Xerox wanted to determine whether their Japanese counterparts' relative costs were as low as their relative prices. The staff compared the operating capabilities and features of the Japanese machines, including those made by Fuji-Xerox, and tore down their mechanical components for examination.

The investigation revealed that production costs in the United States were much higher. Discarding their standard budgeting processes, U.S. manufacturing operations adopted the lower Japanese costs as targets for driving their own business plans. Top management, gratified with the results, directed that all units and cost centers in the corporation use benchmarking.

But distribution, administration, service, and other support functions found it difficult to arrive at a convenient analogue to a product. These nonmanufacturing units began to make internal comparisons, including worker productivity at different regional distribution centers and per-pound transportation costs between regions. Next, they looked at competitors' processes. In logistics that meant comparing the transportation, warehousing, and inventory management of Xerox's distribution function with those of the competition.

Benchmarking against the competition, however, poses problems. For one thing, comparisons with competitors may uncover practices that are unworthy of emulation. For another, while competitive benchmarking may help you meet your competitors' performance, it is unlikely to reveal practices for beating them. Moreover, getting information about competitors is obviously difficult. Finally, we have observed that people are more receptive to new ideas that come from outside their own industry. Noncompetitor benchmarking, then, is the method of choice.

A noncompetitor investigation can give management information about the best functional practices in any industry. These may include technological advances unrecognized in your own industry (like bar coding, which originated in the grocery industry but has since been widely applied). Adoption of these practices can help you achieve a competitive advantage.

The first step in the process is to identify what will be benchmarked — expense-to-revenue ratios, inventory turns, service calls, customer satisfaction — whatever the "product" of the particular function is. Then pinpoint the areas that need improvement.

In Xerox's experience, managers tend to concentrate first on comparative costs. But as they become more knowledgeable about benchmarking, managers discover that understanding practices, processes, and methods is more important because these define the changes necessary to reach the benchmark costs. Moreover, as managers become more confident about benchmarking, they can readily extend it beyond cost reduction to profit-producing factors like service levels and customer satisfaction.

L&D and L. L. Bean

Where do you find well-run noncompetitors for the purpose of comparison? Annual reports and other easily available publications can uncover gross indicators of efficient operation. Universally recognized measures like ROA, revenue per employee, inventory turns, and percent SG&A expenses will help identify the well-managed companies.

To identify superior performance in particular functions, Xerox relies especially on trade journals, consultants, annual reports and other company publications in which "statements of pride" appear, and presentations at professional and other forums. The same well-run organizations keep turning up.

Getting a noncompetitor's cooperation in the venture is usually easier because professionals in a function are eager to compare notes. They want to know how their system stacks up. Indeed, several noncompetitors have agreed to share the expense of benchmarking studies with Xerox.

One of Xerox's most valuable benchmarking experiences, with L. L. Bean, Inc., the outdoor sporting goods retailer and mail-order house, illustrates well how these ventures work. It was carried out by the Xerox Logistics and Distribution unit, which is responsible for inventory management, warehousing, and transport of machines, parts, and supplies.

Historically L&D's productivity increases had been 3 percent to 5 percent per year. By 1981 it was clear that improvement was necessary to maintain profit margins in the face of industry price cuts.

The inventory-control area had recently installed a new planning system, and the transportation function was capitalizing on opportunities presented by deregulation. Warehousing was next in line for improvement, and the distribution-center managers wanted a change. They identified the picking area as the worst bottleneck in the receiving-through-shipping sequence.

A new technology, automated storage and retrieval systems (ASRS) for materials handling, had appeared on the scene and was the subject of hot debate in Xerox's distribution function. The company had just erected a high-rise ASRS warehouse for raw materials and assembly parts in Webster, New York, in the same complex as a large finished-goods distribution center. Internal benchmarking evaluations by L&D showed that heavy investment in capital equipment for ASRS could not be cost justified for finished goods. They needed a different way to boost warehousing and materials handling productivity, but what?

In January 1981 L&D assigned a staff member half time to

come up with a suitable noncompetitor to benchmark in the warehousing and materials handling areas. The staff member combed trade journals and conferred with professional associations and consultants to find the companies with the best reputations in the distribution business. He then targeted those companies with generic product characteristics and service levels similar to Xerox reprographic parts and supplies.

By November the staff member had singled out L. L. Bean as the best candidate for benchmarking. Of particular interest were Bean's warehouse operations. The staff member summed up his impressions in a memo to his boss:

"I was particularly struck with the L. L. Bean warehouse system design. Although extremely manual in nature, the design minimized the labor content, among other benefits. The operation also did not lend itself to automation [of handling and picking]. The design therefore relied on very basic handling techniques, but it was carefully thought out and implemented. In addition, the design was selected with the full participation of the hourly work force. It was the first warehouse operation designed by quality circles."

To the layperson, L. L. Bean products may bear no resemblance to Xerox parts and supplies. To the distribution professional, however, the analogy was striking: Both companies had to develop warehousing and distribution systems to handle products diverse in size, shape, and weight. This diversity precluded the use of ASRS.

Three months later a Xerox team visited Bean's operations in Freeport, Maine. Besides the person in charge of benchmarking in L&D, the team consisted of a headquarters operations manager and a field distribution-center manager. These two people represented the line employees who would ultimately make any changes.

Analysis of the findings back home in Rochester, New York, revealed a broader range of computer-directed activities than Xerox had. These activities included:

- Arranging materials by velocity — that is, fast movers were stocked closest to the picking route.
- Storing incoming materials randomly to maximize warehouse space utilization and minimize forklift travel distance.
- Sorting and releasing incoming orders throughout the day to minimize picket travel distance (known as short-interval scheduling).
- Basing incentive bonuses on picking productivity offset by error rates.
- Automating outbound carrier manifesting by calculating

transportation costs ahead of time.

- Plans for implementing automated data capture through bar coding.

Exhibit I compares the prospective performance of Xerox's most efficient warehouse then being planned with L. L. Bean's performance as of February 1982. Because of the nature of its operations, Xerox often picked several pieces per order, so Xerox had a higher figure for pieces per man-day. But L. L. Bean could pick almost three times as many lines per man-day. (A line, which represents picker travel distance for one trip to a bin, is the crucial measure of productivity.)

The report documenting the findings attracted wide interest within Xerox's L&D organization, particularly because Bean's was a labor-intensive system that could be adapted fairly easily to Xerox's purposes. As a result, L&D incorporated some of L. L. Bean's practices in a program to modernize Xerox's warehouses. These practices included materials location arranged by velocity, to speed the flow of materials and minimize picker travel distance, as well as enhancing computer involvement in the picking operation. Xerox is now putting together a totally computer-managed warehouse.

Exhibit I
Comparison of Key Performance Criteria
in Two Distribution Centers

	L. L. Bean	Xerox
Orders per man-day	550	117
Pieces per man-day	1,440	2,640
Lines per man-day	1,440	497

Further Experience

Benchmarking has become an ongoing practice at Xerox Logistics and Distribution. The requirement to carry on the procedure has been pushed down the organization to individual operations, which now do their own benchmarking rather than have a specialist perform it. Because the process is well understood and because the people who undertake it are the ones who implement the findings, benchmarking is now much easier to carry out than before. L&D has taken the noncompetitor approach to benchmarking many times. Exhibit II shows some of the practices Xerox uncovered using this method.

From these efforts L&D has greatly increased its productivity. Before benchmarking, the organization was making annual productivity gains of 3 percent to 5 percent; now it strives for, and reaches, improvements of 10 percent. Of that figure, some 3 percent to 5 percent is derived from L. L. Bean-type investigations, using competitors as well as noncompetitors. In addition, the people involved in the benchmarking process often find that the work is broadening and furthers their professional growth. They become more useful to the organization.

L. L. Bean, incidentally, has benefited, too. After seeing Xerox's success, the company adopted benchmarking as part of its own planning process.

Exhibit II
Practices Uncovered via Noncompetitive Benchmarking

Type of company	Practice
Drug wholesaler	Electronic ordering between store and distribution center
Appliance manufacturer	Forklift handling of up to six appliances at once
Electrical components manufacturer	Automatic in-line weighing, bar code labeling, and scanning of packages
Photographic film manufacturer	Self-directed warehouse work teams
Catalog fulfillment service bureau	Recording of item dimension and weight to permit order-filling quality assurance based on calculated compared with actual weight

Bibliography

Alster, Norman. "An American Original Beats Back the Copycats." *Electronic Business* 3, No. 19 (October 1987): 52-58.

Beck, Larry. "We Are Successfully Taking on All Competition." *Modern Materials Handling* 41, No. 10 (September 1986):56-59.

Cavinato, Joseph. "How to Benchmark Logistics Operations." *Distribution* 87, No. 8 (August 1988): 93-96.

Daniels, Aubrey C. "Performance Management: The Behavioral Approach to Productivity Improvement." *National Productivity Review,* Summer 1985.

Demers, Mary L. "Team Xerox Ties the Score." *CDIS Newsletter* 2, No. 6.9, Dataquest, San Jose, Calif. (June 1987): 18-19.

DeToro, Irving J. "Strategic Planning for Quality at Xerox." *Quality Progress* 20, No. 4 (April 1987): 16-20.

Drozdowski, Thomas E. "GTE Uses Benchmarking to Measure Purchasing." *Purchasing* 94, No. 6 (March 1983): 21-24.

Dumaine, Brian. "Corporate Spies Snoop to Conquer." *Fortune* 118, No. 11 (November 7, 1988): 68-76.

Furey, Timothy R. "Benchmarking: The Key to Developing Competitive Advantage in Mature Markets." *Planning Review* 15, No. 5 (September/October 1987): 30-32.

Glavin, William F. "Competitive Benchmarking, A Technique Utilized by Xerox Corporation to Revitalize Itself to a Modern Competitive Position." *Review of Business* 6, No. 3 (Winter 1984): 9-12.

Ishikawa, Kaoru. *Guide to Quality Control.* Tokyo: Asian Productivity Organization, 1983.

Jacobson, Gary and John Hillkirk. *Xerox: American Samurai.* New York: Macmillan Publishing Co., 1986.

Kane, Edward J. "IBM's Quality Focus on the Business Process." *Quality Progress* 19, No. 4 (April 1986): 24-33.

Kearns, David T. "Quality Improvement Begins at the Top." Jerry Bowles, Ed. *World* 20, No. 5 (May 1986): 21.

Kelsch, John E. "Benchmarking: Shrewd Way to Keep Your Company Ahead of Its Competition." *Boardroom Reports,* December 15, 1982.

Lewis, Byron C. and Albert E. Crews. "The Evolution of Benchmarking as a Computer Performance Evaluation Technique." *MIS Quarterly* 9, No. 1 (March 1985): 7-16.

Linstone, Harold A. and M. Turoff. *The Delphi Method: Techniques and Application.* Redding, Mass.: Addison-Wesley, 1975.

McComas, Maggie, Christopher Knowlton, and Patricia A. Langan. "Cutting Costs Without Killing the Business." *Fortune* 114, No. 8 (October 1986): 70-78.

Pipp, Frank J. "Management Commitment to Quality." *Quality Progress* 16, No. 8 (August 1983): 12-17.

Prokesch, Steven E. "L. L. Bean Meshes Man and Machine." *New York Times,* December 23, 1985.

Prokesch, Steven E. "People Make Bean's a Modern Marvel — L. L. Bean Warehouse an Industry Standard." *Maine Sunday Times,* December 29, 1985.

Prokesch, Steven E. "Remaking the American CEO." *New York Times,* January 25, 1987.

Prokesch, Steven E. "Xerox Halts Japanese March." *New York Times,* November 7, 1985.

"A Truly Outstanding System for Manual Order Picking." *Modern Materials Handling* 35, No. 3 (March 1980): 66-71.

Tsiantar, Dody and John Schwartz. "George Smiley Joins the Firm." *Newsweek* 111, No. 18 (May 2, 1988): 46-47.

Tucker, Francis G., Seymour M. Zivan, and Robert C. Camp. "How to Measure Yourself Against the Best." *Harvard Business Review* 87, No. 1 (January-February 1987): 2-4.

Tucker, Francis G. and Seymour M. Zivan. "A Xerox Cost Center Imitates a Profit Center." *Harvard Business Review* 65, No. 1 (May-June 1985): 2-4.

Tzu, Sun. *The Art of War.* James E. Clavel, Ed. New York: Delacorte Press, 1983.

Index

gap (*see* Gaps)
generic process, 4
getting started, 20
goals and objectives:
  cascading, 187
  establishment of, 31
historical perspective, 6-8
identifying best firms, 66
  (*see also* Best competitors)
implementation alternatives, 207-210
  line management, 207
  performance teams, 210
  process czar, 208-209
  program management, 207-208
institutionalize, 206, 241
level of detail, 47
logic poster, 165
management involvement, 34
  (*see also* Benchmarking, Expectations, and Senior
    Management Orchestration)
managerial perspective, 8-10
methods, 4
mission statement, 42
  candidates for benchmarking, 42
monitoring programs, 211, 220
need for, questions indicating, 43
newsletter, 165
noncompetitive, 172
objectives, 28
outputs, 41, 46, 48
  appropriateness, 47
performance appraisal, 231
philosophical steps, 4
practice opportunity, 129-135
practices, recognizing, 143
  be benchmarked, 143
  clear superiority, 144
  expert judgment, 145
  large opportunity, 144-145, 125
  practice reviews, 145-146
  sell services (marketplace superiority) 127, 143
    (*see also,* Benchmarking, Tests)
process steps, 17
  action, 19
  analysis, 18

Printed in the United States
101289LV00003B/1-93/A